Northrop Frye and Critical Method

Northrop Frye

and Critical Method

Robert D. Denham

WITHDRAWN

The Pennsylvania State University Press

University Park and London

Library of Congress Cataloging in Publication Data

Denham, Robert D.
  Northrop Frye and critical method.

  Includes bibliographical references and index.
  1. Criticism. 2. Frye, Northrop. I. Title.
PN81.D39   801'.95'0924   78-50001
ISBN 0-271-00546-7 ✓

To Rachel

Preface

The criticism of Northrop Frye represents one of the most impressive achievements in the recent history of critical thought. He is "probably the most influential critic writing in English since the 1950's," according to Walter Jackson Bate. "Certainly in the English speaking world," he says, "Frye's importance since 1957 (the date of his *Anatomy of Criticism*) is unique."[1] Murray Krieger remarks that Frye "has had an influence—indeed an absolute hold—on a generation of developing literary critics greater and more exclusive than that of any one theorist in recent critical history."[2] Frank Kermode says that the *Anatomy* is the one book published within the previous decade that he finds himself returning to most often, adding that Frye has "the best mind in the business except for William Empson's."[3] Harold Bloom observes that Frye "has earned the reputation of being the leading theoretician of literary criticism among all those writing in English today."[4] And the editors of a recent anthology of modern criticism refer to Frye as an indispensable critic, linking him with Eliot, Pound, and Richards as the major critics of our age. "More than any other modern critic," they say, "he stands at the center of critical activity."[5] These are typical expressions of the respect Frye's work commands. His importance as a critic need not be argued: it is one of the givens of modern critical discussion. Although many have disagreed with him, especially with his attempt to formulate a comprehensive and systematic theory of criticism independent of value judgments, few within his own field have ignored him.

But though he has been read, discussed, and debated for a generation, no one has undertaken a systematic and comprehensive study of his work as a whole. The commentary continues to grow, but even the best accounts are limited in one of two ways. On the one hand, students of Frye who have chosen to examine a single topic in his work have provided us only a partial view. On the other hand, when the interpreters' aims have been more universal and inclusive, general statement and summary have preempted detailed analysis. Thus, while a number of commentaries have contributed to our understanding of Frye's work, none has been at once detailed and comprehensive. My own study is based on the conviction that the whole of his criticism merits a closer analysis than has yet been attempted. I have tried therefore to go beyond what others have said about Frye by placing the details of his argument in the context of his total view of literature and criticism.

Frye's work has been subjected to a variety of mistaken interpretations and judgments. These range from distortion at one extreme to a failure of understanding at the other. Lying somewhere between are the many oversimplifications which do injustice to his work in one way or another. My own study does not atone for all the inadequacies. In the first place, although I have aimed at a comprehensive analysis, I have had to be selective at some points. This is especially true of my treatment of Frye's practical criticism. But I have tried to do justice to each *area* of his work—to his theoretical, his practical, and his cultural or social criticism. In any case, an attempt to account for all of Frye's writings would be a monumental and unrealistic task. He has been extraordinarily prolific, having written now some fifteen books and more than 330 essays, reviews, and contributions to books.[6] There are doubtless times when I too have oversimplified, distorted, and failed to understand Frye. I hope that these are few and that I have at least minimized the partial and the erroneous views.

The chief reasons, then, for this study are three: Frye is eminent enough as a critic to deserve a thorough investigation, and the treatment he has thus far received has been either incomplete or misguided. A third reason is personal, springing from my fascination with the quality of Frye's mind and from a desire to know what makes it work. His speculations about literature raise most of the important critical issues: he asks the right questions; and even when his answers are unsatisfactory or unconvincing, the additional questions he forces us to ask are never trivial. His theory is complex and subtle, intricately designed and expansive in scope, forever moving outward from the literary work into a broad series of contexts. It is like a Gothic cathedral, and to ask about the mind of its architect is to ask about the method behind the theory. How can we make clear what Frye has said and, more important, his reasons for saying it? These questions underlie what follows. By examining the problems Frye is trying to solve, the nature of his particular subject matter, the principles and concepts of his critical language, and his mode of reasoning, we can arrive, I think, at a special kind of understanding of his work. These are the four issues I have tried to keep in mind throughout.[7]

Any discussion of Frye which hopes to do justice to his critical theory as a whole must account for *Anatomy of Criticism*. I have taken this as the chief document to be explained. My first four chapters attempt to trace its argument, one chapter being devoted to each of the four theories developed there—the theories of modes, symbols, myths, and genres.

In chapter 5 I examine Frye's ideas about critical and literary autonomy, the scientific nature of criticism, value judgments, and the social function of the critic, all of which are important theoretical questions raised in the *Anatomy* and elsewhere. Chapter 6 is an effort to see how Frye puts his own theories to work. It includes analyses of his practical, historical, and social criticism. In particular, I examine his writings on Milton, his essay on "the age of sensibility," his study of English Romanticism, and *The Critical Path*.

The dangers I have sought to avoid in each of these chapters are the Scylla of the prejudiced opponent whose bias precludes objectivity and the Charybdis of the dogmatic disciple whose exuberance inhibits understanding. The moderate course between these extremes is a proper combination of sympathy and disinterestedness, and that is what I have aimed for. In the final chapter, which is an "essay" in the original sense of the term, I point out some of the problematic areas of Frye's criticism, pose several alternative solutions, and discuss the powers and limitations of his method.

Everyone who has read Frye knows that he is a schematic thinker. The diagrammatic form of his thought, with its multilateral symmetries, has been the object of both praise and censure, and sometimes even of fun. Meyer Abrams remarks, not altogether facetiously, that Frye's division and subdivision of the various modes, symbols, archetypes, and genres "is reminiscent of the mediaeval encyclopaedic tables designed to comprehend the *omne scibile*; instinctively though in vain the reader looks for an appendix that will open out into a square yard of tabular diagram."[8] We should not be misled by the tone here, for the schematic design of the *Anatomy* is clearly an integral part of Frye's purpose and method. He has said, in fact, that he did have specific diagrams in mind when he wrote the *Anatomy*,[9] and he has commented on the similarity between his view of literature and the mandala vision, the mandala being a projection of the way one sees.[10] For these reasons, I have from time to time produced the kind of schematic model Abrams calls for. Because diagrams necessarily oversimplify and suggest a rigidity of thought which is foreign to the whole tone of Frye's work, I offer them only as expository aids.

This book would not have been possible without the encouragement and helpful advice of Wayne C. Booth and Elder Olson. My introduction to criticism came by way of the *Poetics* in the classroom of Elder Olson, and to him I owe a large intellectual debt. It was under the direction of Wayne Booth, however, that this study first took shape, and to him I owe a number of special debts, for helping to provide me with tools of analysis and ways of thinking, as well as all the nameless, unremembered acts. To both teachers I acknowledge my gratitude. I am also grateful to Lawrence I. Lipking, Robert Scholes, and W.T. Jewkes, who read earlier versions of the book, for their astute comments and helpful suggestions.

I express my deep appreciation to Northrop Frye for his generous responses to my inquiries over the years and for granting me permission to quote from his works. To discover and keep track of his long, still-growing list of writings would have been infinitely more difficult without his kind and attentive replies to my queries.

I also wish to thank Emory & Henry College and the National Endowment for the Humanities for research grants which enabled me to complete this study.

Portions of the book have appeared elsewhere in slightly different form. I am grateful to the editors of the following journals for permission to reprint my own work: *Connecticut Review, South Atlantic Bulletin, Xavier University Studies, Centrum, South Carolina Review,* and *Canadian Literature.* The preface and the final chapter incorporate some material from the "Introduction" to my *Northrop Frye: An Enumerative Bibliography* (Metuchen, N.J.: Scarecrow Press, 1974). Portions of chapters 1, 2, and 7 appeared in the "Introduction" to *Northrop Frye on Culture and Literature: A Collection of Review Essays,* ed. Robert Denham (Chicago: University of Chicago Press, 1978). I wish to thank the editors of these two presses for permission to use some of my own words again.

Contents

List of Figures

List of Abbreviations

AC   *Anatomy of Criticism: Four Essays* (1957)

CL   *Northrop Frye on Culture and Literature: A Collection of Review Essays* (1978)

CP   *The Critical Path: An Essay on the Social Context of Literary Criticism* (1971)

EI   *The Educated Imagination* (1963)

FI   *Fables of Identity: Studies in Poetic Mythology* (1963)

FS   *Fearful Symmetry: A Study of William Blake* (1947)

MC   *The Modern Century* (1967)

NP   *A Natural Perspective: The Development of Shakespearean Comedy and Romance* (1965)

RE   *The Return of Eden: Five Essays on Milton's Epics* (1965)

SeS   *The Secular Scripture: A Study of the Structure of Romance* (1976)

SER   *A Study of English Romanticism* (1968)

SM   *Spiritus Mundi: Essays on Literature, Myth, and Society* (1976)

SS   *The Stubborn Structure: Essays on Criticism and Society* (1970)

WTC   *The Well-Tempered Critic* (1963)

1

Theory of Modes

Historical Criticism: Heroic Powers of Action

Because literary critics have often used different words to mean the same thing and the same word to mean different things, understanding critical theory requires close attention to the language critics use. This is especially true in Frye's case: he is not only, to use his own phrase, a "terminological buccaneer," pirating words from the critical tradition and redefining them to suit his own purposes, he is also a terminological innovator, creating his own categories whenever he needs them. Frye's argument in the First Essay of *Anatomy of Criticism* will be better understood, then, if we examine his special terminology and his redefinition of some familiar critical terms. The aim of the First Essay, entitled "Historical Criticism," is to develop a theory of literary modes. It is built upon four fundamental categories:

> *Fictional:* Relating to literature in which there are internal characters, apart from the author and his audience; opposed to thematic.
> *Thematic:* Relating to works of literature in which no characters are involved except the author and his audience, as in most lyrics and essays, or to works of literature in which internal characters are subordinated to an argument maintained by the author, as in allegories and parables; opposed to fictional.
> *Ethos:* The internal social context of a work of literature, comprising the characterization and setting of fictional literature and the relation of the author to his reader or audience in thematic literature.
> *Mode:* A conventional power of action assumed about the chief characters in fictional literature, or the corresponding attitude assumed by the poet toward his audience in thematic literature. Such modes tend to succeed one another in historical sequence.[1]

The opposition between "fictional" and "thematic" provides the basis not only for the general organization of the First Essay but also for the two meanings which the word "mode" comes to assume in this section. "Mode" is a category defined broadly in relation to what Frye calls the ethical elements, or the *ethos,* of a literary work. The *ethos,* an expansion of Aristotle's "character," refers on the one hand to the literary hero and his society and on the other to a writer and his audience. The constant term, then, in Frye's definition of both fictional and thematic modes is *ethos,* though the meaning in each case is different, since the point of reference is either the hypothetical characters or the author-audience relationship. "Fictional" works are those in which the characters are internal, existing primarily as functions of a plot. And a "fictional mode" refers to the power of action which a character possesses.

This distinction enables Frye to classify fictional works according to the position of the hero on a *spoudaios-phaulos* continuum, beginning with the hero as a god and ending with him as inferior to ourselves. He then develops an elaborate pattern through which his five fictional modes (myth, romance, high mimesis, low mimesis, and irony), in both their tragic and comic forms, are said to have cyclically moved.

Since "every work of literature has both a fictional and a thematic aspect" (AC, 53), "fictional" and "thematic" are relative terms. Lying behind Frye's elaboration of the various *fictional* modes, for example, is always an awareness of the author-audience relationship (*ethos* in the second sense). "In literary fictions," he says in the first paragraph of the First Essay, "the plot consists of somebody doing something. . . . The something he does or fails to do is what he can do, or could have done, on the level of the postulates made about him by the author and the consequent expectations of the audience" (AC, 33). These "postulates" and "expectations," which indicate a concern for both the creative process and the audience's response, are rhetorical considerations, or what Frye would refer to as "thematic" aspects of a literary work; for they depend on choices the author must make to manipulate his reader's response. But the important point for the dialectic of Frye's categories is that they are *internally* rhetorical: their essential reference is to the way an author causes his audience to respond not to the external world but to the self-contained world of the fictional hero. The values obtained from the response are therefore primarily final rather than instrumental.

This is not the case, however, with works in the "thematic mode," for here the internal characters more or less disappear, having been subordinated to the *dianoia* of the writer's argument. Works in the thematic mode are therefore *external* fictions in which the dominant "ethical" relationship is between the writer and his society, rather than between the hero and his. "Poetry may be as completely absorbed in its internal characters," Frye remarks, "as it is in Shakespeare, or in Homer. . . . But as soon as the poet's personality appears on the horizon, a relation with the reader is established which cuts across the story, and which may increase until there is no story at all apart from what the poet is conveying to his reader" (AC, 52). Whereas the typical question asked about a fictional work is, Frye claims, "How is this story going to turn out?" the question for thematic works becomes "What's the *point* of this story?" (AC, 52). In the latter mode, therefore, *mythos* and *ethos* (in the first sense) are subordinated to *dianoia*, as Frye's definition of "thematic" indicates.

At times the primary criterion underlying the fictional-thematic dichotomy appears to be one of ends, so that Frye's division of literature into two basic modes comes to resemble the mimetic-didactic categories of the Chicago Neo-Aristotelians.[2] At other times, however, his criteria become so far-ranging as to amount to a distinction between aesthetic systems themselves. This is the case at the end of the First Essay where he aligns Aristotle's view of art with the fictional mode and Longinus's with the thematic. Such a distinction then permits him to set up a series of dialectical opposites which he sees as corresponding in a general way with his two modal categories: literature as product versus literature as process, artifact versus quality, *catharsis* versus *ecstasis*, detachment versus absorption (AC, 66–67). Here the method used to define the fictional and thematic categories has gone far beyond "ethical" relationships and rhetorical ends, for it involves the juxtaposition and then the merging of different critical methods, even of entire critical traditions. This syncretic tendency, as we shall see, occurs throughout Frye's criticism.

From Myth to Irony: The Taxonomy of Fictional Modes

Having set down the principle that fictions may be classified according to the power of action possessed by the fictional hero, Frye proceeds to develop his theory of fictional modes. His principle for differentiating the modes is the relationship of the hero both to other men and to his natural environment, a principle which yields the five categories that appear throughout *Anatomy of Criticism:* (1) *myth,* in which the hero's superiority is different in kind from that of other men and their environment; (2) *romance,* in which the hero's superiority is one of degree; (3) *high mimesis,* where the hero is superior in degree to other men but not superior to nature; (4) *low mimesis,* in which the hero is more or less equal to other men and not superior to his environment; and (5) *irony,* where the hero's power of action is inferior to that of ordinary men (AC, 33–34). The relationship of the hero to society provides the basis, moreover, for a further distinction between tragic and comic aspects of fictions. "Tragic," in the First Essay, refers to those stories in which we witness the death, fall, or isolation of the hero; and "comic," to those in which the hero is somehow integrated into society. Thus Frye is able to differentiate ten fictional modes, each of the five primary categories possessing what he calls a "general distinction" between tragic and comic aspects of plot. Each of these modes, furthermore, can be said to

	TRAGIC FORMS	COMIC FORMS
MYTH	Dionysiac stories: about dying or isolated gods Effect: "solemn sympathy" of nature Theme: imaginative alignment between man and nature Naive examples: stories about Hercules, Orpheus, Balder, Christ Sentimental examples: *The Dream of the Rood*, Kingsley's ballad in *Alton Locke*	Apollonian stories: about heroes accepted by society of gods Effect: experience of imaginative vision of eternal world Theme: integration of society, salvation, acceptance, assumption Naive examples: stories about Mercury, Hercules Sentimental example: *The Paradiso*
ROMANCE	Nature reduced largely to animal and vegetable world Effect: elegiac; pity and fear absorbed into pleasure Naive examples: *Beowulf, Song of Roland*, stories of martyred saints Sentimental example: Tennyson's *The Passing of Arthur*	Nature as pastoral world Effect: idyllic mood Naive examples: modern popular westerns Sentimental example: pastoral poems
HIGH MIMESIS	Combination of heroic and ironic, of the incongruous and the inevitable Effect: catharsis of pity and fear Naive examples: Greek tragic drama, *The Mirror for Magistrates* Sentimental examples: tragic drama of Shakespeare, Racine	Combination of heroic and ironic (in Old Comedy) Effect: catharsis of sympathy and ridicule Naive example: Old Comedy of Aristophanes (*The Birds*) Sentimental example: *The Tempest*
LOW MIMESIS	Effect: pity and fear communicated externally as sensations; pathos Typical character: the *alazon* Naive examples: Gothic thrillers, popular fiction with its mad scientists Sentimental examples: *Lord Jim, Madame Bovary, Pierre*, Balzac, Dickens	Effect: resolution involving social promotion Typical character: the *picaro* Naive examples: New Comedy of Meander, Cinderella, Horatio Alger stories Sentimental examples: Shaw's Sergius, Synge's playboy, Balzac, Stendhal
IRONY	Hero as *pharmakos* Effect: dispassion (pity and fear not raised) Two poles: archetypes of Adam and Christ Naive examples: Plato's *Apology*, Job Sentimental examples: *The Trial, Crime and Punishment*	*Pharmakos* driven out Effect: relief; experience of the element of "play" Two poles: enemy either inside or outside society Naive examples: *The Clouds*, detective stories, Graham Greene, comedy of manners Sentimental examples: *Volpone, Tartuffe, Merchant of Venice*

Figure 1. Fictional modes.

have naive (primitive or popular) and sentimental (later or more so-phisticated) forms (AC, 35). Frye also refers to the "comic" and "tragic" categories as "tendencies," one toward integrating the hero into society, the other toward isolating him (AC, 54). These principles of differen-tiation will yield, to organize the matter visually, the simplified diagram of Figure 1. This chart, however, even if it were to include all of Frye's examples, would scarcely account for the subtle and complex nature of his argument. The principles of differentiation outlined thus far oper-ate only at the highest level of generality; but when Frye turns to elaborate the various kinds of fictional works appropriate to each broad category, his argument calls upon a number of other criteria.[3]

This can be illustrated by a closer look at his discussion of tragic fictional modes, where the argument depends not so much upon the bare fact that the hero and his environment can be found to exist in varying relationships as it does upon the kinds of effects which these relationships produce. Frye observes that in the Dionysian stories of dying gods, the "association of a god's death with autumn or sunset does not, in literature, necessarily mean that he is a god 'of' vegetation or the sun, but only that he is a god capable of dying, whatever his department" (AC, 36). But because of the god's superiority to nature, the effect of his death is often shown in what happens to nature as a result: an effect captured by such expressions as the "solemn sympathy" of nature or "all creation weeping at the death of Christ." "Effect" here does not refer to what an audience feels but rather to what is shown, internally in a myth, to be the "natural" result of a god's death. The so-called pathetic fallacy, in other words, can indicate that we are in the presence of the tragic mythical mode when the alignment between man and nature comes from an aspect of the plot which is tragic (AC, 36).

In his discussion of tragic romance Frye uses "effect" in a some-what different sense. The death or isolation of the romantic hero, he says, "has the effect of a spirit passing out of nature, and evokes a mood best described as elegiac. . . . The elegiac is often accompanied by a diffused, resigned, melancholy sense of the passing of time, of the old order changing and yielding to a new one" (AC, 36–37). This melan-cholic mood, created by the death of the hero, is a fact of *emotional* importance, so that Frye is here speaking not of internal effects but of the affective significance which the death of the hero has upon us as readers. In fact, Frye's discussion of both tragic romance and tragic high and low mimesis dwells more upon principles relating to affective response than upon any other principle. He turns to Aristotle once again, taking the traditional concept of catharsis to express the central position of high-mimetic tragedy within the five modes; and he ex-pands this doctrine, applying it to tragic romance and to low-mimetic tragedy, through a discussion of the "two general directions in which emotion moves." In high-mimetic tragedy, pity and fear are the emotions representing these two directions, the former moving us toward an object, the latter away from it (AC, 37). There are, Frye claims, two parallel affective movements in tragic romance:

> Naive romance [e.g., *Beowulf* and *The Song of Roland*], being closer to the wish-fulfillment dream, tends to absorb emotion and communicate it internally to the reader. Romance, therefore, is characterized by the acceptance of pity and fear, which in ordinary life relate to pain, as forms of pleasure. It turns fear at a distance, or terror, into the adventurous; fear at contact, or horror, into the marvellous, and fear without an object, or dread (*Angst*) into pensive melancholy. It turns pity at a distance, or concern, into the theme of chivalrous rescue; pity at contact, or tenderness, into a languid and relaxed charm, and pity without an object (which has no name but is a kind of animism, or treating everything in nature as though it had human feelings) into creative fantasy. (AC, 37)

Low-mimetic tragedy, on the other hand, depends on still different emotions. Here Frye argues that "pity and fear are neither purged nor absorbed into pleasures, but communicated externally, as sensations" (AC, 38). Pity becomes pathos, because we sympathize with the isolated hero who is one of us; and fear becomes "a kind of pathos in reverse," the sensational response we have to the tradition of such characters as Heathcliff and Dickens's villains (AC, 38–39). Finally, in ironic tragedy pity and fear completely disappear, as we respond dispassionately to the typical victim, the *pharmakos* or scapegoat. As in the case of tragic myth, Frye appeals to principles other than effects in defining tragic irony. The point to be emphasized, however, is that a simple combination of his general definition of tragedy, coupled with his definition of any one of the modes, is not sufficient to account for the nature of a given kind of tragic work. Kenneth Burke maintains that such concepts as pity and fear are incidental to the development of Frye's argument about tragic modes.[4] But such categories as these, rooted in our affective response, give a more specific content to the various modes than permitted by Frye's general framework in this part of the First Essay. In addition, other important criteria enter Frye's discussion; the categories of hamartia, inevitability, and incongruity, for example, are used to define high-mimetic tragedy. Frye gives extended accounts, moreover, of the various kinds of heroes peculiar to each mode, accounts which employ a host of examples as well as the character-type terms which he helped to popularize: *alazon, miles gloriosus, eiron,* and *pharmakos*—about which more later.

Frye does not employ a single method for defining the tragic fictional modes. Nor does he always base his definitions upon the same categories. Although some of his principles are more important than others, he can without warning change the categories which underlie his definitions. He can move easily, for example, from a discussion of the literary effects of low-mimetic tragedy into an account of the writer himself when the subject becomes ironic tragedy (AC, 39–40). Specifically, the difference between *alazon* and *eiron* as the respective names for the low-mimetic and ironic heroes of tragedy appears initially to be a distinction for making the various relations between a hero and his society more explicit. Yet the self-deprecating *eiron* refers in this context not to the fictional hero but to the ironic writer himself (AC, 40). In other words, the criteria which underlie the terms *alazon* and *eiron* and the objects to which they refer are different: one is a matter of character type; the other, of rhetorical technique.

Frye's account of the five comic fictional modes follows a pattern similar to that of the tragic, each of the tragic principles being represented by a corresponding comic one. The death of a god, which in mythical tragedy was called Dionysiac, becomes Apollonian, or "the story of how a hero is accepted by a society of gods" (AC, 43). The elegiac effect of romantic tragedy becomes, in romantic comedy, the idyllic. The catharsis of pity and fear in high-mimetic tragedy becomes the catharsis of sympathy and ridicule, the corresponding comic emotions. The two poles of tragic irony, the archetypes of Adam and Christ, become the two poles of comic irony, or the internal and external social enemies. Since Frye devotes twice as much space to discussing ironic comedy as he does to the other four modes combined, I have singled out this last comic mode for more detailed analysis.

"In studying ironic comedy," Frye says, "we must start with the theme of driving out the *pharmakos* from the point of view of society" (AC, 45). That we *must* begin here, apparently, is because ironic comedy offers a special problem. If, on the one hand, the theme of the comic is the integration of society, how is it, on the other hand, that in the ironic phase of this mode one of the typical characters is shown to be driven out of society, rather than integrated into it? Frye's answer to this problem is largely in terms of effects, or how we respond to ironic comedy. We respond with relief, for example, when a character like Tartuffe is hauled off to prison. But unless such a conclusion is handled deftly by the poet, our sense of social revenge may become so great as to preclude comedy altogether. The same feeling can arise when the comic entertainer like Falstaff or Charlie Chaplin is rejected, a feeling that can produce "one of the most terrible ironies known to art" (AC, 45). There is a point, in fact, where comedy approaches the world of hate and fear which we know in the real world as savagery; and when ironic comedy actually reaches this point—the nadir of its cycle—we have passed beyond the bounds of art into existential reality. But, Frye argues, what keeps art and life separated at this point is the element of play. "Playing at human sacrifice," he says, "seems to be an important theme of ironic comedy" (AC, 46). Thus, whereas in tragic irony the detachment of the audience's response results from the catharsis of pity, in comic irony it results from barriers which play throws up between the *pharmakos* and our response to his rejection. Ridicule, in other words, is purged in comic irony because the element of play delivers the audience from unpleasantness. We see this process at work in such currently popular forms as the detective story and melodrama, both of which aim to expel the enemy from society, yet neither of which can be taken seriously because, in Frye's words, the "protecting wall of play is still there" (AC, 47).

The nature of the enemy of society is Frye's principle for distinguishing three basic forms of ironic comedy: melodrama, the parody of melodrama, and the comedy of manners. In naive melodrama the enemy is the villain. The very act of our hissing the villain, however, is a mark of his absurdity, or of our unwillingness to take him seriously as a threat to society. Thus the irony results from the game we play at being serious. In the second stage the enemy is not so much the villainous person as it is a malignancy within society itself. When viciousness of this sort is viewed ironically it produces comic parody and ridicule. Melodramatic formulas can be parodied, as in Graham Greene; or the melodramatic spirit itself can be the butt of ridicule, as in Jonson, Congreve, Wilde, and Shaw. Finally, a third stage can be seen in works where a kind of standoff results between the comic fool and his slanderous or snobbish society. The villain here is society itself, and thus we sympathize with the comic hero, who, however much a fool, possesses something more valuable than his society does.

We have seen that throughout his discussion of ironic comedy Frye appeals most often to criteria relating to the audience's response. Unless we can recognize and respond to the element of play, Frye is saying, the irony will pass us by. But the three types of comic irony are also distinguished on the basis of affects—how we respond to the varying relationships between the ironic hero and his society.

We must conclude then that Frye's method of defining the tragic and comic modes is not a simple one. When dealing with the large categories, those on the two axes of the chart, he works with broad genus-differentiae distinctions. But when he elaborates the ten modes themselves a number of other categories are pressed into service, including literary effects, typical forms and characters, various representations of nature, plus a long list of illustrations for each of the ten fictional modes. The point needs emphasizing because critics of Frye's modal taxonomy, by ignoring all but the large categories, have made his definitions simpler than they in fact are.[5]

From Myth to Irony: The Taxonomy of Thematic Modes

As already indicated, thematic modes are external fictions in which the dominant "ethical" relationship is between the poet and his society or his audience. Although Frye's modes are distinct from genres or literary species, he does see a correlation on the one hand between fictional modes and novels, epics, and plays, and on the other between thematic modes and essays and lyrics. Another way Frye makes the distinction is to adapt Aristotle's terminology once again, referring to the primary interest of thematic works as *dianoia*, a term he translates here as "theme" or "conceptual interest" (AC, 52). (The word takes on a variety of other meanings in the Second Essay.)

"Thematic" is a term which operates in Frye's argument at the highest level of generality. Even though all works of literature have both fictional and thematic interests, there is often no satisfactory way, he admits, of determining which is the constitutive principle of a given work. One may try to determine the primary interest or end, or the main emphasis, or the dominant "ethical" relationship, but whether the fictional or the thematic interest is finally more important "is often simply a matter of opinion or emphasis in interpretation" (AC, 53). Thus Frye's "thematic" category is a highly relative one, as indicated by the following comparative exercise:

> *The History of Tom Jones, a Foundling,* is a novel named after its plot; *Sense and Sensibility* is named after its theme. But Fielding has as strong a thematic interest (revealed chiefly in the introductory chapters to the different books) as Jane Austen has in telling a good story. Both novels are strongly fictional in emphasis compared to *Uncle Tom's Cabin* or *The Grapes of Wrath,* where the plot exists primarily to illustrate the themes of slavery and migratory labor respectively. They in turn are fictional in emphasis compared to *The Pilgrim's Progress,* and *The Pilgrim's Progress* is fictional in emphasis compared to an essay of Montaigne. (AC, 53)

Frye's discussion of the various thematic modes follows a pattern similar to that of his analysis of the fictional modes. Corresponding to the "tragic" and "comic" aspects of fictional modes are the "episodic" and "encyclopaedic" tendencies of thematic literature.[6] To define these two types of works, Frye once again employs several criteria:

> [Episodic] [1] In thematic literature the poet may write as an individual, emphasizing the separateness of his personality and the distinctness of his vision. [2] This attitude produces most lyrics and essays, a good deal of satire, epigrams, and the writing of "eclogues" or occasional pieces generally. [3] The frequency of the moods of protest, complaint, ridicule, and loneliness (whether bitter or serene) in such works may perhaps indicate a rough analogy to the tragic modes of fiction.
>
> [Encyclopaedic] [1] Or the poet may devote himself to being a spokesman of his society, which means, as he is not addressing a second society, that a poetic knowledge and expressive power which is latent or needed in his society comes to articulation in him. [2] Such an attitude produces poetry which is educational in the broadest sense: epics of the more artificial or thematic kind, didactic poetry and prose, encyclopaedic compilations of myth, folklore, and legend like those of Ovid and Snorri, where, though the stories themselves are fictional, the arrangement of them and the motive for collecting them is thematic. [3] In poetry which is educational in this sense, the social function of the poet figures prominently as a theme. (AC, 54)

Although the isolation-integration (or tragic-comic) distinction may be implicit in some parts of these definitions, only in a vague way can it be said to differentiate the two categories, for, to take only one example, a poet can emphasize his distinctive vision without being isolated from society. Rather, the principles here are more specific. The bracketed numbers in the passage above indicate that Frye bases his distinction on three principles: first, the role of the poet (personal versus social); second, examples of the kinds of works he produces (lyrics, essays, etc., versus artificial epics, didactic works, compilations of myth, etc.); and third, the prominent mood or theme which is communicated (complaint and protest versus social and educational integration). These distinctions, rather than being neat formulas for sharply differentiating between thematic works, represent simply Frye's attempt to distinguish what he sees as two main tendencies in nonfictional literature. Communicating as an individual, the poet *tends,* he says, to produce discontinuous forms; and as a social spokesman, he *tends* to produce more extended patterns (AC, 55). That this is more than a simple distinction between short and long works of literature is clear from Frye's more detailed discussion of thematic modes.

Because the ethical relationship of thematic literature is between poet and reader, Frye's point of departure for defining the five thematic modes is to distinguish the several functions which poets have traditionally served. Where the poet, for example, is an inspired visionary, serving as a vehicle for the voice (or will) of a god, we are in the presence of the mythical mode. Where his function is chiefly one of memory, we have thematic romance. In the high-mimetic mode, he is seen principally as the courtier or counselor, the preacher or orator, functioning in some relation to the theme of leadership. The poet as his own hero, or as an extraordinary personality like the "fictional" hero of romance, is typical of the low-mimetic mode. And finally, when the poet is seen essentially as a craftsman with the literal function of making poems, the resulting mode is irony. The nature or function of the poet, in short, is the chief, though by no means the exclusive, criterion Frye uses to differentiate among the thematic modes. Some of the other principles he employs, like stipulating the central or typical theme of each mode, are indicated in Figure 2.

One matter, however, deserves special commentary: the principle of analogy, which figures so importantly at other places in Frye's system. The encyclopaedic form of the mythical mode is sacred scripture, and Frye maintains that "in the other modes we should expect to find encyclopaedic forms which constitute a series of increasingly human *analogies* of mythical or scriptural revelation" (AC, 56). That we should *expect* to find them is only because of Frye's prior assumption that in the cyclical sequence of modes the center of gravity moves progressively from the divine toward the human world. What Frye is saying, in other words, is that as myth moves toward romance and then toward the two mimetic modes we continue to encounter something which corresponds, in the less-than-mythical literary worlds, to divine revelation: thus the expression "human analogies." For example, the encyclopaedic knowledge found in thematic romance (catalogues of kings and tribes, genealogies of gods, historical traditions, etc.) is not scriptural revelation; but, because this knowledge can be regarded as a kind of sacramental testament by the poet whose function is to remember, it can be seen as a "human analogy of divine knowledge" (AC, 57; see also pp. 315–24). Similarly, in the literary Platonism of the high-mimetic mode, the human analogy of myth is the ideal world, the poetic *dianoia* which, as Sidney says, "the poets only deliver." In the low-mimetic, where the typical aim is to communicate certain psychological or subjective states of mind, the human analogy of myth is the act of individual creation (AC, 59). And finally, in the ironic mode, the analogy is the nondidactic revelation of the epiphany, the *Augenblick*, the *illumination* of *symbolisme*, or "the repetitions of certain experiences at widely scattered intervals [which] create these

	ENCYCLOPAEDIC	EPISODIC
MYTH	Poet: functions as inspired visionary, voice of god Example: sacred scripture Develops from oracle	Examples: oracle, commandment, parable, prophecy, aphorism
ROMANCE	Poet: function is to remember Central theme: marvellous journey Centrifugal perspective: distant quest Human analogy of myth: divine knowledge Examples: *Divine Comedy,* Gower, *Cursor Mundi*	Poet: passes from one world to another Central theme: boundary of consciousness Examples: *Widsith;* poems of exile (memory vs. experience), of vision (experience vs. dream), of revelation (old dispensation vs. *vita nuova*)
HIGH MIMESIS	Poet: preeminently a courtier, orator, counselor, preacher; functions in relation to theme of leadership Central theme: centripetal perspective Human analogy of myth: ideal world (literary Platonism) Examples: *Faerie Queene, The Lusiad, Jerusalem Delivered, Paradise Lost*	Central theme: cynosure, centripetal gaze Examples: metaphysical poetry
LOW MIMESIS	Poet: becomes his own subject, becomes the fictional hero of romance, the extraordinary person Central theme: psychological or subjective states of mind Human analogy of myth: individual creation Examples: *Faust,* Blake's prophecies, mythological poems of Shelley, Keats	Central theme: analysis of subjective mental state Examples: Rousseau, Romantic lyrics
IRONY	Poet: literal function of making poems; a craftsman Central theme: vast panorama of history (*temps perdu*) Human analogy of myth: the epiphany Examples: Proust, *The Waste Land,* Woolf's *Between the Acts*	Central theme: pure but transient vision; the aesthetic or timeless moment Examples: Rimbaud's *illumination,* the German *Augenblick,* imagism, *symbolisme*

Figure 2. Thematic modes.

timeless moments" out of *temps perdu,* as in Proust (AC, 61). "Analogies of revelation," as we shall see, figure importantly in the Fourth Essay, where the thematic mode becomes a part of Frye's definition of specific encyclopaedic forms.

The conception of the cyclical nature of literature enters briefly into the discussion of thematic modes. Irony, Frye says, returns to myth in the fictional modes. There is a parallel movement in the thematic modes where the craftsman of irony completes the cycle by becoming the oracular visionary of myth. As examples of this tendency, Frye points to Yeats's cyclical history, Joyce's Viconian theories, the oracular, internal voice of Rilke, the Promethean persona of Rimbaud, and Nietzsche's notion of the new divinity of man (AC, 62).

One final principle of Frye's discussion of thematic modes relates to what he calls the "fallacy of existential projection." The initial distinction here is another set of dialectical poles. At the fictional end of Frye's continuum, writers in every mode are seen as imposing the same kind of mythical form on their content: the same stories get told and retold, only in different modes. At the other pole is the writer who imitates *dianoia,* but only in the sense of imposing a literary form on whatever his "theme" or conceptual interest happens to be. What Frye in effect is trying to work out here is a relationship between form and content which frees him from the claim that poets directly express *dianoia.* To take this position, he argues, is to risk the fallacy of projecting back upon a thematic work whatever we might discover the poet's actual thought or beliefs to be. This problem can arise also in our response to fictional works. We have already noticed how the element of play functions to control our reaction to ironic comedy. If we are oblivious to the play, however, then we will tend to view this particular mode as an existential projection of something neither comic nor ironic, but of pure savagery or maliciousness. It is natural, Frye observes, for tragic and comic forms "to throw their shadows" into philosophies of fate and providence. But as the critic is concerned only with the literary form imposed on a work, he commits the fallacy of existential projection if he argues back from the poem's *dianoia* to the philosophy which lies beyond it. The *dianoia* actually projected in thematic works like *The Faerie Queene* and *Faust,* for example, is not the personal beliefs of Spenser and Goethe but two forms of "as if" thought, one "a quasi-Platonic philosophy of ideal forms" and the other "a philosophy of genesis and organicism" (AC, 64, 65). And it is the literary mode imposed in these projections, not their truth, which is the business of the literary critic. The form-content dualism here, as old as Horace himself, coupled with the solution to the problem of poetry and belief, which is reminiscent of Coleridge's doctrine of suspension, is one of the clearest expressions in the First Essay of Frye's kinship with the New Critics.

Recurrence in Literary History

As the title of the First Essay suggests, literary modes tend to succeed one another in time. But Frye does not use the expression "historical criticism" conventionally; his concern is not to show that literature is related to particular social and political events but rather to suggest that the five modes correspond to five epochs of both Greco-Roman and Western European writing. He argues that there is a noteworthy correlation, for example, between myth and premedieval works, and between romance and the literature of the Middle Ages; and this correlation is seen as continuing through the high-mimetic development of the Renaissance, the low-mimetic of the nineteenth century, and the ironic of the twentieth. The most explicit indication of the mode-period correlation is in the section on thematic modes where Frye uses the words "mode" and "period" synonymously. He speaks, for example, of the "literary Platonism of the high mimetic *period*." He practically equates the low mimetic with Romanticism, and he refers to the modes as "epochs" and "ages." Frye's point, however, is not merely that litera-ture, on a linear scale of modes, "has steadily moved its center of gravity down the list" (AC, 34) but also that the modal paradigm is cyclical. "Our five modes," he says, "evidently go around in a circle" (AC, 42). In writers like Kafka and Joyce, tragic irony moves toward the emergence once more of the mythical mode. The same kind of movement is seen in the comic modes where works such as science fiction frequently try to imagine "what life would be like on a plane as far above us as we are above savagery. . . . It is thus a mode of romance with a strong inherent tendency to myth" (AC, 49). Historical criticism thus refers to the sequence of modes, the movement being a circular rather than a strictly linear succession.

The metaphor of the cycle (or circle) derives chiefly from Speng-ler, whose theory of the organic growth of cultures attracted Frye early in his career.[7] According to this theory

> cultures behave exactly like organisms: they grow, mature, de-cline, and die; and they all last about the same length of time. . . . The culture to which we belong is a "Western" one, which had its spring in the Middle Ages, its summer in the Renaissance, its autumn in the eighteenth century, and began its winter with the French Revolution. Previously there had been a classical culture which went through the same stages. The heroes of Homer correspond to those of our own age of chivalry; the era of the Greek city-states to our Renaissance, and the last glories of Athens to our age of Bach and Mozart. With Alex-ander the "civilization" phase of world empires begins, for Alex-ander corresponds to our Napoleon.[8]

This view is analogous to Frye's theory of the parallel phases of cultural history. "I have never been very clear about the shape of the history of literature," he says, "apart from the shape of history in gen-eral."[9] Frye acknowledges that Spengler "provided the basis for the conception of modes" outlined in the *Anatomy* (SM, 113), but it is not so much Spengler's cyclic view that is important for him as it is the idea of an organic cultural growth and aging. In fact, while the seasonal metaphor might lead us to call the parallel phases "cycles," it is actually inappropriate, Frye points out, to label Spengler's view of history a cyclical one, even though he sometimes gives the illusion of holding such a view. "Spengler has no theory of cycles at all."[10] Frye prefers to say simply that modes tend to move toward or return to earlier forms; thus he avoids the fatalistic overtones which have frequently been sounded by cyclical theories of history. In an earlier version of the First Essay, he observes that his survey does not "justify us in predicting that the cycle of modes will go around again."[11] But the history of literature does show us that the broad modal patterns Frye describes have occurred, and it is the idea of recurrence he prefers, so long as it is dissociated from suggestions of mechanistic and inevitable repetition. Spengler helped Frye to see that the linear, progressive view of history was dead, that recurrence is to be understood as organic rhythm, and that cultures age rather than decline.[12]

The Purpose of Modal Taxonomy

The principles of the First Essay now before us, we can inquire into the function of Frye's modal taxonomy, beginning with the several claims Frye himself makes. The first is that an understanding of the cyclical nature of modes can help explain the structure of modern literature. "Irony," says Frye, "descends from the low mimetic: it begins in realism and dispassionate observation. But as it does so, it moves steadily towards myth, and [in the tragic mode] dim outlines of sacrificial rituals and dying gods begin to reappear in it" (AC, 42). This manner of argument permits Frye to combine the first and last vertical elements of the modal scale, so that for him it is not inconsistent to speak of "ironic myth" as one of the fictional modes; after all, he claims that we must learn to recombine the modes once we have learned to distinguish them (AC, 50). The point is that if we try to judge (say) *The Altar of the Dead* by the low-mimetic standards of those nineteenth-century realists from whom James learned his craft, then we will have to call his story "a tissue of improbable coincidence, inadequate motivation, and inconclusive resolution." But if we look at it from the perspective of fictional modes "as ironic myth, a story of how the god of one person is the *pharmakos* of another, its structure becomes simple and logical" (AC, 42–43). In other words, the study of modern fiction cannot rely solely upon the critical procedures which were developed to study the realistic novel. And insofar as the novel-centered view of narrative structures has recently become something of a norm (what Frye calls the low-mimetic prejudice), then his claim that the study of all narrative need not follow the canons of nineteenth-century realism is an effort to encourage a more pluralistic set of norms for critical inquiry.[13]

This is related to a second function which the sequence of fictional modes is designed to achieve. It should do something, Frye says, "to give a more flexible meaning to some of our literary terms" (AC, 49). He points out that the words "romantic" and "realistic" are relative terms, with little exactness as descriptive adjectives; and then, by way of illustration, he observes that "if we take the sequence *De Raptu Proserpinae, The Man of Law's Tale, Much Ado About Nothing, Pride and Prejudice, An American Tragedy,* it is clear that each work is 'romantic' compared to its successors and 'realistic' compared to its predecessors" (AC, 49). The implication here is not that the vocabulary of Frye's own scheme is *not* relative or that his own terms can be used descriptively with exactness, but that he despairs of such terms ever being used with exactness. Rather, he is recommending for such terms as "romantic" and "realistic" a wider and less judicial frame of reference than has traditionally been the case. The purpose of this flexibility is to help us distinguish among conventions; and if we can learn to recognize the several modes—so runs Frye's argument—then we will be less likely to impose value judgments on those works which do not conform to our own social norms. The fact that the ironic mode, for example, is less reticent than the low-mimetic about accepting stable social values is no reason for attacking either low-mimetic conventions as prudish or hypocritical, or ironic conventions as unwholesome or elitist. Rather we should be content only to observe "that the low mimetic is one step more heroic than the ironic, and that low mimetic reticence has the effect of making its characters, on the average, more heroic, or at least more dignified, than the characters in ironic fiction" (AC, 50). In short, Frye wants his modes to be descriptively flexible and free from the constrictions he sees in judicial criticism.

In the third place, Frye observes that the theory of modes can be applied to the principles of selection used by writers of fiction. The claim is based upon an interesting illustration about the various uses of ghosts in fiction. In the low-mimetic mode, for example, a writer would be unlikely to represent a ghost because, as Fielding observed, it would tax the reader's credulity. But in the high-mimetic mode he can easily choose to introduce such spirits because the fictional world is on a plane above our own, where they do not violate the canons of plausibility. Similarly, there is no problem in myth, where ghosts and human beings inhabit the same world (AC, 50). Thus the conventions that a writer adopts depend on the particular mode he has selected. And Frye believes his system will help us correlate and thus better understand the relationship between general modes and particular conventions.

A fourth function of modal analysis, according to Frye, is that it helps us to realize both the traditional and the contemporary aspects of a work of art. Whereas the tone of a given work is characterized by a primary mode, the others may also be present. *The Canterbury Tales,* for instance, is chiefly a romance, but Chaucer is also a master of techniques peculiar to the low-mimetic and ironic modes. Through an analysis of the various modes simultaneously present in fictional works—what Frye calls "modal counterpoint"—we can better understand "that the two essential facts about a work of art, that it is contemporary with its own time and that it is contemporary with ours, are not opposed but complementary facts" (AC, 51). Thus the analysis of modes serves to remind us—and this is the point Frye never tires of emphasizing—that the literature of any period is both conventional and traditional, a part of "the total order of words."

The analysis of fictional modes thus illustrates this central principle in Frye's theory: although there are two poles of literature (the mimetic and mythical), the structural principles of narrative remain constant. The social context of a literary form may tend toward realism and accurate description at one pole or toward myth, with no concern for plausibility, at the other; but low-mimetic and ironic formulas are "plausible adaptations" of fictional conventions which are rooted in the earliest of stories (AC, 51). "Displacement" is the term Frye uses to describe the tendency of fictions progressively to move, throughout the sequence of modes, from myth toward verisimilitude. Although this term is meant to describe rather than explain the phenomenon of progressive plausibility, it is another of Frye's important critical principles (about which more later). Frye believes that the analysis of fictional modes provides a kind of inductive proof for his claim that narrative structure is always a conventional, displaced form of an earlier story.[14]

Finally, the analysis of modes represents Frye's plea for a less provincial attitude among critics. "As for the inferences," he says, "which may be made from the [survey of modes], one is clearly that many current critical assumptions have a limited historical context" (AC, 62). The era of the New Criticism he sees as a time of "ironic provincialism, which looks everywhere in literature for complete objectivity, suspension of moral judgements, concentration on pure verbal craftmanship, and similar virtues." And he implies that there are critics who use as their norm for interpreting all literature the principles peculiar to a given mode; all of this leads to the conclusion "that no set of critical standards derived from only one mode can ever assimilate the whole truth about poetry" (AC, 62).

Modal Theory and Literary History

Frye argues that "there is a place for classification in criticism, as in any other discipline" (AC, 29). His classification of modes, like the other taxonomies developed in the *Anatomy,* is based on the assumption that in order to talk sensibly about literary texts we need a systematic ordering of the properties they share with each other. In this respect, his taxonomies represent an approach to the study of literature which has long been fundamental to criticism. Yet among the various attempts to classify heroes and character types, on the one hand, and the relationship of the poet to his audience, on the other, Frye's effort is unique. The uniqueness results from his providing not simply a set of synchronic distinctions about heroic powers of action but also a diachronic interpretation of these powers. In other words, Frye's theory of modes—as the title of the First Essay suggests—is also a theory of literary history.

The word "mode," however, is not an unequivocal term in contemporary criticism, having come to signify so much in some cases as to signify almost nothing. Allan Rodway, drawing ostensibly upon Frye's First Essay to develop his own theory of modes, concludes finally that a "work's mode . . . is whatever it seems to be in its most general aspect." "[It is] largely a matter of attitude or tone rather than style or form of writing." Although Rodway finds Frye's modal schema to be "useful as well as beautiful" and almost successful, his own imprecise definition of "mode" is quite different from Frye's.[15] Because Frye employs several criteria to distinguish each of his five modes, his use of the term, though multireferential, is more specific. His usage, moreover, depends upon the original meaning of the word: the *measure* is man, whether "man" is taken fictionally as the hero or thematically as the poet. Such usage, as Angus Fletcher reminds us, is appropriate, "because in each of the five [modes] the hero is a protagonist with a given strength relative to his world, and as such each hero—whether mythic, romantic, high mimetic, low mimetic, or ironic—is a *modulor* for verbal architectonics; man is the measure, the *modus* of myth."[16] Frye's own claims about the value of modal criticism are borne out by the uses which others have made of the First Essay. These can be separated into three general, though not unrelated. areas: the theoretical, the practical, and the historical.

Among contemporary critics, Robert Scholes has devoted the most attention to Frye's modal criticism. His earliest treatment of the topic is in *The Nature of Narrative,* and in several later works he expands his analysis of modes into a theory of literary types which is similar to Frye's.[17] Both critics provide a framework for clarifying literary simi-

larities and differences; both are able to discover a limited number of
ideal literary types; both develop a theory with a diachronic and a
synchronic thrust; both recognize the value of organizing their categories schematically. The chief difference between the two theories is the
principle used to differentiate the various modes. For Frye, the principle is the hero's power of action (for fictional works) and the poet's
attitude toward his audience (for thematic works). Scholes distinguishes
his modes, however, on the basis of the differing relationships between
the fictional and the external worlds. "All fictional works," he says, "are
reducible to three primary shades. These primary modes of fiction are
themselves based on three possible relations between any fictional
world and the world of experience. A fictional world can be better than
the world of experience, worse than it, or equal to it. These fictional
worlds imply attitudes we have learned to call romantic, satirical, and
realistic."[18]

Scholes refines this simple scheme, producing finally a spectrum of
seven fictional possibilities: satire, picaresque, comedy, history, senti-
ment, tragedy, and romance. Although he refers to these ideal types as
"forms," he is careful to point out that they do not refer "to any form
of story customarily associated with the term." They refer rather to the
ethical quality or value of the fictional world. "Our 'real' world," he
says, "(which we live in but never understand) is ethically neutral. Fictional worlds, on the other hand, are charged with values. They offer
us a perspective on our own situation, so that by trying to place them
[by using a theory of modes] we are engaged in seeking our own
position." Thus for Scholes the difference in quality or value between
the real world and fictional representations is what distinguishes the
modes in his synchronic chart of theoretical literary types. But his
starting point is quite different from the *basic* principles underlying
Frye's modal taxonomy, where the relative power of the hero is mea-
sured not by the real world but by his own fiction. In addition to Frye,
Auerbach looms large behind Scholes's theory of modes, for the variations in "the representation of reality" form his modal differentiae.
Nonetheless, he depends heavily on the First Essay, which, along with
the Fourth, he sees as having provided "a major contribution to one of
the most interesting critical enterprises in recent years—the attempt to
organize a system of narrative genres."[19]

While acknowledging his debt to Frye's system (one that rings
"deeply true in its essence"), Scholes views the system as "being plainly
wrong in much of its substance." He finds Frye's classification of heroic
powers of action to be unsystematic and internally inconsistent.[20] The
thrust of his critique, however, is directed not so much at what Frye's
theory contains as at what it doesn't, and he considers his own theory,

the details of which are omitted here, to be superior mainly because "it is more aware of specific and historical generic considerations."[21] He means that Frye's modal criticism remains at too high a level of generality, that Frye is reluctant to discuss the historical relationships of specific literary types, and that his theory of genres (Fourth Essay) is not well enough integrated with his theory of modes. In an effort to improve on Frye's scheme, Scholes proposes that the act of critical reading should pass *from* modal criticism (an awareness of the ideal types, essentially a deductive procedure) *through* generic criticism (an inductive organization of the empirical phenomena which make the ideal types possible) *to,* finally, a criticism which accounts for the unique qualities of the individual work.

Although Scholes speaks of modal criticism as "heady, conceptual wheeling and dealing," he is firmly convinced of its value. In fact, the claims he makes for his modal scheme are not unlike Frye's own. It "can help to tell us where we are and to explain how we got there. In doing so, it should serve to make us more sympathetic and open to the varieties of fiction, old and new. It can also serve us pedagogically as a way of teaching literary history as a living and ongoing process, and as a way of putting historical learning in the service of interpretation. . . . No student has finished a proper initiation into a generic poetics of fiction until he has experienced the gap between generic knowledge and modal ideas, and has some notions of his own about how to re-shape modal theory to close that disturbing space."[22]

Taking issue with Frye's theory of modes, Tzvetan Todorov proposes that we distinguish between historical genres (those which "result from an observation of literary reality") and theoretical genres (those which result "from a deduction of a theoretical order"). The latter are based on an abstract hypothesis which assumes one element of literary works to be fundamental; this element then becomes the basis for dif-ferentiating among theoretical genres. For Todorov, Frye's modes are abstract, theoretical genres and thus not altogether satisfactory; like Scholes, Todorov believes that an adequate modal and generic theory must give more emphasis than Frye's does to the practical, empirical order, that it should work back and forth between the theoretical and the historical. "The genres we deduce from the theory," says Todorov, "must be verified by reference to the texts. . . . [and] the genres which we encounter in literary history must be subject to the explanation of a coherent theory."[23]

Frye's theory of modes may not meet the requirements for an ideal theory of literary types: after all, the First Essay is restricted to one kind of convention.[24] But to suggest that he gives little attention to the empirical order is inconceivable. Frye says he has been "rigorously selective in examples and illustrations" (AC, 29), but even so, his grasp of literary history is immense. On the other hand, Frye *has* proceeded deductively. All that need be acknowledged here is that the *bases* of his classification of fictional modes do constitute important elements in literary works. Christine Brooke-Rose argues that Todorov's criticism is unjustified because Frye's theory is a theory of historical rather than theoretical modes.[25] Still, it is clear that Frye does work back and forth between the historical and the theoretical. Bruce Bashford is closer to the truth in saying that the First Essay "is primarily a formal history in that, beginning with certain formal features of literature, it works out the permutations of their various components, and then looks at the empirical history of literature to see how the resultant categories actually turn up."[26] Frye's modes exist at a high level of generality, and they may come to be refined as we learn more about literary history. But a knowledge of ideal types, whether described as modal or generic or pregeneric, is, as E.D. Hirsch convincingly argued, essential to interpretation. Types serve both a constitutive and a heuristic function.[27] They have the power to determine how we understand the meaning of a text by fulfilling our expectations and helping us to perceive individual literary traits as components of whole works. They help to *establish* meaning on the one hand and to *discover* it on the other.

The test of Frye's theory of modes is that it has had practical consequences for what he calls "specific criticism" (AC, vii)—the analysis and interpretation of individual literary works. Scores of critics have been able to use his modal and generic distinctions in their practical criticism. The most fully developed application is in Robert Foulke and Paul Smith's *An Anatomy of Literature,* an anthology which takes its principles of organization directly from Frye.[28] Like Frye, they conceive of modes in analytic and historical (rather than in descriptive or structural) terms:

> We will define the term *mode* as a conventional assumption about the nature and limits of a central character's power of action. The definition implies something like an agreement between the author's preliminary ideas and the reader's consequent expectations of a fictional world. When we read a literary work and respond to its mode, we attempt to reconstruct the conditions or terms under which such a concept of action is possible. We become part of that audience contemporary with the writer to the extent that we understand and for the moment assent to his assumptions about what men can do or think that they can do. Partly because these assumptions are first principles and partly because they are so deeply embedded in the historical ground on

which the work rests, they are like those unspoken beliefs the author can count on his audience knowing and to which he need do no more than allude—perhaps the surest indication of their cultural importance.[29]

Foulke and Smith reduce Frye's five modes to four: the romantic (Frye's mythic and romantic combined), the formal (Frye's high-mimetic), the natural (Frye's low-mimetic), and the ironic. Their description of each of the modes is a simplified version of Frye's complex analysis, yet their account of the hero's power of action remains essentially the same as his. They do add, however, that the definition of a mode should include, in addition to the central character's power of action, "his relationship to society and nature, and the underlying concepts or models that give shape and coherence to his world."[30]

Unlike Scholes and Todorov, who seek a correlation between Frye's modal and generic theories, Foulke and Smith concentrate on the affinities between the modes and Frye's pregeneric narrative patterns (romance, comedy, tragedy, and irony). Moreover, they understand modal criticism, as Frye does, both synchronically and diachronically. Altogether, their discussion of literary modes is the most complete account to date of the principles of Frye's First Essay. One of Scholes's complaints about Frye's system is, as indicated above, that it remains too distant from the intractable realities of specific literary works and their historical relationships. While the complaint against Frye may remain (even though it lies outside his purpose), Foulke and Smith do show how Frye's modal categories can be used practically. In the "General Introduction" of *An Anatomy of Literature,* in the introductory essays to each of the four sections of the book, and in their analyses of eight separate works, they illustrate how a modal awareness can help to organize some of our intuitions about literature and clarify the conceptions of action, society, and nature we encounter in literary works. Foulke and Smith argue, finally, that "the most effective use we can make of the concept of mode is to think of it as representing those general historical presuppositions that modify or shape narrative patterns to the tastes of a particular period."[31] They emphasize, even more strongly than Frye, the historical character of the sequence of modes, which brings us to the third use of modal criticism—what Scholes refers to as "a way of teaching literary history" and "a way of putting historical learning in the service of interpretation."[32]

Literary history, Foulke and Smith remind us, has two principal meanings: (1) literature in history, a centrifugal concept relating to external history—temporal and spatial contexts in which literary works are written; and (2) history in literature, a centripetal concept relating to internal history—the dynamic and evolutionary aspects of literature itself. Literature in *history* "directs our attention outward from the work to the world that produced it, and we consider such questions as the influence of Coleridge on Wordsworth or of Elizabethan theatrical conventions on Shakespeare"; whereas history in *literature* directs our attention "through periods of time and usually within the limits of some literary form or genre; then we entertain such problems as the development of the pastoral ode or the novel or 'nature poetry.' " Foulke and Smith argue that an awareness of literary modes can help us see the intricate relationship between literature in history and history in literature: "The modes fix our attention on the intersection of two lines of critical interest, one outward to the history that surrounds literature and one inward to the history of literature itself. That point of intersection is, of course, the literary work, where we witness the effects of its historical environment and its modal heredity."[33]

Foulke and Smith are aware, just as Frye is, of the dangers of using the modal scheme too rigidly, thereby imposing on literature an artificial history. They are aware also that the modes can be understood synchronically: they "may transcend, or in some way be independent of, history."[34] Nevertheless, it is what they have learned from the theory of literary history in the First Essay which causes them to emphasize the affinities among the four modes, the four narrative patterns, and the kinds of works characteristic of the major periods of English literary history: the romantic mode and the epics and narrative poems of the medieval period, the formal mode and the tragic dramas of the Renaissance, the natural mode and the comic novels and dramas of the eighteenth and nineteenth centuries, and the ironic mode and the fiction and drama of the modern age.

Todorov claims, as we have seen, that the system of the First Essay is composed of theoretical rather than historical modes. The number of modes—five in Frye's case—are fixed, he says, not because Frye has observed them but because the principles of his system impose that number.[35] But this is to overstate the case. Frye's many illustrations indicate that in his inductive survey of literature he has in fact observed the modes. And the attention he devotes in the First Essay to displacement and to the historical sequence of modes does not support Todorov's neat disjunction between theoretical and historical categories. Foulke and Smith have a more balanced understanding of Frye's modal theory and its application, because they recognize both the diachronic and the synchronic thrusts of the First Essay. Angus Fletcher, who has written the most illuminating account of Frye's theory of history, recognizes this too. "Theoretical networks like the *Anatomy*," he remarks, "are always called 'antihistorical,' since they openly resist the uncontrolled evolution of historically changing cityscape, on which they impose a simpler, reductive, more efficient system of intercommunication." But Fletcher argues in general that the *Anatomy* does present an intelligible view of history and in particular that the theory of the First Essay is not "too schematic or rigid to allow for actual human history." He concludes that Frye's theory of modes is "no less a type of history for combining induction and deduction,"[36] even though the deductive framework of Frye's modes, in his view, emerges as a utopian informing pattern, creating what Frye calls that "final unification of material which is the mark of a completely realized history" (CL, 155).

Fletcher alludes several times to various critics—they remain unnamed—who claim that Frye's modal system denies "the fluid texture of history." His rebuttal is twofold. On the one hand, he claims that the First Essay

> can be described as a prolegomena to a more meticulous periodization of literary history, and it remains deliberately rough, without giving up the hope that each mimetic phase could be distinguished and analyzed in great detail. The theocentric basis of medieval thought could be closely handled, to test its bearing on romance; the courtly cult of the prince in the Renaissance could be related to the methods of high mimetic; the rationalism of modern science to the canons of low mimetic; and so on, through much subtler inquiries than these. In principle there is no reason why Essay I could not form the basis for a freely conducted practical investigation of historical fact.[37]

In other words, the deductive foundations of Frye's view of literary history can be tested, revised, and completed by a series of inquiries into historical fact. This is his immediate answer to the objection that Frye is not writing a properly detached, inductive literary history.

On the other hand, Fletcher argues that a purely inductive history is impossible anyway and that by using a metahistorical plot to develop his view of the literary past Frye is simply engaging in a procedure followed by any other historian. To be sure, some historians are more universalizing and theoretical than others. But the notion that there is a purely inductive history, Fletcher suggests, is a chimera. Frye, then, is no less a historian for engaging in speculative or philosophical historiography, the kind of history where, in the words of Isaiah Berlin, "the pattern, and it alone, brings into being and causes to pass away and confers purpose, that is to say, value and meaning, on all there is. To understand is to perceive patterns."[38] Frye has "always suffered from acute historical consciousness," according to William Rueckert; he has "freed himself from history in order that he might, from within and by

means of the timeless coordinates of his system, reenter history, properly, powerfully equipped to study it, cope with it, move around in it,
and protect himself from being so mercilessly victimized by it."[39] History, for Frye, is the direct verbal imitation of *praxis*, the world of
events, just as philosophy and science are the primary or direct verbal
imitations of *theoria*, the world of images and ideas. History, therefore,
is set over against poetry, which is the secondary imitation of action
(*mythos*) and of thought (*dianoia*). As Frye says, "the historical is the
opposite of the mythical."[40] This is true, however, only as it relates to
what Frye calls the "historian proper," that is, the historian who "works
inductively, collecting his facts and trying to avoid any informing patterns except those that he sees, or is honestly convinced he sees, in the
facts themselves" (FI, 54). Frye's historical consciousness has been influenced not so much by the historians proper as by the metahistorians,
those whose accounts of human action are carried along by the comprehensive mythical patterns they impose upon their material. When
such patterns occur, the distance between the historical and the poetic
tends to collapse. Frye observes that "there are romantic historical
myths based on a quest or pilgrimage to a City of God or a classless
society; there are comic historical myths of progress through evolution
or revolution; there are tragic myths of decline and fall, like the works
of Gibbon and Spengler; there are ironic myths of recurrence or casual
catastrophe" (FI, 54). The study of such metahistorical patterns becomes especially appropriate for the literary critic because the informing principles behind them are akin to those of poetry and myth. This
is why Spengler has been a formative influence on Frye's thought. "If
The Decline of the West were nothing else," he says, "it would still be one
of the world's great Romantic poems" (SM, 187). The reason for Spengler's appeal, then, is the poetic imagery upon which his vision of history
is constructed. Frye is drawn toward the work of Toynbee and Vico for
the same reason. Metahistorians such as Spengler and Vico are important for him not simply because he can read their expansive narrative
patterns in the same way that he reads the plots of an epic, novel, or
historical romance, thereby demonstrating the resemblance between
the metahistorical and the poetic universes. They are important also
because of the ways in which they enter and inform his own critical
theory.

Yet the difference between the inductive "historian proper" and
the deductive metahistorian is a distinction which Fletcher, drawing on
contemporary historiographers, suggests is untenable. Similarly, Hayden White observes that critics of historiography as a discipline have
gone "so far as to argue that historical accounts are *nothing but* interpretations, in the establishment of the events that make up the chronicle of

the narrative no less than in assessments of the meaning or significance of those events for the understanding of the historical process in general." White, himself a historian, believes that although Frye wants to support the distinction between proper history and metahistory, "on his own analysis of the structures of prose fictions, he must be prepared to grant that there is a mythic element in 'proper history' by which the structures and processes depicted in its narratives are endowed with meanings of a specifically fictive kind." White, in fact, finds Frye's ideas about pregeneric plot structures (romance, comedy, tragedy, and satire) useful in "identifying the specifically 'fictive' element in historical accounts of the world."[41]

The diachronic thrust of the First Essay appears to have raised more questions than the synchronic: Todorov claims that Frye's modes are theoretical, not historical, and Fletcher refers to those who believe the First Essay to be historically naive. Some of the force is taken from these objections, however, not only by those critics, such as Foulke and Smith, who have found Frye's modal scheme to be genuinely useful but also by those, such as Fletcher, who believe that the diachronic elements in the First Essay rest firmly in a tradition of interpretation championed by many historiographers. With Hayden White we come full circle, for here is a historian who finds in a literary critic a model for analyzing not literary history but historical interpretations in general. White's essay offers an excellent example of the uses to which others have put Frye's ideas and of the ways thinkers continue to engage him in dialogue—a dialogue which has moved far beyond the ironic provincialism Frye saw in the criticism of the 1940s and 1950s.

Frye's view of history, literary and otherwise, is an integral part of his continuous vision of culture, which is a vision that does not make radical distinctions among the products of culture. What most attracts Frye are the metaphors which historians project upon the flux of human events in order to make sense of them. When such metaphors are absent, as in, say, Bonamy Dobrée's history of eighteenth-century British literature, the historian's account suffers. Dobrée covers the subject (a revealing metaphor itself), but what one misses in his book, Frye says, is "that final unification of material which is the mark of the completely realized history in whatever field" (CL, 155). Such final unification, however, may frequently take forms which are unacceptable because deterministic or one-sided. Thus just as Frye rejects progressive histories of literature, which manifest themselves in the cult of the original, so he rejects those attitudes toward history based solely upon metaphors of growth-toward-perfection. At the other extreme, he has little use for ironic views of history, especially the deterministic one he has sometimes described as the Great Western Butterslide: "the doctrine of a coordinated synthesis in medieval culture giving place, at the Renaissance, to a splitting and specialized schizophrenia which has got steadily worse until it has finally landed us all in that Pretty Pass in which we are today" (CL, 132).

Frye's own view of history is founded upon an organic and rhythmic metaphor of cultural aging. Its philosophical foundation, like that of Spengler's own analogical schema, is Romantic, which means that the realities of time, life, and history are to be discovered "by feeling, intuition, imaginative insight, and, above all, by symbolism" (SM, 180). But its ultimate source is Blake, who believed that history, like daily sense experience, has to be ordered by the imagination. For Blake, as well as for Frye, "history is imaginative material to be synthesized into form."[42] The First Essay of the *Anatomy* is one such formal synthesis of imaginative material.

Pluralism and the Question of Frye's Aristotelian Debt

Attacks on critical provincialism, as well as the claim that an adequate criticism must employ a variety of principles, appear throughout Frye's work. Although critical pluralism makes the same kind of claim, Frye's status as a pluralist is more apparent than real. The implication of saying "that no set of critical standards derived from only one mode can ever assimilate the whole truth about poetry" (AC, 62) is that a number of different sets of standards might achieve such a goal. But the underlying assumptions in this passage, partially betrayed by the word "assimilate," are those of a critical syncretist, not a pluralist. Syncretism implies that there are several partially valid critical systems and that the best elements from each approach can be welded into a meta-criticism able to deal adequately with any work. The syncretist, unlike the pluralist, does not hold that the critical method one uses depends upon the kind of question asked. Frye's syncretic tendency is seen clearly in a passage from the end of the First Essay:

> Just as catharsis is the central conception of the Aristotelian approach to literature, so ecstasis or absorption is the central conception of the Longinian approach. This is a state of identification in which the reader, the poem, and sometimes, at least ideally, the poet also, are involved. We say reader, because the Longinian conception is primarily that of a thematic or individualized response: it is more useful for lyrics, just as the Aristotelian one is more useful for plays. Sometimes, however, the normal categories of approach are not the right ones. In *Hamlet,* as Mr. Eliot has shown, the amount of emotion generated by the hero is too great for its objects; but surely the correct conclusion

to draw from this fine insight is that *Hamlet* is best approached as a tragedy of *Angst* or of melancholy as a state in itself, rather than purely as an Aristotelian imitation of an action. On the other hand, the lack of emotional involvement in *Lycidas* has been thought by some, including Johnson, to be a failure in that poem, but surely the correct conclusion is that *Lycidas,* like *Samson Agonistes,* should be read in terms of catharsis with all passion spent. (AC, 67)

What Frye is saying is that some works are best approached by using the assumptions and method of Aristotle, and some by using those of Longinus. Frye extends the approaches of these critics to represent the two chief views which run throughout the history of criticism (AC, 66), and what he hopes to do by assimilating them is to erect an inclusive system for interpreting all literature: whatever poems cannot be accounted for by the Aristotelian approach are adequately handled by the Longinian. The critical pluralist, however, maintains that one's approach depends upon the kind of problem he is seeking to solve. If one wants to analyze the plot of *Hamlet,* for example, then the *Poetics,* the pluralist would argue, provides a useful method for doing so. But if one wants to isolate the peculiar qualitative mood of the play, then perhaps the principles of Longinus's essay can be of assistance. In other words, the pluralist would claim, disregarding altogether the question of whether Eliot's judgment of *Hamlet* is right, that the play is not "best approached" at all, and that the correct conclusion to be drawn from both Eliot's and Johnson's judgments can be determined only in relation to the questions they are asking.

The argument for a pluralism of critical methods has been best articulated by the Chicago Aristotelians, particularly R.S. Crane, whose observations about critical method lead him to conclude that no one critical theory "can be completely subsumptive of the truth about literature."[43] Crane argues that there are many valid sets of methodological principles, each of which has its own powers and limitations; and that critical methods themselves are "immune to theoretical questioning," since a critic's choice of a subject matter and his method of reasoning are, more than anything else, practical decisions, stemming from his own interests and from the kinds of problems he wants to solve. The pluralistic critic holds, therefore, that the principles and methods of critical discourse "are tools of inquiry and interpretation rather than formulations about the 'real' nature of things."[44] Perhaps the clearest statement of Crane's position is in *The Languages of Criticism and the Structure of Poetry* where he proposes as his major premise that literary criticism is "a collection of distinct and more or less incommensurable 'frameworks' or 'languages,' within any one of which a question like poetic structure necessarily takes on different meaning and receives a different kind of answer from the meaning it has and the answer it is properly given in any of the rival critical languages in which it is discussed."[45] Crane and Frye are in agreement, then, that no one approach can answer all critical questions, but they differ in the directions they move after having made this assumption. Frye wants an interpenetration of critical approaches. Crane, using Aristotelian principles, wants sharply to separate critical approaches on the basis of what each of them can specifically do.

Frye has frequently been labeled an Aristotelian. Many of his readers have seen him as a modern-day Aristotle, systematically laying out a new *Poetics*. As already indicated, the presence of Aristotle is felt throughout the First Essay. Frye calls upon Aristotle's distinction between *spoudaios* and *phaulos* to provide the basis for his classification of fictional modes. Aristotle's *mythos, ethos,* and *dianoia* are used to help differentiate between fictional and thematic modes. Frye draws upon catharsis, which he refers to as Aristotle's "central conception" (AC, 66), to help define the tragic fictional modes. The First Essay in fact is replete with references and allusions to the *Poetics* (see AC, 34, 40, 41, 44, 65–67). But the omnipresence of Aristotle does not represent as significant a debt as it may at first seem; for neither does Frye draw upon the philosophic method of the *Poetics,* nor are the problems he confronts Aristotelian. The real influence of the *Poetics* is one of critical vocabulary. Yet even this influence may be misleading unless we realize not only that a word like *dianoia* functions one way in the *Poetics* and another way in the *Anatomy* but also that most of the language itself which Frye has appropriated from Aristotle has a *meaning* different from the original. The following examples will illustrate the differences.

The first, found in the Polemical Introduction, raises the question of general method. Frye says that "a theory of criticism whose principles apply to the whole of literature and account for every valid type of critical procedure is what I think Aristotle meant by poetics" (AC, 14). It is not at all clear, however, that Aristotle is seeking to arrive at principles which "apply to the whole of literature." Only some works of art, he says in chapter 1 of the *Poetics,* "happen to be imitations." And since Aristotle nowhere attempts to define *all* art or even *all* literature, it would be more accurate to say that the principles in the *Poetics* are specific principles: they apply to Aristotle's inductive study of literary kinds. He is concerned with knowledge not about "poetry" in general but about poetic species. Nor is it clear that the *Poetics* is an attempt to account for "every valid type of critical procedure." Such a claim overlooks the crucial principle in Aristotle's work of a sharp division among the sciences; so that "poetics" deals only with questions which have to do with the making or construction of literary works. This means that for Aristotle other valid types of critical procedure, which would be used to solve different literary problems, are reserved for other disciplines.[46]

A second illustration comes from Frye's use of the Aristotelian distinction relating to character, the distinction between *spoudaios* and *phaulos*. Whereas in Aristotle these words refer specifically to an ethical quality of the object imitated, indicating whether the agent is morally better or worse than ordinary man, in Frye the terms are used to refer quite generally to the relationship of a character to other men and to his environment. The distinction which serves as the basis of Aristotle's usage all but disappears in Frye, who, recognizing the *figurative* meaning of the two words (AC, 33), changes their reference from a moral application to one of natural law.

A third example is Frye's use of the word "catharsis," one of the central concepts he employs to differentiate tragic modes on the basis of their effects. His use of the word to define the high-mimetic mode appears closely to approximate the *meaning* which the term has in the *Poetics,* though, again, the function of the word in the two discourses is not at all similar. The main point of difference is that Frye believes the principles of catharsis can be applied to fictional forms other than tragedy, such as comedy and satire. Thus, whereas in Aristotle the word stands for the quality or power (*dynamis*) peculiar to a given poetic species, in Frye it comes to mean "emotional or intellectual detachment" characteristic of literary kinds in general (AC, 66).

Frye's debt to the *Poetics,* as we shall continue to see in what follows, is more apparent than real. The Aristotelian influence is not one of doctrine, still less of method. It is primarily one of terminology, but even here, despite the continuing deference to Aristotle, most of the resemblances are superficial.[47] To anticipate a part of my later argument, the more important figure looming behind *Anatomy of Criticism* is Plato, both his philosophical idealism and his analogical method. If Plato is not the organizing force behind the First Essay, at least his treatment of art, in Frye's view, is completely consistent with a theory of modes, for it was Plato who saw literature as myth (in the *Phaedrus*), as romance (in the *Ion*), as high mimesis (in the *Symposium*), as low mimesis (in the *Republic*), and as irony (in the *Cratylus*) (AC, 65).

2

Theory of Symbols

Ethical Criticism: The Contexts of Literary Symbols

In Part I of *The Critical Path,* where Frye gives an account of his own intellectual history in moving from the study of Blake to writing *Anatomy of Criticism,* he remarks that his theory of literature was developed from an attempt to answer two questions: What is the total subject of study of which criticism forms a part, and how do we arrive at poetic meaning? (CP, 14–15). The Second Essay, "Ethical Criticism: Theory of Symbols," addresses itself to the latter question. Frye's starting point is to admit the principle of "polysemous" meaning, a version of Dante's fourfold system of interpretation. This principle can be called an "established fact," he says, because of the "simultaneous development of several different schools of modern criticism, each making a distinctive choice of symbols in its analysis" (AC, 72). Once the principle is granted, there are two alternatives: "We can either stop with a purely relative and pluralistic position, or we can go on to consider the possibility that there is a finite number of valid critical methods, and that they can all be contained in a single theory."[1]

Frye develops his argument by first placing the issue of meaning in a broader context:

> The meaning of a literary work forms a part of a larger whole. In the previous essay we saw that meaning or *dianoia* was one of three elements, the other two being *mythos* or narrative and *ethos* or characterization. It is better to think, therefore, not simply of a sequence of meanings, but of a sequence of contexts or relationships in which the whole work of literary art can be placed, each context having its characteristic *mythos* and *ethos* as well as its *dianoia* or meaning. (AC, 73)

Context, then, rather than meaning becomes the organizing principle; and the term Frye uses for the contextual relationships of literature is "phases," which becomes the organizing category for the taxonomy of the Second Essay.

The word "ethical" in the title of this essay obviously does not derive from the meanings which *ethos* had in the First Essay: Frye does not intend to expand the analysis of characterization found there. Nor is he concerned with something else "ethical" might imply, judicial evaluations or the moral element of literature. The word refers rather to the connection between art and life which makes literature a liberal yet disinterested ethical instrument. Ethical criticism, Frye says in the Polemical Introduction, refers to a "consciousness of the presence of society. . . . [It] deals with art as a communication from the past to the present, and is based on the conception of the total and simultaneous possession of past culture" (AC, 24). It is the archetype, as we shall see in chapter 3, which provides the connection between the past and the present. Unlike the other essays in the *Anatomy,* Frye's theory of symbols is directed toward an analysis of *criticism.* "Phases" are contexts within which literature has been and can be interpreted: they are primarily, though not exclusively, meant to describe critical procedures rather than literary types, which is to say that the phases represent methods of analyzing symbolic meaning. Frye's aim is to discover the various levels of symbolic meaning and to combine them into a comprehensive theory.

"Symbol" is the first of three basic categories Frye uses to differentiate the five phases. Here we encounter once again the breadth of reference and unconventional usage which many of Frye's terms have, for in the Second Essay symbol is used to mean "any unit of any literary structure that can be isolated for critical attention" (AC, 71). This includes everything from the letters a writer uses to spell his words to the poem itself as a symbol reflecting the entire poetic universe. This broad definition permits Frye to associate the appropriate kind of symbolism with each phase, and thereby to define the phase at the highest level of generality. The symbol used as a sign results in the descriptive phase; as motif, in the literal phase; as image, in the formal phase; as archetype, in the mythical phase; and as monad, in the anagogic phase.

The other primary categories which underlie Frye's definition of the phases are narrative (or *mythos*) and meaning (or *dianoia*). These terms also have a wide range of reference, much wider even than in the First Essay. One can only indicate the general associations they have in Frye's usage. *Narrative* is associated with rhythm, movement, recurrence, event, and ritual. *Meaning* is associated with pattern, structure, stasis, precept, and dream. The meaning of "narrative" and the meaning of "meaning," then, always change according to the context of Frye's discussion. The central role which this pair of terms comes to assume in the *Anatomy,* as well as in Frye's other work, cannot be overemphasized.

The correlation which Frye makes between the five phases and their respective symbols, narratives, and meanings, as well as the relation among the phases and several other categories, is set down, as a kind of visual shorthand for the discussion which follows, in Figure 3.

The Taxonomy of Symbolism

The Literal and Descriptive Phases The first two of Frye's contexts, the literal and descriptive phases, are linked together in his discussion because, unlike the other three phases, they are defined in relation to each other. The method is one of dichotomous division whereby Frye sets up a series of opposing terms within the triadic framework (symbol-narrative-meaning), outlined above. The opposing sets of categories are then used to define, or give content to, the terms "literal" and "descriptive."

The opposing terms of the first category (symbol) are motif and sign, which represent the kinds of signification which the literal and descriptive phases respectively embody. These two words are defined in turn by another series of opposing qualities. When the symbol is a sign, the movement of reference is centrifugal, as in descriptive or assertive works; and when the symbol is a motif, the movement is centripetal, as in imaginative, or in what Frye calls "hypothetical" works. Similarly, in the former case, where allegiance is to the reality principle, value is instrumental and priority is given to instruction; and in the latter, where allegiance is to the pleasure principle, value is final and priority is given to delight.

Underlying Frye's distinction between the "narrative" and "meaning" poles of the dichotomy is an assumption, fundamental to other parts of *Anatomy of Criticism,* that all art possesses both a temporal and a spatial dimension. Frye refers to the temporal or narrative dimension of the literal phase as rhythm, and the narrative movement of the descriptive phase is the relation which the order of words has to external reality. Similarly, when the spatial aspect is more important in our experience of a work, we tend to view it statically as an integrated unit, or to use Frye's chief metaphors, as pattern or structure. Thus he is led to describe a poem's meaning in the literal phase as "its pattern or integrity as a verbal structure. Its words cannot be separated and attached to sign-values: all possible sign-values of a word are absorbed into a complexity of verbal relationships." On the other hand, a poem's meaning in the descriptive phase is "the relation of its pattern to a body of assertive propositions, and the conception of symbolism involved is the one which literature has in common, not with the arts, but with other structures in words" (AC, 78).

As indicated in Figure 3, each of the phases of symbolism has an

affinity to both a certain kind of literature and a typical critical procedure. This relation for the descriptive and literal phases of *literature* can
be represented by a continuum running from documentary naturalism
at one pole to *symbolisme* and "pure" poetry at the other. Although
every work of literature is characterized by both these phases of symbolism, there can be an infinite number of variations along the descrip-
tive-literal axis, since a given work tends to be influenced more deeply
by one phase than the other. Thus when the descriptive phase predominates, the narrative of literature tends toward realism, and its
meaning toward the didactic or descriptive. The limits, at this end of
the continuum, would be represented by such writers as Zola and
Dreiser, whose work "goes about as far as a representation of life, to be
judged by its accuracy of description rather than by its integrity as a
structure of words, as it could go and still remain literature" (AC, 80).
At the other end, as a complement to naturalism, is the tradition of
writers like Mallarmé, Rimbaud, Rilke, Pound, and Eliot. Here the
emphasis is on the literal phase of meaning: literature becomes a "centripetal verbal pattern, in which elements of direct or verifiable statement are subordinated to the integrity of that pattern" (AC, 80). Criticism, says Frye, was able to achieve an acceptable theory of literal
meaning only after the development of *symbolisme* (AC, 80).

In a similar fashion, the literal and descriptive phases are reflected
in two chief types of *criticism*. Related to the descriptive aspect of a
symbol, on the one hand, are the various kinds of documentary criticism which deal with sources, historical transmission, the history of
ideas, and the like. Such approaches assume that a poem is a verbal
document whose "imaginative hypothesis" can be made explicit by assertive or propositional language. A literal criticism, on the other hand,
will find in poetry "a subtle and elusive verbal pattern" that neither
leads to nor permits simple assertive statements or prose paraphrases.
As Frye's language here suggests, this tendency is represented by New
Criticism, an approach which is based

> on the conception of a poem as literally a poem. It studies the
> symbolism of a poem as an ambiguous structure of interlocking
> motifs; it sees the poetic pattern of meaning as a self-contained
> "texture," and it thinks of the external relations of a poem as
> being with the other arts, to be approached only with the Hora-
> tian warning of *favete linguis,* and not with the historical or the
> didactic. The word texture, with its overtones of a complicated
> surface, is the most expressive one for this approach.[2]

Frye's indebtedness to the terms and distinctions of contemporary
poetics is obvious here. In fact, the principal assumption underlying his

	LITERAL	DESCRIPTIVE	FORMAL	MYTHICAL	ANAGOGIC
TYPE OF SYMBOL	Motif	Sign	Image	Archetype	Monad
NARRATIVE (*MYTHOS*)	Rhythm or movement of words; flow of particular sounds	Relation of order of words to life; imitations of real events	Typical event or example Shaping principle	Ritual: recurrent act of symbolic communication	Total ritual of man, or unlimited social action
MEANING (*DIANOIA*)	Pattern or structural unity; ambiguous and complex verbal pattern	Relation of pattern to assertive propositions; imitation of objects or propositions	Typical precept Containing principle	Dream: conflict of desire and reality	Total dream of man, or unlimited human desire
RELATED KIND OF ART	*Symbolisme*	Realism and naturalism	Neoclassical art	Primitive and popular writing	Scripture, apocalyptic revelation
RELATED KIND OF CRITICISM	"Textural" or New Criticism	Historical and documentary criticism	Commentary or interpretation	Archetypal criticism (convention and genre)	Anagogic criticism (connected with religion)
MEDIEVAL LEVEL		Literal or historical	Allegorical	Moral or tropical	Anagogic
PARALLEL MODE	Thematic irony	Low mimesis	High mimesis	Romance	Myth

Figure 3. The phases of symbolism.

analysis of the descriptive and literal phases is one he shares with the major proponents of the New Criticism, those whose concern has been to locate the meaning of poetry in the nature of its symbolic language. Frye's distinction between assertive and hypothetic meaning is closely akin, for example, to Cleanth Brooks's opposition between factual and emotional language; to I.A. Richards's emotive-referential dialectic; to the distinction in John Crowe Ransom between rational and poetic meaning, or in Philip Wheelwright between steno-language and depth-language; to the opposition in William Empson between clarity and ambiguity; or, finally, to the procedure running throughout contemporary criticism, which attempts to separate poetic language from that of either ordinary usage or science on the basis of the more complex, ambiguous, and ironic meaning of the former. The characteristic method of inference in each of these procedures, as R.S. Crane observes, is based on a similar dialectic; for they all, Frye included, employ a process of reasoning *to* what the language and meaning of poetry are *from* what assertive discourse and rational meaning are not.[3]

Frye would like to refute the semantic analysis of logical positivism, that is, the reduction of all meaning to either rational or emotional discourse.

> Some philosophers who assume that all meaning is descriptive meaning tell us that, as a poem does not describe things rationally, it must be a description of an emotion. According to this the literal core of poetry would be a *cri de coeur,* . . . the direct statement of a nervous organism confronted with something that seems to demand an emotional response, like a dog howling at the moon. . . . We have found, however, that the real core of poetry is a subtle and elusive verbal pattern that avoids, and does not lead to, such bald statements. (AC, 81)

While it is true that the subtlety and the range of reference in Frye's discussion of the literal phase will not permit a simple equation between the meaning expressed by symbols in this phase and the nondescriptive meaning of the analytic philosophers, it is no less true that he still remains within the framework of the theory he opposes; what he does is to convert his denial of the principles of linguistic philosophy into the principles of his own poetic theory. The primary assumptions remain the same: poetry, in the literal and descriptive phases, is primarily a mode of discourse and there is a bipolar distribution of all language and thus of all meaning.[4]

The first section of Frye's theory of symbols results in an expansion and rearrangement of the medieval scheme of four levels of interpretation, according to which literal meaning is discursive or representational meaning. Its point of reference is centrifugal. When Dante interprets scripture literally, he points to the correspondence between an event in the Bible and a historical event, or at least one he assumed to have occurred in the past. In this sense, literature signifies real events. The first medieval level of symbolism thus becomes Frye's descriptive level. His own literal phase, however, has no corresponding rung on the medieval ladder. The advantage of rearranging the categories, Frye believes, is that he now has a framework to account for a poem literally as a poem—as a self-contained verbal structure whose meaning is not dependent upon any external reference. This redesignation is simply one more way that Frye can indicate the difference between a symbol as motif and sign. As a principle of Frye's system, it reveals the dialectical method he uses to define poetic meaning. He is not satisfied, however, with the dichotomy, calling it a "quizzical antithesis between delight and instruction, ironic withdrawal from reality and explicit connection with it" (AC, 82). Therefore, in his discussion of the third phase of symbolism he attempts to move beyond these now-familiar distinctions of the New Criticism.

The Formal Phase This phase of symbolism relates specifically to the imagery of poetry. Yet formal criticism can be seen as studying literature from the point of view, once again, of either *mythos* or *dianoia*. The meaning of these two terms remains fairly close to the meaning they had in Frye's discussion of the literal and descriptive phases, though here they function differently. In the first two phases, narrative (*mythos*) and meaning (*dianoia*) tended to diverge, in Frye's argument, toward opposite poles. In the formal phase, however, his interest is in making them converge until they are somehow unified, for it is the essential unity of a work of art which the word "form" is usually meant to convey.

Frye's explanation of this point involves a highly complex dialectic. First of all, he uses the concept of imitation to contravene the form-content dichotomy. *Mythos*, he says, is a secondary imitation of an action because it describes typical rather than specific human acts. And *dianoia* is a secondary imitation of thought because it also is concerned with the typical, in this case, "with images, metaphors, diagrams, and verbal ambiguities out of which specific ideas develop" (AC, 83). The assumption underlying the argument, apparently, is that the concept of secondary imitation, because it represents the typical, is a principle which unifies formal criticism and thus permits the discussion of poetry on this level always to remain internal. In formal imitation, Frye says, "the work of art does not reflect external events and ideas, but exists between the example and the precept" (AC, 84). Or again, "The central principle of the formal phase, that a poem is an imitation of nature, is . . . a principle which isolates the individual poem" (AC, 95). Frye's argument depends on using the concept of typicality to avoid the antithesis implicit in the literal and descriptive phases. Yet Frye's use of the word "typical" is equivocal: more philosohical than history on the one hand, and more historical than philosophy on the other.

The second argument for the unity of formal criticism is based upon the movement-stasis dichotomy, analogized once again to the terms *mythos* and *dianoia*. Every detail of a poem is related to its form, Frye claims, and this form remains the same "whether it is examined as stationary or as moving through the work from beginning to end" (AC, 83). His main point is that we need to balance the ordinary method of studying symbolism, which is solely in terms of meaning, with the study of a poem's *moving* body of imagery. "The form of a poem is the same whether it is studied as narrative or as meaning, hence the structure of imagery in *Macbeth* may be studied as a pattern derived from the text, or as a rhythm of repetition falling on an audience's ear" (AC, 85). The method of definition here continues to rely upon the principle of dichotomous division: *mythos* versus *dianoia*, movement versus stasis, narrative versus meaning, structure versus rhythm, shaping form versus containing form (AC, 82–85). Yet the way these pairs of opposites function, as compared with their use in the previous section, is that they do not point to realities outside the poem. Poets do not directly imitate either nature or thought; they create potential, hypothetical, and typical forms. It is this conception of art which Frye also sees as helping to resolve the split between delight and instruction, form and content.

Criticism in the formal phase is called commentary, "the process of translating into explicit or discursive language what is implicit in the poem" (AC, 86). More specifically, it tries to isolate the ideas embodied in the structure of poetic imagery. This produces allegorical interpretation, and, in fact, commentary sees all literature as potential allegory (AC, 89). The range of symbolism in the formal phase ("thematically significant imagery") can be classified according to the degree of its explicitness. All literature, in other words, can be organized along a continuum of formal meaning, from the most to the least allegorical, as in Figure 4.

Naive   Continuous   *Freistimmige*   Doctrinal   Implicit   Ironic   Indirect

Figure 4. Degrees of allegorical explicitness (formal phase).

The criterion here is the degree to which a writer insists on relating his imagery to precepts and examples. Naive allegory is so close to discursive writing that it can hardly be called literature at all. It "belongs chiefly to educational literature on an elementary level: schoolroom moralities, devotional exempla, local pageants, and the like" (AC, 90). Even though such naive forms have no real hypothetical center, they are considered allegorical to some degree since they occasionally rely upon images to illustrate their theses.

The two types of actual or formal allegory, continuous and *freistimmige*, show an explicit connection between image and idea, differing only in that the former is more overt and systematic. Dante, Spenser, and Bunyan, for example, maintain the allegorical connections throughout their work, whereas in writers like Hawthorne, Goethe, and Ibsen the symbolic equations are at once less explicit and less continuous.[5] If the structure of the poetic imagery has a strong doctrinal emphasis, so that the internal fictions become exempla, as in Milton's epics, a fourth kind of allegorical relation is established. And to the right of this, located at the "center" of the scale, are "works in which the structure of imagery, however suggestive, has an implicit relation only to events and ideas, and which includes the bulk of Shakespeare" (AC, 91). All other poetic imagery tends increasingly toward the ironic and paradoxical end of the continuum; it includes the kind of symbolism implied by the metaphysical conceit and *symbolisme*, by Eliot's objective correlative and the heraldic emblem. Frye refers to this latter kind of imagery (e.g., Melville's whale and Virginia Woolf's lighthouse) as ironic or paradoxical because as units of meaning the symbols arrest the narrative, and as units of narrative they perplex the meaning. Beyond this mode, at the extreme right of the continuum, are indirect symbolic techniques, like private association, Dadaism, and intentionally confounding symbols.

What Frye has done is to redefine the word "allegory," or at least greatly expand its ordinary meaning; for he uses the term not only to refer to a literary convention but also to indicate a universal structural principle of literature. It is universal because Frye sees all literature in relation to *mythos* and *dianoia*. We engage in allegorical interpretation, in other words, whenever we relate the events of a narrative to conceptual terminology. This is commentary, or the translation of poetic into discursive meaning. In interpreting an "actual" or continuous allegory like *The Faerie Queene*, the relationship between *mythos* and *dianoia* is so explicit that it prescribes the direction which commentary must take. In a work like *Hamlet* the relationship is more implicit. Yet commentary on *Hamlet*, for Frye, is still allegorical: if we interpret *Hamlet*, say, as a tragedy of indecision, we begin to set up the kind of moral counterpart (*dia-*

noia) to the events of its narrative (*mythos*) that continuous allegory has as a part of its structure. We should expect, then, that as allegory becomes more implicit, the direction that the commentary must go becomes less prescriptive. And this is precisely Frye's position: an implicit allegory like *Hamlet* can carry an almost infinite number of interpretations.[6]

The Mythical Phase If in the formal phase a poem is considered as representing its own class, a unique artifact lying midway between precept and example, in the mythical phase it is seen generically, one of a whole group of similar forms. The fundamental principle here is Frye's assumption regarding the total order of words, for the study of poetry involves not simply isolating the poem as an imitation of nature but also considering it as an imitation of other poems. And since literature shapes itself out of the total order of words, the study of genres becomes important. Frye reserves his treatment of genres for the Fourth Essay, concentrating here upon convention, the principle which ultimately provides the basis for the study of genres. He emphasizes the conventionalized aspect of art not only because it is close to his own interests, both as a theoretical and a practical critic, but also because he believes literary convention has been neglected by criticism. Thus he spends some time elaborating a number of his basic convictions: the more original art is, the more profoundly imitative it is of other art; we have all been schooled in low-mimetic prejudices about the creative process; the conventional aspect of poetry is as important as what is distinctive in poetic achievement.

The symbol which characterizes the fourth phase is, of course, the conventional symbol, or what Frye calls the "archetype." Poetry, he says in a passage that points directly toward the Third and Fourth Essays, is not simply

> an aggregate of artifacts imitating nature, but one of the activities of human artifice taken as a whole. If we may use the word "civilization" for this, we may say that our fourth phase looks at poetry as one of the techniques of civilization. It is concerned, therefore, with the social aspect of poetry, with poetry as the focus of a community. The symbol in this phase is the communicable unit, to which I give the name archetype: that is, a typical or recurring image. I mean by an archetype a symbol which connects one poem with another and thereby helps to unify and integrate our literary experience. And as the archetype is the communicable symbol, archetypal criticism is primarily concerned with literature as a social fact and as a mode of communication. By the study of conventions and genres, it attempts to fit poems into the body of poetry as a whole. (AC, 99)

The study of convention is based upon analogies. In the case of genres, it is analogies of form; in the case of archetypes, analogies of symbolism. To see Moby Dick, for example, as an archetype is to recognize an analogy between Melville's whale and other "leviathans and dragons of the deep from the Old Testament onward" (AC, 100). He is but one of a recurring tradition of such creatures which are clustered together in our experience of literature; such images come together in our imaginative experience, Frye argues, because of their similarities. Another example is the use of a dark and light heroine, a common convention of nineteenth-century fiction. The dark heroine, he says, "is as a rule passionate, haughty, plain, foreign or Jewish, and in some way associated with the undesirable or with some kind of forbidden fruit like incest. When the two are involved with the same hero, the plot usually has to get rid of the dark one or make her into a sister if the story is to end happily" (AC, 101). Frye sees this archetype recurring in countless stories, including those of Sir Walter Scott, James Fenimore Cooper, Wilkie Collins, Poe, Melville, and Hawthorne; there is even a male version of the convention in *Wuthering Heights* (AC, 101).

Frye observes that the function of signs also depends on conventional associations. But the difference between signs and archetypes is that the latter are complex variables, which means that a given archetype may symbolize a variety of objects, ideas, or emotions. "Green," for example, "may symbolize hope or vegetable nature or a go sign in traffic or Irish patriotism as easily as jealousy, but the word green as a verbal sign always refers to a certain color" (AC, 102). Some archetypal associations are more obvious than others, even though there are no necessary connections, "no intrinsic or inherent correspondences which must invariably be present" (AC, 103). But archetypes are not only complex; they also vary in explicitness. Frye sees these relations as a scale, running from pure convention at one extreme to pure variable at the other, as in figure 5. This range of conventions should not be confused with the scale of allegorical meanings in the third phase; the two scales are parallel only insofar as their common principle is the degree of explicitness which images and archetypes, respectively, have. As Figure 5 indicates, the most highly conventionalized literature is likely to be naive (i.e., primitive or popular). It would follow then that archetypes are easiest to study, because more obvious and explicit, in naive forms; which is one reason for Frye's frequent attention to primitive and popular forms of art.[7]

The symbol as archetype is the first principle underlying Frye's definition of the fourth phase. How do the categories *mythos* and *dianoia* function in this definition? The pairs of opposites in his dialectic now become *recurrence* and *desire,* and *ritual* and *myth.* Relating these

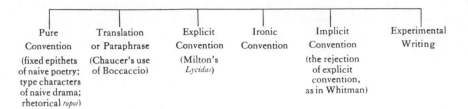

Figure 5. Degrees of archetypal convention (mythical phase).

terms to *mythos* and *dianoia* depends once more on some highly abstract reasoning. The transition comes in this passage:

> Every phase of symbolism has its particular approach to narrative and to meaning. In the literal phase, narrative is a flow of significant sounds, and meaning an ambiguous and complex verbal pattern. In the descriptive phase, narrative is an imitation of real events, and meaning an imitation of actual objects or propositions. In the formal phase, poetry exists between the example and the precept. In the exemplary event there is an element of *recurrence*; in the precept, or statement about what ought to be, there is a strong element of *desire,* or what is called "wish-thinking." These elements of recurrence and desire come into the foreground in archetypal criticism, which studies poems as units of poetry as a whole and symbols as units of communication.
>
> From such a point of view, the narrative aspect of literature is a recurrent act of symbolic communication: in other words a ritual. . . . [and] the significant content is the conflict of desire and reality which has for its basis the work of the dream. Ritual and dream, therefore, are the narrative [*mythos*] and significant content [*dianoia*] respectively of literature in its archetypal aspect. (AC, 104–5)

The method of reasoning by which Frye reaches the "therefore" in the final sentence is analogical. That ritual is the narrative aspect of the archetypal phase follows only because ritual is defined as a recurrent act of symbolic communication. The quality of recurrence, in other words, is what narrative and ritual have in common. How then does Frye arrive at the principle of recurrence? To a degree it is present in his initial definition of narrative in the literal phase, where *mythos* is seen as rhythm, or the recurrent movement of words. But in the formal phase, recurrence as an aspect of *mythos* disappears altogether from his discussion. One might argue that the principle of recurrence is implicit, in the formal phase, in Frye's account of typical actions; but this hardly explains why *typical* is used to characterize both narrative and meaning. The "example" is the formal aspect of narrative, and the temporal association Frye makes is to see *mythos* as a *moving* body of imagery. But in order to keep his categories consistent, that is, to make "recurrence" a principle of narrative throughout each of the phases, Frye must find some way of reintroducing it into the formal phase, for this will provide a means of transition to ritual. He does this by simply asserting that in "the exemplary event there is an element of recurrence," which is true insofar as we desire the exemplary event to be imitated again and again. The point is, however, that recurrence is maintained as the basic category by an analogical leap from the literal to the mythical phase, bypassing the formal phase.

Frye employs the same kind of dialectic in moving from the precept of the formal phase to the dream of the mythical. Here the transition is based on the assertion that there is a strong element of desire associated with the precept, so that desire becomes the mediating category between the third and fourth phases. Putting it straightforwardly, the form of the argument is this: Desire is related to precept; precept is the *dianoia* of formal criticism. Desire is related to dream; dream is the *dianoia* of archetypal criticism. The relationship, of course, is again analogical.

Once Frye has distinguished ritual and dream, which on the archetypal level represent *mythos* and *dianoia* respectively, he seeks to unite them under the category of myth. The archetypal study of narrative, he says, deals with "the generic, recurring, or conventional actions which show analogies to rituals: the weddings, funerals, intellectual and social initiations, executions or mock executions, the chasing away of the scapegoat villain, and so on"; whereas the archetypal study of *dianoia* treats the generic, recurring, or conventional "shape" of a work, "indicated by its mood and resolution, whether tragic, comic, ironic, or what not, in which the relationship of desire and experience is expressed" (AC, 105). Specific illustrations of this kind of study are found in the Third Essay. At this point Frye wants to show the relationship between ritual and dream, neither of which is literary, to a single form of verbal communication. This form is myth, which explains the title of the fourth phase. From the perspective of the mythical phase, Frye argues, we see the same kinds of processes or rhythms occurring in literature that we find in ritual and dream. There are two basic patterns; one cyclical, the other dialectical. Ritual imitates the cyclical process of nature: the rhythmic movement of the universe and the seasons, as well as the recurring cycles of human life; and literature in the archetypal phase imitates nature in the same way. The dialectical pattern, on the other hand, derives from the world of dream, where desire is in constant conflict with reality. Liberation and capture, integration and expulsion, love and hate are some of the terms we apply to this moral dialectic in ritual and dream.[8] The same pattern, when it is expressed hypothetically, is to be found in poetry. Archetypal criticism, Frye concludes, is based upon these two organizing patterns (AC, 105–6).

Frye's indebtedness to contemporary anthropology and psychology is apparent in these distinctions, resonating as they do with the language of Frazer, Freud, and Jung. But Frye is careful to emphasize the distinction between the aims of criticism and those of these other disciplines. The critic, he says, "is concerned only with ritual or dream patterns which are actually in what he is studying, however they got there" (AC, 109). Some archetypal critics, he adds, do not recognize this, having been misled into searching for the origins of the ritual elements of literature. His point is not that such studies have no place in criticism but that they belong on the descriptive rather than the archetypal level. What is at stake here is distinguishing clearly between the history of literary works and the genre to which they belong. Frye apparently has his eye on scholars like Gilbert Murray, who maintained that in tragedy there survives an ancient ritual involving a combat between the old year-spirit and the new; or F.M. Cornford, who extended Murray's thesis to Greek comedy, arguing that the basic pattern of the Aristophanic play can be directly traced to primitive seasonal rituals, such as the Combat, Sacred Marriage, and Beanfeast. Frye is not saying that Murray and the Cambridge anthropologists were wrong, even though it may be incorrect to assume that a given Greek play actually descends from a ritual libretto. He is saying, rather, that for the archetypal critic the question is irrelevant. On the other hand, Frye would not deny that a Greek play could have been conditioned by standard patterns of ritual or that its conventions were determined by actual performances. What is at issue, in other words, is not the dependence of a given play upon an actual performance, but simply a parallelism between narrative and ritual patterns, or between the conventions and genres of literature and those of ritual ceremony. The archetypal critic, Frye would say, is concerned only with this latter question. The historical critic may be concerned with the former.[9]

Frye's position on the application of psychology to literature is similar: the archetypal critic will not want to confuse biography with criticism. The repetition of a certain pattern in Shakespeare's plays, he says, may be studied in various ways. "If Shakespeare is unique or anomalous, or even exceptional, in using this pattern, the reason for his use of it may be at least partly psychological" (AC, 111), and critics may, at the descriptive level, resort to psychological theory in attempting to explain it.

The archetypal critic, however, can pursue the problem only when the same pattern is recognized in Shakespeare's contemporaries or in the dramatists of different ages and cultures, in which case convention and genre become the important considerations (AC, 111).

In an early essay on the nature of symbolism Frye says that "wherever we have archetypal symbolism, we pass from the question 'What does this symbol, sea or tree or serpent or character, mean in this work of art?' to the question 'What does it mean in my imaginative comprehension of such things as a whole?' Thus the presence of archetypal symbolism makes the individual poem, not its own object, but a phase of imaginative experience."[10] Archetypal symbolism works in two directions for Frye. On the one hand, because the language of myth and symbol enters and informs all verbal culture, he uses what he has learned about symbolism as a literary critic to understand and interpret texts in philosophy, psychology, history, and comparative religion. On the other hand, he sees these disciplines as informing literary criticism itself. Thus he can approach Toynbee's *Study of History* from the centrifugal perspective, seeing it as "an intuitive response based on an imaginative grasp of the symbolic significance of certain data" (CL, 80). The book can be read, then, not as a factual chronicle which is trying to prove something by its massive accumulation of data but as a grand imaginative vision. Similarly, Frye approaches Frazer's *Golden Bough* as if it were an encyclopaedic epic or a continuous form of prose fiction. It is, he says, really "about what the human imagination does when it tries to express itself about the greatest mysteries" (CL, 89).

But Frye also works in a centripetal direction. Cassirer, Spengler, Frazer, Jung, and Eliade are themselves students of symbolism whose works provide us with a grammar of the human imagination. Cassirer's symbolic forms, like those found in literature, take their structure from the mind and their content from the natural world. And Frazer's expansive collections of material, because they give us a grammar of unconscious symbolism on both its personal and its social sides, will be of greater benefit to the poet and literary critic than to the anthropologist. Thus *The Golden Bough*, like Jung's *Psychology of the Unconscious*, becomes primarily a work of literary criticism. Similarly, Eliade's studies in *Religionsgeschichte* are especially important for the literary critic because they provide a grammar of initiatory and comparative symbolism.

The two perspectives—the centrifugal and the centripetal—do not finally move in opposite directions in Frye's work. They interpenetrate, to use his familiar metaphor. In a review of Jung's *Psychology of the Unconscious*, Frye develops a view of criticism which makes its way later, some of it verbatim, into his account of the archetypal phase of symbolism in the *Anatomy*. But this is not to say that Frye is a Jungian. His view has always been that criticism needs to be independent from externally derived frameworks—what he calls "determinisms." "Critical principles," he says, "cannot be taken over ready-made from theology, philosophy, politics, science, or any combination of these" (AC, 7). Yet Frye himself, as the Second Essay bears ample witness, has appropriated a number of concepts from other disciplines, especially from psychology and anthropology.

The choice of metaphors used to describe the relation of one subject to another is, Frye says, "a fateful choice" (SM, 106). His own choice of "interpenetration" avoids the determinism implicit in such vertical metaphors as "founded upon" and in such horizonal ones as "connected" or "united." The first "means that we have to get something established in another subject 'before' we can study literature, which of course means that we never get to study literature at all"; whereas the second means that by trying to build bridges between different subjects we destroy the context of them both (SM, 106–7). There should be no problem, then, in understanding Frye's relation to someone like Jung.

> I am continually asked . . . about my relation to Jung, and especially about the relation of my use of the word "archetype" to his. So far I have tended to resist the association, because in my experience whenever anyone mentions it his next sentence is almost certain to be nonsense. . . . It seems strange to overlook the possibility that the arts, including literature, might just conceivably be what they have always been taken to be, possible techniques of meditation, in the strictest sense of the word, ways of cultivating, focussing and ordering one's mental processes on the basis of symbol rather than concept. (SM, 117)

This is the reason that Frye can say that Jung's work is "a grammar of literary symbolism which for all serious students of literature is as important as it is endlessly fascinating" (CL, 129).

To see archetypal criticism as concerned with the social aspects of poetry is, as Frye says, to emphasize the relationship of the individual poem to other poems. But this is only half of what should properly be emphasized, for a poem is also a "part of the total human imitation of nature that we call civilization" (AC, 105; see also 99, 112–13). What does it mean to say that civilization is a total human imitation of nature, an idea which recurs frequently in Frye's work? He himself refers to it metaphorically as "the process of making a total human form out of nature" (AC, 105, 112). He means that as civilization develops, the natural world is transformed from the nonhuman into something with human shape and meaning. This process is given direction by desire. Because man is not satisfied, for example, with roots and caves, his civilization creates "human forms of nature" in farming and architecture. This kind of desire, Frye says,

> is thus not a simple response to need, for an animal may need food without planting a garden to get it, nor is it a simple response to want, or desire *for* something in particular. It is neither limited to nor satisfied by objects, but is the energy that leads human society to develop its own form. Desire in this sense is the social aspect of what we met on the literal level as emotion, an impulse toward expression which would have remained amorphous if the poem had not liberated it by providing the form of its expression. The form of desire, similarly, is liberated and made apparent by civilization. The efficient cause of civilization is work, and poetry in its social aspect has the function of expressing, as a verbal hypothesis, a vision of the goal of work and the forms of desire. (AC, 105–6)

Criticism on the archetypal level therefore is concerned not just with genre and convention. Because it views the symbol as a natural object with a human meaning, its scope is expanded to include civilization. And from this perspective, poetry becomes a product of a vision of the goals of human work. (The Blakean influence behind these ideas, especially the concept of civilization as a "human form," is a point to which we shall return shortly.)

This view, says Frye, makes it tempting for the archetypal critic to see art as an ethical instrument whose function is to serve society by visualizing its goals. Similarly, in the descriptive phase we are likely to encounter truth as an external goal for art, and in the literal and formal phases, beauty. But, Frye argues, as none of these external standards can ultimately determine the value of literature, we need to move beyond the archetypal phase and the goals of civilization, where art is not an end in itself, "to culture, where it is disinterested and liberal, and stands on its own feet" (AC, 115). By such passage, we climb to the anagogic level.

The Anagogic Phase   The anagogic phase is Frye's beatific critical vision. Its argument is more difficult because more visionary. Its Blakean language has caused the response of some readers to sound like Pound's dismissal of the medieval fourth level: "Anagogical? Hell's bells, '*nobody*' knows what THAT is."[11] This kind of reaction is perhaps understandable if Frye's statements about the anagogic phase are taken out of context, as the following quotations should illustrate:

> Nature is now [in the fifth phase] inside the mind of an infinite man who builds his cities out of the Milky Way. This is not reality, but it is the conceivable or imaginative limit of desire, which is infinite, eternal, and hence apocalyptic. By an apocalypse I mean primarily the imaginative conception of the whole of nature as the content of an infinite and eternal living body which, if not human, is closer to being human than to being inanimate. (AC, 119)

> Anagogically, then, the symbol is a monad, all symbols being united in a single infinite and eternal verbal symbol which is, as *dianoia,* the Logos, and, as *mythos,* total creative act. (AC, 121)

> The study of literature takes us toward seeing poetry as the imitation of infinite social action and infinite human thought, the mind of man who is all men, the universal creative word which is all words. (AC, 125)

Unless seen in context, these passages approach the limits of intelligibility. The problem, then, is to understand these statements in the framework of Frye's discourse.

Frye begins by drawing an analogy between his anagogic phase and the medieval fourth level. He defines anagogy as "universal meaning," a definition which, although not exactly consistent with medieval usage, is important in Frye's description of the anagogic symbol.[12] The second analogy is a parallel between the fifth phase and fifth mode of Frye's own framework. Both are concerned with the mythopoeic aspect of literature, that is, with "fictions and themes relating to divine or quasi-divine beings and powers." These two analogies should alert us to expect a description of the anagogic phase which draws upon religious or visionary language.[13]

The analogy to myth having been drawn, Frye can now move toward the principle upon which the fifth phase is said to rest, namely, that there is a *center* to the order of words. That such a center exists is predicated on the assumption that our "greatest" literary experiences derive from works which are the most mythopoeic (AC, 117). These are, at one end, primitive and popular works, both of which afford "an unobstructed view of archetypes," and, at the other, the learned and recondite mythopoeia in writers like Dante, Spenser, James, and Joyce. "The inference," Frye says, "seems to be that the learned and the subtle, like the primitive and the popular, tend toward a center of imaginative experience" (AC, 117). The crux of the matter comes in this heavily value-laden statement:

> In the greatest moments of Dante and Shakespeare, in, say *The Tempest* or the climax of the *Purgatorio,* we have a feeling of

converging significance, the feeling that here we are close to seeing what our whole literary experience has been about, the feeling that we have moved into the still center of the order of words. Criticism as knowledge, the criticism which is compelled to keep on talking about the subject, recognizes the fact that there *is* a center of the order of words. (AC, 117–18)

Frye realizes the difficulties attendant on such a view; he therefore faces the problem of defining the norm for the order of words—the "still point" around which his literary universe revolves.

The first and most obvious basis for Frye's position is his own literary experience, the feeling he has of being at the center of significance when in the presence of the greatest works of literature.[14] In the second place, the idea of a center to the order of words is consistent with, even a logical consequence of, the imagery Frye has already used to describe the structure of literature. If the literary modes are cyclical and if the critical phases are parallel to the modes, then it stands to reason that the cycle must have a center. In short, the notion of "converging significance" does not fit well into a strictly linear paradigm. More important than this, however, is the idea of order itself. If literature does constitute a total order, then there must be some principle holding it together. We have already seen Frye assert that the function of the archetypal critic (in the fourth phase) is to search out those principles of structure which works of literature have in common. This kind of study, however, tells us nothing about the structure of literature as a whole; therefore, unless we can find some unifying principle for the total order, the study of genres and conventions will be nothing more than "an endless series of free associations" (AC, 118). In other words, one can never arrive at the self-contained whole, which is literature itself, simply by studying archetypes, for as symbols they represent only parts of the whole. The existence of a total order among *all* literary works is the prior assumption, therefore, which makes it necessary for Frye to establish a norm underlying the order. And this norm is the center, the "still point" around which his literary universe revolves.

Having asserted the existence of a unifying principle, Frye's problem becomes trying to define it. His first recourse is to the categories which have been used continually, though not univocally, throughout the Second Essay: symbol, *mythos,* and *dianoia.* The symbols of the anagogic phase are "universal symbols": "I do not mean by this phrase," Frye says, "that there is any archetypal code book which has been memorized by all human societies without exception. I mean that some symbols are images of things common to all men" (AC, 118). This being the case, then some symbols have a limitless range of reference:

their power to communicate is not bound by nature or history. It is this illimitable aspect of the anagogic symbol that Frye's definition fastens upon. The *dianoia* and *mythos* of the mythical phase were respectively dream and ritual. Expanding these categories to define the symbol of the anagogic phase, Frye says that "literature imitates the total dream of man, and so imitates the thought of a human mind which is at the circumference and not at the center of its reality" (AC, 119). This is the "meaning" pole of Frye's dialectic. At the other pole, representing "narrative," poetry is said to imitate "human action as total ritual, and so [to imitate] the action of an omnipotent human society that contains all the powers of nature within itself" (AC, 120). Unlimited social action (or total ritual) and unlimited individual thought (or total dream) are the dialectical opposites, therefore, which unite to produce the macrocosmic aspect of the anagogic phase. This centrifugal movement, extending indefinitely outward toward a periphery where there are no limits to the intelligibility of a symbol, is but one of the aspects of the anagogic symbol, the macrocosm of total ritual and dream. The other, as we have seen, is the centripetal movement, turning inward toward the center of the literary universe, or toward the microcosm, which is "whatever poem we happen to be reading" (AC, 121). Seen together, these two movements produce the anagogic symbol, or what Frye calls the "monad" (AC, 121). This is a paradoxical concept, but only in the sense that an expression like "concrete universal" is also paradoxical, for "monad" refers to the individual poem which manifests or reflects within itself the entire poetic universe.

The Blakean Influence

The figure of William Blake looms large behind Frye's thought in this section, a more important influence than the one brief allusion to him might suggest. In a prefatory note Frye tells us that he learned his principles of literary symbolism and Biblical typology from Blake in the first place (AC, vii). And when Frye refers to the "imaginative limit of desire" and to the apocalypse as "the imaginative conception of the whole of nature as the content of an infinite and eternal living body" (AC, 119), he is using the same kind of language he used in *Fearful Symmetry* to describe the implications of Blake's view of poetry. In Frye's understanding of Blake, in fact, we begin to strike close to the heart of a number of his fundamental convictions: his Romantic aesthetic, his conviction that critical principles derive ultimately from poetic vision, his belief in the possibility of a cultural synthesis. An understanding of Frye's indebtedness to Blake should help illuminate what he means by the fifth phase of symbolism.

In the history of discourse about literature most critics have derived the deductive foundations of their critical theories from philosophers, or from other critics, or from what might be called broadly the speculative and discursive currents of thought prevalent at the time.[15] Frye is a notable exception to this tendency, having derived a number of his most important critical principles from the study of poets themselves. This fact is apparent at a number of places in his writings, not the least of which is in his discussion of fifth-phase symbolism. "Anagogic criticism," he says, "is usually found in direct connection with religion, and is to be discovered chiefly in the more uninhibited utterances of poets themselves" (AC, 122). It is important not to overlook what is being proposed here. Frye is not saying that anagogic symbols can be found in uninhibited poetry, though doubtless he would make this claim in another context. He is saying rather that if we really want to know what anagogic *criticism* is, then we have to turn to the *poetry* of the more uninhibited writers. In other words, at the anagogic level poetry *is* criticism and criticism *is* poetry. We find anagogic criticism, to give some of Frye's examples, "in those passages of Eliot's quartets where the words of the poet are placed within the context of the incarnate Word . . . in Valery's conception of a total intelligence which appears more fancifully in his figure of M. Teste; in Yeats's cryptic utterances about the artifice of eternity . . . in Dylan Thomas's exultant hymns to a universal human body" (AC, 122). Frye does not include Blake among his examples at this point, but ten years earlier in his book on Blake's prophecies he had come to the same conclusion, namely, that the solution to deciphering Blake's symbolic code lay within *literature* itself. Some of the principles of this book, *Fearful Symmetry,* will provide a useful commentary on Frye's discussion of the anagogic phase.

"I had not realized, before this last rereading," Frye says in the preface to a 1962 reprint of *Fearful Symmetry,* "how completely the somewhat unusual form and structure of my commentary was derived from my absorption in the larger critical theory implicit in Blake's view of art. Whatever importance the book may have, beyond its merits as a guide to Blake, it owes to its connection with the critical theories that I have ever since been trying to teach, both in Blake's name and in my own."[16] Frye's purpose in *Fearful Symmetry* is to study the relationship between Blake's mature thought and the literary tradition. He assumes that Blake is best understood when the entire canon, from the early lyrics to the late and incomplete prophecies, is viewed as a unified achievement. The total vision is what is important. He assumes, furthermore, that the most enlightening kind of commentary on Blake will seek to place his work in its historical and cultural contexts (FS, 3–5).

By showing Blake's relationship to the Western humanistic tradition, he intends "to establish Blake as a typical poet and his thinking as typically poetic thinking" (FS, 426). But placing Blake in this context does not mean locating the sources of his art in, say, the writings of Swedenborg or Plotinus; nor does it mean trying to uncover those events of history or of Blake's personal life which seem to lie behind at least some of his poems. "In the study of Blake," Frye argues, "it is the analogue that is important, not the source" (FS, 12). The study of these analogues turns out to constitute the bulk of Frye's commentary, as he locates one Blakean parallel after another in the prose Edda, Chaucer, Spenser, Milton, the post-Augustans, the Ossian poems. Frye's subject matter then is the speculative and symbolic aspects of Blake's work and the relationship of both to the history of thought.

The starting point of his exegesis is not with individual poems but with Blake's theory of knowledge; for it is only by understanding and then surrendering ourselves to the epistemological foundations of Blake's thinking, Frye argues, that we can face squarely both the material and the pattern of his vision. Blake's epistemology is that of a visionary, one who "creates, or dwells in, a higher spiritual world in which the objects of perception in this one have become transfigured and charged with a new intensity of symbolism" (FS, 8). Thus Frye devotes the first part of the book to placing Blake's unitary theory of the imagination over against the separation of subject and object in the "cloven fiction" of Locke's philosophizing. By following Blake's own allegorical method and interpreting him in an imaginative rather than in a historical way, we are confronted with "the doctrine that all symbolism in all art and all religion is mutually intelligible among all men, and that there is such a thing as an iconography of the imagination" (FS, 420). The "grammar" of this iconography, or the way Blake represents his vision of reality by means of his special yet traditionally rooted symbolism, is what Frye charts in *Fearful Symmetry*. And he believes that by learning this grammar we can develop a key to the art of reading poetry. In *Anatomy of Criticism* that part of the grammar which Frye learned from Blake appears chiefly in the Second and Third Essays.

The most important Blakean idea in the Second Essay has to do with the principles of simile and metaphor, Frye's discussion of these coming at the end of his theory of symbols. In a system so firmly dependent upon the method of analogy as Frye's, where argument progresses by associative leaps, we might expect to find frequent references to these two grammatical forms of association. Frye is not so much interested, however, in the rhetorical use of simile and metaphor as he is in the modes of thought which underlie them. These are analogy and identity, principles which represent the two processes by which the imaginative power of the mind transforms the nonhuman world (Nature) into something with human shape and meaning (Culture). This is the point at which we begin to see the strong influence of Blake. In one of his autobiographical essays, Frye recounts the intuition that came to him as he was contemplating the fact that Milton and Blake were connected by their use of the Bible: "If [they] were alike on this point, that likeness merely concealed what was individual about each of them, so that in pursuing the likeness I was chasing a shadow and avoiding the substance. Around three in the morning a different kind of intuition hit me. . . . The two poets were connected by the *same* thing, and sameness leads to individual variety, just as likeness leads to monotony" (SM, 17).

Blake opposed his own view of reality to the commonsense view of Locke, who conceived of subject and object as only accidentally related: the subjective center of perception exists at one pole; the objective world of things at the other. In order to classify objective things, one points to their resemblances. Thus Locke's "natural" epistemology was based on the principles of separation and similarity. And the process of perceiving similarities, according to Blake, must always move from the concrete to the abstract. Thus in what Blake calls "Allegory" or "Similitude" we have a relationship of abstractions. Frye's illustration of these Blakean terms is as follows:

> The artist, contemplating the hero, searches in his memory for something that reminds him of the hero's courage, and drags out a lion. But here we no longer have two real things: we have a correspondence of abstractions. The hero's courage, not the hero himself, is what the lion symbolizes. And a lion which symbolizes an abstract quality is not a real but a heraldic lion. . . . Whenever we take our eye off the image we slip into abstractions, into regarding qualities, moral or intellectual, as more real than living things. (FS, 116–17)

Now what Blake opposes to the natural view of Locke, or to similitude in this sense, is the imaginative or visionary view of "Identity," the literary form of which is metaphor.

The process of identity, according to Blake, "unites the theme and the illustration of it" (FS, 117). There are two kinds of identity perceived by the imagination. When Blake says a thing is identified *as* itself, he means to point not to its abstract quality but to its experienced reality. He calls this reality its "living form" or "image." And all of Blake's images and mythological figures, according to Frye, "are 'minute particulars' or individuals identified with their total forms."[17] In the second kind of identity things are seen as identical *with* each other. Here the Lockian view is turned upside down, since the perceiving subject is now at the circumference and not the center of reality. All perceivers, since they are identical and not separate, are one perceiver, who, in Blake's view, is totally human and totally divine. Blake's image for this, in Frye's words, is "the life of a single eternal and infinite God-Man," in whose body all forms or images are identical.[18] Thus, in the imaginative world of Blake, things are infinitely varied, because identified *as* themselves; at the same time, all things are of one essence, because identical *with* each other.

In the *Anatomy* Frye associates analogy with both descriptive meaning and realism, and identity with poetic meaning and myth, a separation based on Blake's distinction between Locke's natural epistemology and his own imaginative one. But the relationship as it is developed in the *Anatomy* is more complex than this. The conception one has of simile and metaphor depends upon the level of criticism he is engaged in, so that the meaning which metaphor has for a critic at the descriptive level will be different from its meaning at the anagogical.

At the *descriptive* level, metaphor and simile have the same function. To say "A is B" or "A is like B" is to say only that A is somehow comparable to B. "Descriptively," as Frye says, "all metaphors are similies" (AC, 123). On the *literal* level, both metaphor and simile are distinguished by the absence of a predicate. A and B are simply juxtaposed with no connecting link, as in imagistic poetry. "Predication," Frye says, "belongs to assertion and descriptive meaning, not to the literal structure of poetry" (AC, 123). At the *formal* level, where images are the content of nature, metaphors and similes are analogies of natural proposition, thus requiring four terms, two of which have some common factor. Thus "A is B" or "A is like B" means at the formal level that A:X::B:Y, where the common factor is an attribute of B and Y. "The hero was a lion" is Frye's example, and we recognize in this illustration that formal metaphor is close to what Blake meant by the abstract similitude. In the *archetypal* phase, the metaphor "unites two individual images, each of which is a specific representative of a class or genus" (AC, 124). Dante's rose and Yeats's rose, while symbolizing different things, nevertheless represent all poetic roses. Archetypal metaphor is thus related to the concrete universal, and its Blakean analogue is the first kind of identity, identification *as*. Finally, at the *anagogic* level the most important analogical principle is metaphor in its radical form. To say that "A is B" means not that they are uniform or that they are separate and similar but that they are unified. Since literature at this level is seen in its totality, everything is potentially identical with everything else. This, of course, corresponds to Blake's second kind of identity, identity *with*.

"A work of literary art," Frye says, "owes its unity to this process of identification *with,* and its variety, clarity, and intensity to identification *as*" (AC, 123). His own interests direct him most often to search out the former of these analogies. The world of mythology lies at the center of his predilections, and this is the world of implicit metaphorical identity: to speak of a sun-god in mythology is to say that a divine being in human shape is identified with an aspect of physical nature. On the other hand, the world of realism, which lies at the periphery of Frye's own interests, is the world of implicit simile. To say that something is "lifelike" is to comment on its "realism," a term Frye once referred to as that "little masterpiece of question-begging" (FS, 420). So important is the principle of identity to Frye that he sometimes quite explicitly uses it to distinguish poetry from discursive thought or to define the formal principle of poetry.[19]

Analogy and identity, then, are the two important concepts by which nature and human forms are assimilated. Analogy and simile establish the similarities between human life and nature, whereas identity and metaphor show us an imaginative world where things attain a human, rather than merely a natural, form. "If we ask what the human forms of things are," says Frye, "we have only to look at what man tries to do with them. Man tries to build cities out of stones, and to develop farms and gardens out of plants; hence the city and the garden are the human forms of the mineral and vegetable world respectively."[20] We will see how Frye applies the principle of radical metaphoric identification when we come to the Third Essay. At this point it is important for us to recognize that the radical form of metaphor "comes into its own," as Frye says, in the anagogic phase. Both anagogy and radical metaphor, as principles of literature at the highest imaginative level, show us a poetic world completely possessed by the human mind.

Apocalyptic reality is for Frye, as it was for Blake, reality in its highest form. It is what the human imagination can conceive at the extreme limits of desire. Frye's conception of apocalypse is based upon a radical disjunction between the phenomenal and noumenal worlds, between what is perceived by sensory perception and what is apprehended by the reach of imagination, or between the "fallen" and "unfallen" worlds. Apocalypse is synonymous with the latter of these categories, and it has been represented variously as the Revelation at the end of the Bible or the Paradise at the beginning, to use the Christian metaphors; or as the Golden Age, to use the image of classical antiquity. It is only in the apocalyptic world, according to Frye, that nature can be humanized and man liberated—and both are achieved at the same time by the principle of radical metaphor. "This is apocalypse," says Frye, "the complete transformation of both nature and human nature into the same form."[21]

It took Frye twenty years to articulate the contrast between similarity and identity, which he calls "one of the most difficult problems in critical theory" (CP, 23). Identity is clearly a principle of literary structure for him, and in a number of places he has described the various forms which the drive toward identity takes. But in his later writings Frye has been more intent on making clear that the drive toward identity is a process engaged in by readers as well as by literary characters. There are recognition and self-recognition scenes in life as well as in literature. The latter, Frye says, have much to do in helping us in the journey toward our own identity. In *The Secular Scripture* he speaks of the highest form of self-identity as coming from one's vision of the apocalyptic world, the original world from which man has fallen, a world of revelation and full knowledge which exists mysteriously between "is" and "is not" and in which divine and human creativity are merged into one.[22] In such a state, the distinction between subject and object disappears in favor of a unified consciousness. In poetry, identity-with, as opposed to identity-as, means that the poet and his theme become one. The religious analogue of such a relation is the symbolic act of communion. Another analogue is the relation between lovers, who, like poets, identify themselves with what they make. Frye says that artists like Beckett and Proust

> look behind the surface of the ego, behind voluntary to involuntary memory, behind will and desire to conscious perception. As soon as the subjective motion picture disappears, the objective one disappears too, and we have recurring contacts between a particular moment and a particular object, as in the epiphanies of the madeleine and the phrase in Vinteuil's music. Here the object, stripped of the habitual and expected response, appears in all the enchanted glow of uniqueness, and the relation of the moment to such an object is a relation of identity. Such a relation, achieved between two human beings, would be love. . . . In the relation of identity, consciousness has triumphed over time. (CL, 220)

For Frye, such a relation is the singular way of regaining, in literature and life, that apocalyptic vision of the paradise which has been lost.

The Phases of Symbolism Synthesized

What purpose, finally, is served by Frye's analysis of the phases of symbolism? This question should be seen in the context of Frye's aim, which is to argue that a finite number of valid critical emphases can all be synthesized into one system. Thus he is led to maintain, to take one example, that historical scholarship and the New Criticism should be seen as complementary, not antithetical, approaches. Frye's attempt to synthesize these and other legitimate methods into a broad theory of contexts means that his attention is always directed away from the peculiar aims and powers of a given critical method. And even though the differences among approaches provide the basis for his classifying in the first place, these differences are always related to a single category or set of concepts, the most important in this essay being symbol, narrative, and meaning. In other words, Frye translates the principles of other methods into the language of his own discourse; and this, along with the breadth of reference of his special categories, expanded far beyond the particular meaning they have in Aristotle, greatly facilitates his achievement of the synthetic end.

The question then becomes: What function is served by the synthesis? A part of Frye's answer is found in his discussion of the formal phase where he claims that knowledge of the "whole range of possible commentary" will help "correct the perspective both of the medieval and Renaissance critics who assumed that all major poetry should be treated as far as possible as continuous allegory, and of the modern ones who maintain that poetry is essentially anti-allegorical and paradoxical" (AC, 92). In other words, there is no need for the critic to restrict himself to one approach.[23] "The present book," Frye says in the "Tentative Conclusion," "is not designed to suggest a new program for critics, but a new perspective on their existing programs, which in themselves are valid enough. The book attacks no methods of criticism, once that subject has been defined: what it attacks are the barriers between the methods. These barriers tend to make a critic confine himself to a single method of criticism, which is unnecessary, and they tend to make him establish his primary contacts, not with other critics, but with subjects outside criticism" (AC, 341).

Frye's theory of phases, however, has a function beyond that simply of universalizing the critical perspective and thus serving to lessen critical differences. As we move up the critical ladder to the last two phases, we arrive finally at that kind of criticism upon which the unification of critical thought depends. "In this process of breaking down barriers," says Frye, "I think archetypal criticism has a central role, and I have given it a prominent place" (AC, 341). Thus Frye's theory of phases serves to indicate where he himself stands as a critic. His conception of the archetype is absolutely central to his entire theory, not only because it is a steppingstone to the ultimate critical enterprise of the anagogic phase, but also because it is the basis for his theories of myth and genre. The first of these is archetypal criticism itself.

3

Theory of Myths

"Standing back" from the *Anatomy,* as Frye urges us to do when looking at a literary work, reveals that his theories of myths and genres are extensions of the last two phases of his theory of symbols. Figure 6 presents the organization diagrammatically. This asymmetry is a logical outcome of both Frye's aim and his prior assumptions. His purpose is to give an account of the structural principles of literature, and he has assumed that these principles cannot be derived except as literature is conceived as a total order of words. Since archetypal and anagogic criticism are the only kinds which assume this larger context, Frye explores them in his search for the most basic structural principles.

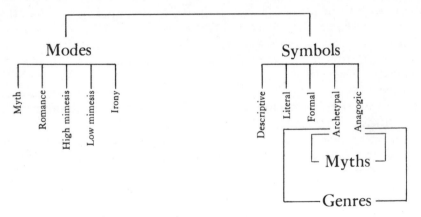

Figure 6. General structure of *Anatomy of Criticism.*

Frye says in the "Introduction" to the Third Essay:

> In this book we are attempting to outline a few of the grammatical rudiments of literary expression, and the elements of it that correspond to such musical elements as tonality, simple and

compound rhythm, canonical imitation, and the like. . . . We are suggesting that the resources of verbal expression are limited, if that is the word, by the literary equivalents of rhythm and key, though that does not mean, any more than it means in music, that its resources are artistically exhaustible. (AC, 133)

Rhythm and key are Frye's metaphors for the conventions of literature; and the particular conventions he explores in the Third Essay are archetypes.[1]

Another analogy Frye draws is between literature and the pictorial arts. When speaking of a painting, he observes, we often make the distinction between its design or stylization, on the one hand, and its content or subject, on the other. The former categories are analogous to the structural principles of literature, and we are better able to observe them when some distance separates us from the realistic details of content. "In looking at a picture," Frye says,

> we may stand close to it and analyze the details of brush work and palette knife. This corresponds roughly to the rhetorical analysis of the new critics in literature. At a little distance back, the design comes clearer into view, and we study rather the content represented: this is the best distance for realistic Dutch pictures, for example, where we are in a sense reading the picture. The further back we go, the more conscious we are of the organizing design. At a great distance from, say, a Madonna, we can see nothing but the archetype of the Madonna, a large centripetal blue mass with a contrasting point of interest at its center. (AC, 140)

Similarly, if we "stand back" from works of literature we can observe their archetypal shapes and mythopoeic designs.[2]

Frye's starting point in the Third Essay is the principle that archetypal patterns are most clearly discernible in myth, for in mythical stories we are in a world of pure and abstract literary design. Myth is the first of three organizations of archetypal symbols; it lies at the pole of total metaphorical identity, and it assumes the form either of a desirable apocalyptic world or an undesirable demonic one. At the other extreme is the world of verisimilitude or naturalism, embodying the *same* archetypes found in myth, except they are now displaced in the direction of plausibility. Lying between these two poles is the whole area of romance. Here the archetypes of art resemble human experience more closely than in myth, although at the same time the content of art is more conventional, having been analogized to the ideal, mythical world (AC, 136–40). The term "romance" does not refer here, as it did in the First Essay, to a historical mode. It refers rather to the dialectical tendency, inherent in those forms of literature which are neither undisplaced myth nor pure naturalism, to move toward the real or the plausible, in one direction, and toward the ideal or mythical, in the other. Whenever this tendency is present, we have romance.

Frye's analogy between the structural principles of literature and their equivalents in music (key and rhythm) provides a convenient means for seeing the bipolar organization of the Third Essay. The literary equivalent of musical key is the structural pattern of imagery. To apply Frye's terminology to the structure of archetypal meaning, the literary equivalent of musical key is the *dianoia* or static pattern formed by imagery, as well as its pattern of ideas. Corresponding to musical rhythm, at the other pole, is the *mythos* of imagery, or the narrative movement from one structure of imagery to another (AC, 136, 140, 158). The organization of the Third Essay therefore rests upon the formulation of the now-familiar distinction between *dianoia* and *mythos.*

The Dianoia *of Archetypal Imagery*

Frye's analysis of archetypal meaning is organized along two axes of reference. The first might be called simply "types of imagery." Although he divides archetypal imagery into three basic kinds—apocalyptic, demonic, and analogical—there are in effect five basic categories, since analogical imagery is further divisible into three types. Located along the other axis are the "categories or levels of reality," metaphorically referred to as "worlds." There are seven of these, forming a kind of paradigm of the Great Chain of Being. We conceive of reality, according to Frye, as existing on various levels: the divine world, the human world, the animal world, and so on. These two axes can be seen as forming a matrix on which it is possible to locate the different kinds of archetypal imagery. Figure 7 represents a simplified version of this matrix. While such a literal charting makes Frye's thought appear simpler and more rigid than it in fact is, the diagram has the advantage of providing a quick overview of the categories he uses to distinguish archetypal images.

Since apocalyptic imagery exists at the level of undisplaced myth, we can expect the principle of radical metaphor to figure importantly in Frye's discussion. This principle, when applied to apocalyptic imagery, will yield the concrete universal, which means, as we have already observed, that any apocalyptic image is not only unique in itself but also potentially *identical* with any other apocalyptic image. The argument here is difficult and needs to be examined in some detail.

	APOCALYPTIC	ROMANTIC	HIGH MIMETIC	REALISTIC	DEMONIC
DIVINE WORLD	Society of gods Trinity	Parental, wise old men with magical powers Prospero Raphael	King idealized as divine Mistress of courtly love as goddess	Spiritual vision anchored in empirical psychological experience	Stupid powers of nature, machinery of fate Blake's Nobodaddy, etc.
HUMAN WORLD	Society of men Men as members of one body	Children and innocence Chastity Dante's Matelda Spenser's Britomart	Idealized human forms	Common, typical human situations, parody of idealized romance	Society of egos in tension Tyrant-leader *Pharmakos*
ANIMAL WORLD	Lamb of God Sacrificial horse Dove	Pastoral lamb, horses and hounds of romance, ass, unicorn, dolphin, birds	Eagle, lion, horse, swan, falcon, peacock, phoenix	Ape, tiger	Beasts of prey: tiger, wolf, vulture, dragon
VEGETABLE WORLD	Paradisal garden and tree Arcadian imagery of green world Rose, lotus	Garden of Eden (Milton, Bible) Spenser's Garden of Adonis *Locus amoenus*	Formal gardens (in background)	Farms, painful labor of man Peasants	Sinister forest or enchanted garden Tree of forbidden knowledge
MINERAL WORLD	Jerusalem Highway and road "The Way"	Tower, castle	Capital city with court at center	Labyrinthine modern city Stress on loneliness and lack of communication	Deserts, rocks, waste land
FIRE WORLD	Seraphim and cherubim Ritual sacrifice by fire Saint's halo Burning trees	Fire as purifying symbol Spenser's castle of Busirane Dante's purgatory	King's crown Lady's eyes	Fire as ironic and destructive Prometheus	Malignant demons, will-o'-the-wisps, spirits broken from hell Burning cities
WATERY WORLD	Water of life Fourfold river of Eden Baptism	Fountains, pools Fertilizing rains Lethe	The disciplined river (Thames) ornamented by royal barge	Sea as destructive element Humanized leviathans, Moby Dick, Shelley's open boat	Water of death Spilled blood Sea monsters

Figure 7. Structures of archetypal imagery.

In the Second Essay, Frye maintains that unlimited individual thought and action, existing at the conceivable boundaries of desire, are most likely to be encountered in apocalyptic revelation. The central poetic image for expressing this concept is in classical mythology a god or society of gods, and in the Christian tradition one God. Since both a society of gods and one God are, anagogically, symbolic forms of the *same* unlimited human desire, they can be said to be identical. Everything at the divine level, we recall, is identical in the sense of being unified. Therefore, in the Third Essay Frye's own tabular equation among the divine world, a society of gods, and one God (AC, 141) follows from his theory of anagogic metaphor.

This, however, is but half of Frye's argument. He makes the additional and even more paradoxical claim that, at the apocalyptic level, a relation of identity also exists among the seven different categories of reality (divine, human, animal, vegetable, etc.). This means, to take only one example, that the sheep, or the "human form" imposed upon the animal world (the sheep having traditional priority as a domesticated animal), is *identical* at the apocalyptic level with the city, which, as built from stone, is the traditional image imposed by human work upon the mineral world. It is possible to understand this relationship of identity only at the level of apocalypse or revelation, and the perfect conception for illustrating the idea of radical identification is Christ, who is metaphorically God, man, the lamb, the tree of life, the temple, and the light and water of life, all at the same time. The doctrine of transubstantiation also illustrates the identification of apocalyptic images. This doctrine is nothing less than a radical metaphor which identifies the bread and wine of the vegetable world with "the body and blood of the Lamb who is also Man and God, and in whose body we exist as in a city or temple" (AC, 143).

Once Frye has established the categories which constitute his vertical axis, he then lists the various kinds of images which can be discovered in apocalyptic, demonic, and analogical works. Examples of archetypal imagery are represented in Figure 7. The general pattern of Frye's discussion, however, is not linear, as the outline in Figure 7 implies. Archetypal criticism, Frye says in his analysis of fourth-phase symbolism, "rests on two organizing rhythms or patterns, one cyclical, the other dialectic" (AC, 106). We should therefore expect to find Frye using these patterns in his theory of myths. Indeed, both are present. The cyclical pattern underlies the second half of this theory, whereas the dialectical rhythm organizes the first.

The dialectic of archetypal *dianoia*, which is our present concern, is most obviously apparent in the two pairs of opposite categories underlying Frye's chapter headings: apocalyptic versus demonic, romantic versus realistic. Thus we find apocalyptic imagery, representing the world of unlimited desire and projected as Paradise or Eden, opposed by demonic imagery, symbolizing the world of existential hell, "the world of the nightmare and the scapegoat, of bondage and pain and confusion; the world as it is before the human imagination begins to work on it and before any image of human desire, such as the city or the garden, has been solidly established; the world also of perverted or wasted work, ruins and catacombs, instruments of torture and monuments of folly" (AC, 147). Apocalyptic imagery, because it recreates a visionary or divine world, is associated with myth. Demonic imagery, on the other hand, because it so often depends upon parody (cannibalism as a mocking image of the Eucharist, for example), is associated with irony and satire. Thus Frye is making a correlation between the archetypal imagery of his apocalyptic and demonic worlds and the first and last categories in his theory of modes. He completes the correlation in his analysis of analogical imagery, introducing his discussion in these terms:

> Most imagery in poetry has of course to deal with much less extreme worlds than the two which are usually projected as the eternal unchanging worlds of heaven and hell. Apocalyptic imagery is appropriate to the mythical mode, and demonic imagery to the ironic mode in the late phase in which it returns to myth. In the other three modes these two structures operate dialectically, pulling the reader toward the metaphorical and mythical undisplaced core of the work. We should therefore expect three intermediate structures of imagery, corresponding roughly to the romantic, high mimetic, and low mimetic modes. (AC, 151)

This passage implies what Frye means by "analogical imagery." If there is a dialectic which pulls us toward the world of myth, it will represent those kinds of literary works in which the *dianoia* is but an analogy of an undisplaced world. Or, to put the matter in different terms, it will represent a human form of myth. And since there are three modes of literature lying between the two undisplaced worlds, there are three kinds of analogical imagery. Moreover, each form can be said to embody what Frye calls "organizing ideas." This triad of relationships is outlined in Figure 8.

Imagery	Romantic	Realistic	
Mode	Romance	High mimetic	Low mimetic
Analogy	Innocence	Nature and reason	Experience
Organizing Ideas	Chastity and magic	Love and form	Genesis and work

Figure 8. Categories of analogical imagery.

The kinds of imagery which are typically found in each of these intermediate structures are indicated in Figure 7. Regarding the procedure of Frye's argument, his method of classifying these images characteristically begins at the level of literary mode. This permits him to isolate certain types of works. At the romantic end of the continuum, for example, he selects a series of works from the medieval age, the Renaissance, and the nineteenth century. Having done this, he searches for certain clusters or "significant constellations" of romantic imagery, which he then lists as characterizing the analogy of innocence. In actual practice, Frye's method was certainly more inductive than implied by this outline. I mean only to call attention to those stages of the argument which the sequence of his discussion suggests.

Displacement

To this point Frye's account of indirect mythologizing, or what he calls "displacement," has been in terms of credibility. Writers adapt or modify their stories so as to make them follow the laws of probability; thus the movement away from myth is a movement toward verisimilitude. As a result, these stories appear to us as plausible forms of undisplaced myth. But displacement can also move in the direction of *moral* acceptability. At the level of radical metaphor, there is no correlation between what is desirable or undesirable and what is moral. The imagery of the demonic vision, for example, is sinister not because it is morally unacceptable but because it cannot be made an object of desire. Or, to put the matter differently, in apocalyptic symbolism human lust and ambitions are projected onto the gods and thereby identified with them. At this level there is no concern for making the moral and desirable coincide; thus we find such things in mythology as the creation of the world by masturbation. As we move away from the apocalyptic world, however, imagery tends to follow the laws of what is morally acceptable. In other words, civilization, or the human form of desire, tries to collapse the distance between the moral and the desirable. Thus in the analogy of innocence we find that apocalyptic sexual imagery, to take one example, has been displaced as the matrimonial or the virginal (AC, 155–57). But this kind of displacement is typical only of poetry which is closely associated with religion, as in Dante. Frye says that literature "continually tends to right its own balance, to return to the pattern of desire and away from the conventional and moral" (AC, 156). We are most likely to encounter this tendency in the analogy of experience, where morally undesirable imagery often finds its rightful expression "only through ingenious techniques of displacement" (AC, 156).

What function can an understanding of these relationships between poetry and morality serve? On the one hand, it can show us that literature is more flexible than morality, and thus we are prevented from making easy equations between the two. An archetype with typically immoral connotations can be deliberately reversed by the poet through the technique that Frye calls "demonic modulation" (AC, 156). This means that an image or concept from the demonic world, like a serpent or incestuous relations, can be displaced in the direction of the moral. It means also that symbols take their meaning from their context.

> The serpent, because of its role in the garden of Eden story, usually belongs on the sinister side of our catalogue in Western literature; the revolutionary sympathies of Shelley impel him to use an innocent serpent in *The Revolt of Islam.* Or a free and equal society may be symbolized by a band of robbers, pirates, or gypsies; or true love may be symbolized by the triumph of an adulterous liaison over marriage, as in most triangle comedy; by a homosexual passion (if it *is* true love that is celebrated in Virgil's second eclogue) or an incestuous one, as in many Romantics. (AC, 157)

This kind of modulation, Frye would claim, should make us aware that the meaning of imagery, because displaced, can violate its customary moral associations; it follows, then, that the failure to take displacement of this sort into account can cause faulty interpretations, based on the incorrect notion that the moral reference of archetypes is inflexible.

This is but half of Frye's claim, for he suggests also that a "full critical analysis" (AC, 158) will always want to take account of the latent content lying behind the manifest (i.e., displaced) content. As in Freudian analysis, the latent content is likely to be, if not repugnant, at least morally disagreeable. Frye's illustration is from tragedy. This form shows, among other things, that man's acceptance of inevitability is a displacement of his bitter resentment against the obstacles that thwart his desires. "A Christian who believed the Greek gods to be nothing but devils would, if he were criticizing a tragedy of Sophocles, make an undisplaced or demonic interpretation of it. Such an interpretation would bring out everything Sophocles was trying *not* to say; but it could be a shrewd criticism of its latent or underlying demonic structure for all that" (AC, 157–58). In other words, the manifest content of Sophocles' plays is a morally plausible form of what our latent, and therefore deepest, desires are. And it is this latent content which is structurally important for Frye because it lies in or near the realm of undisplaced myth. To be able to see this is to see "the factor which lifts a work of literature out of the category of the merely historical" (AC, 158). Thus

Frye has made two claims about the value of seeing displacement as moral plausibility. On the one hand, it can help us to understand the meaning of individual archetypes, especially when their relation to some moral norm is unconventional. On the other hand, it can help us to see the mythical patterns, both apocalyptic and demonic, which are structural principles of entire works.[3]

The Mythos *of Archetypal Imagery*

We have seen that the bipolar organization of the Third Essay is based upon the distinction between *dianoia* and *mythos*. To use Frye's musical analogy once again, the structural pattern of imagery is the literary equivalent of *key*, whereas the narrative pattern of poetry corresponds to musical *rhythm*. Thus we find that in the second half of Frye's theory of myths, movement or process is the fundamental category. His major concern here is to make explicit the structures of archetypal imagery from the perspective of *mythos*. Movement, as one of the distinguishing traits of *mythos*, has already been anticipated in the analysis of analogical imagery, where there is a dialectical tendency for imagery to be pulled toward one or the other pole of the apocalyptic-demonic continuum. This is one form of process. But an even more basic form, as we shall now see, is cyclical movement.

Frye first shows how the seven categories of imagery, viewed in the previous section from the static perspective of *dianoia*, can also be seen as process. The basic shape of this movement is cyclical, showing "the alternation of success and decline, effort and repose, life and death which is the rhythm of process" (AC, 158). The cyclical form of each category of imagery is outlined in Figure 9.

Moreover, within the several cycles, Frye observes four main phases:

Seasons of the year:	Spring	Summer	Fall	Winter
Periods of the day:	Morning	Noon	Evening	Night
Aspects of water:	Rains	Fountains	Rivers	Sea, snow
Periods of life:	Youth	Maturity	Old age	Death

It is even possible to quadrisect the periods of Western culture into the Medieval Age, the Renaissance, the Eighteenth Century, and the Modern Period (AC, 160). The fourfold division has important consequences for the subsequent structure of Frye's argument. Schematically, the cyclical paradigm is located within the order of nature, whereas the dialectical one moves from the order of nature toward or into the higher apocalyptic realm.

Divine World	Death and rebirth of a god, associated with cyclic process of nature Birth-death-rebirth continuum of identity
Fire World of Heavenly Bodies	Day-night cycle (sun god) Solstitial cycle of solar year Lunar cycle
Human World	Imaginative cycle of waking and dreaming life (experience and innocence) Ordinary cycle of life and death (generic rebirth)
Animal World	Usually a tragic process (violent death by accident, sacrifice). Continuity comes through the life itself
Vegetable World	Annual cycle of seasons Adonis, Proserpine
Water World	Cycle from rains, to springs, to rivers, to sea, to clouds, to snow or rains
Mineral World	Assimilated to organic cycle Golden age, wheel of fortune, meditations over ruins, collapse of empires, *ubi sunt* elegy, etc.

Figure 9. Cyclical imagery for each level of "Reality."

The existence of these broad cyclical and dialectical movements within *mythos* leads Frye to conclude that there are "narrative categories of literature broader than, or logically prior to, the ordinary literary genres" (AC, 162). He calls these pregeneric elements *mythoi,* another fundamental distinction in Frye's master design, for the cyclical and dialectical movements of *mythoi* underlie the entire second half of *Anatomy of Criticism.* In terms of the origin of his most basic categories, *mythoi* derive ultimately from poetic imagery or, more accurately, from the movement of poetic imagery which is a part of our experience of literature.

Frye's method of argument at this point is based upon the similarities of "movement" between the seven categories of reality and the cyclical and dialectical processes of archetypes. Cyclically, the analogy produces four *mythoi*: comedy, romance, tragedy, and irony or satire (this latter also called "realism"). Dialectically, it produces an upward and downward movement between innocence and experience, apocalypse and nature, the ideal and the actual, the comic and the tragic. A diagrammatic representation of these movements is found in Figure 10. We have already encountered a rudimentary form of the dialectical part of this design in the First Essay, where Frye uses "comic" and "tragic" in a similar pregeneric sense to describe aspects of *mythos* in general.

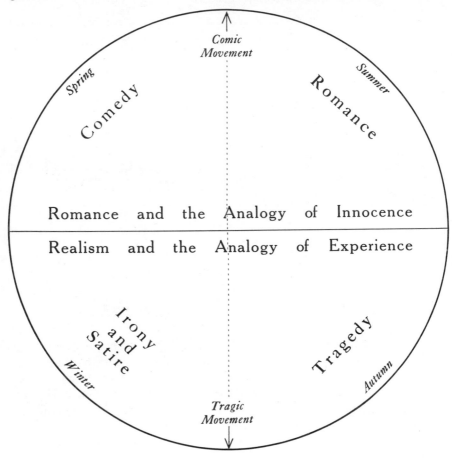

Figure 10. Cyclical and dialectical pattern of the four *mythoi.*

Figure 10, showing the quadrantal and cyclic pattern of the four *mythoi* and the dialectical arrangement of the mythical and realistic worlds, provides only the skeletal outline for Frye's taxonomy. The *mythos* of archetypes is a complex theory, the fullest and most elaborately conceived section of the *Anatomy.* While it accounts for but one-half of Frye's theory of archetypes, it comprises practically one-fourth of the entire book. The elaborateness of its design results chiefly from the theory of phases, the word referring in this context to the variety of literary structures which can be isolated in any one *mythos*.[4] Frye is able to discover six phases for each of the pregeneric *mythoi*; this yields, of course, twenty-four separate structures.

The argument is made more complex, however, by the fact that adjacent *mythoi* tend to merge. "If we think of our experience of these *mythoi*," Frye says, "we shall realize that they form two opposed pairs. Tragedy and comedy contrast rather than blend, and so do romance and irony, the champions respectively of the ideal and actual. On the other hand, comedy blends insensibly into satire at one extreme and into romance at the other; romance may be comic or tragic; tragic extends from high romance to bitter and ironic realism" (AC, 162). To this should be added the fourth possible relation, namely, that irony merges insensibly into tragedy and comedy. We shall examine these correspondences in more detail below.

The procedure used to define each of the *mythoi*—comedy, romance, tragedy, and irony and satire—follows a similar pattern throughout and derives from Frye's attempt to answer three questions: What is the structure of each *mythos*? What are the typical characters of each? And what are the six phases within each category?[5] It is more convenient, I think, to look at the method and structure of Frye's argument from the viewpoint of these three questions than from the perspective of the *mythoi* considered seriatim. My aim is not to summarize the content of his lengthy exposition but to observe the kinds of criteria he employs to define such concepts as plot and character and to see how he uses these categories to differentiate the *mythoi*. Underlying his definitions of each of these is a method which remains fairly constant throughout. The procedure can be illustrated by a passage from the discussion of comedy. The passage refers to *dramatic* comedy simply because Frye, for convenience (AC, 163), has restricted his discussion of comic theory chiefly to drama.

> In drama, characterization depends on function; what a character is follows from what he has to do in the play. Dramatic function in its turn depends on the structure of the play; the character has certain things to do because the play has such and such a shape. The structure of the play in its turn depends on the category of the play; if it is a comedy, its structure will require a comic resolution and a prevailing comic mood. (AC, 171–72)

The main presupposition in this passage is that pregeneric categories like comedy and tragedy do exist, their existence depending, as we have observed, on Frye's analogical and dialectical arguments (AC, 158–62). The next assumption is that this general category will determine the resolution and mood of a given work. Together these constitute its structure, which is the central concept Frye uses to discuss the typical form of each *mythos*. Character, finally, in Frye's Aristotelian argument, does not determine structure but is determined by it.

Structure The following analysis of the archetypal structure of the *mythoi* is based on two of the four typical patterns that Frye isolates: his treatment of comedy and romance. The normal pattern for comedy, he says, comes from the "plot structure of Greek New Comedy, as transmitted by Plautus and Terence. . . . What normally happens is that a young man wants a young woman, that his desire is resisted by some opposition, usually paternal, and that near the end of the play some twist in the plot enables the hero to have his will" (AC, 163). The action of this simple comic pattern has two centers of interest: the obstruction of the hero's desire by certain usurpers or blocking characters who dominate the internal society of the play; and the overcoming of these obstacles in the comic resolution, out of which is created a new society, often signaled by such festive rituals as weddings, dances, banquets, and the like. The way a comedy is developed depends on which of these two centers of interest is heightened. If the interest falls mainly upon the blocking characters, and therefore upon the conflict, then ironic, satiric, realistic, or mannered forms of comedy tend to result. On the other hand, if the emphasis moves toward the comic *anagnorisis* and the reconciliation, then the resultant form is romantic comedy of the Shakespearean kind (AC, 164–67).

Whichever ethical interest predominates, the typical comic structure shows the triumph of reality over illusion. In defining this theme, Frye draws upon two terms from the *Tractatus Coislinianus,* the fragmentary Greek treatise in which, he says, are set down "all the essential facts about comedy in about a page and a half." The terms are *pistis* (opinion) and *gnosis* (proof), and they "correspond roughly to the usurping and the desirable societies respectively" (AC, 166). The author of the *Tractatus* subdivides the latter term into five categories (oaths, compacts, witnesses, ordeals, and laws)—the five material forms of legal proof in Aristotle's *Rhetoric*. This leads Frye to draw an analogy between the action of comedy and the action of a lawsuit, for in both actions a judgment is made which separates the real from the illusory. Thus, he says, "the movement from *pistis* to *gnosis,* from a society controlled by habit, ritual bondage, arbitrary law and the older characters to a society controlled by youth and pragmatic freedom is fundamentally, as the Greek words suggest, a movement from illusion to reality" (AC, 169).

What is real in the comic ending, then, is actually the ideal, even though the nature of the ideal is seldom precisely specified. We can best understand this, Frye says, as the negative of whatever the now-defeated blocking characters have stood for, which is some form of the absurd. This is why our reaction to the typical comic ending involves not so much a moral condemnation of these characters (they are not villains) as it does a social judgment against their absurdity (AC, 167–68). The question of dramatic resolution, then, lies at the heart of Frye's analysis of comic structure; his discussion keeps returning to the issue of what the comic action moves toward: the new society created at the end. We shall see the reason for this emphasis on the *anagnorisis* shortly.

A final and important principle of comic action is that what we actually see presented in a given work is but a part of the total *mythos* of comedy, an idea which Frye compares to the ternary form in music. Just as a comic action leads toward a Saturnalia, the birth of a new but undefined world, so it also leads from the memory of a golden age in the past. This memory is not represented in the action itself: "The audience simply understands an ideal state of affairs which it knows to be better than what is revealed in the play, and which it recognizes as like that to which the action leads" (AC, 171).

Frye's analysis of romance draws upon the same criteria to define the typical romantic form: plot, conflict, development, theme, resolution, and total *mythos*. The essential element in the plot of romance, he maintains, is adventure, and what gives shape to the adventure, thus preventing it from becoming a series of endless repetitions, is the quest. Moreover, the most complete forms of romance show a successful conclusion to the plot, which is typically represented in three stages: "the stage of the perilous journey and the preliminary minor adventures; the crucial struggle, usually some kind of battle in which either the hero or his foe, or both, must die; and the exaltation of the hero" (AC, 187). These stages are called respectively the *agon* (conflict), the *pathos* (death-struggle), and the *anagnorisis* (recognition). In Frye's definition of the typical romantic plot, the first two stages assume a central importance, for they relate to the conflict between the hero and his antagonist; and the *agon*, as we shall see, is the basis (i.e., the archetypal theme) of romance.

Frye sees the typical form of the quest-romance as embodying the dragon-killing theme. His discussion of this draws heavily upon illustrations from the Bible, where metaphorical identifications are readily observed because of its highly mythopoeic form. Thus the dragon, appearing as the antagonist in romance, is a displaced archetype of Satan. Satan is *identified* in the Bible *as* the leviathan, the serpent, the behemoth, these in turn being identified as the source of social sterility (Egypt, Babylon), the fallen order of nature, death—everything, in short, which is opposed to Christ the hero.[6]

An important qualification enters Frye's argument at this point. "If the leviathan," he says, "is the whole fallen world of sin and death and tyranny into which Adam fell, it follows that Adam's children are born, live, and die inside his belly. . . . If we are inside the dragon, and the hero comes to help us, the image is suggested of the hero going down the monster's open throat, like Jonah" (AC, 190). The hero, in other words, disappears. Jesus, like his prototype Jonah, descends into hell. Theseus disappears into the labyrinth. Moses gets lost in the desert. Or, to take a more displaced version, Tom Sawyer climbs down into the cave. This disappearance of the hero is what leads to the qualification of Frye's three-stage romantic plot; for there are not three distinguishable aspects of the quest-myth after all, bur four. Thus to the *agon*, the *pathos*, and the *anagnorisis* Frye now adds the *sparagmos* or the tearing to pieces of the hero—which is the form his disappearance frequently takes (AC, 190–92).

We have seen how the comic plot is but one aspect of the total *mythos* of comedy. In a similar though more expansive way the conflict of romance is but a part of a larger *mythos* which neatly binds together all the *mythoi*. It is not insignificant that Frye's own version of the "monomyth" is presented in connection with his theory of romance:

> The four *mythoi* that we are dealing with, comedy, romance, tragedy, and irony, may . . . be seen as four aspects of a central unifying myth. *Agon* or conflict is the basis or archetypal theme of romance, the radical of romance being a sequence of marvellous adventures. *Pathos* or catastrophe, whether in triumph or in defeat, is the archetypal theme of tragedy. *Sparagmos,* or the sense that heroism and effective action are absent, disorganized or foredoomed to defeat, and that confusion and anarchy reign over the world, is the archetypal theme of irony and satire. *Anagnorisis*, or the recognition of a newborn society rising in triumph around a still somewhat mysterious hero and his bride, is the archetypal theme of comedy. (AC, 192)

That each of these four aspects of the "central unifying myth" appears also in the quest-myth, which has a romantic structure, indicates that Frye conceives of romance, formally speaking, as the fullest or most comprehensive literary type.[7] We shall return to Frye's predilection for romance later in this study. What is important to observe now is that the definition of the structure of a given *mythos* depends essentially on isolating one part of its narrative movement: in comedy it is the discovery; in romance the conflict. While these are elements of the structure of plot, Frye also refers to them as "themes." The two words are in fact synonymous at one level, the action of a comedy, for example, being embodied in the thematic movement from illusion to reality. In another context Frye says that "narrative in literature may also be seen as theme, and theme *is* narrative, but narrative seen as a simultaneous unity. At a certain point in the narrative, the point which Aristotle called *anagnorisis* or recognition, the sense of linear continuity or participation in the action changes perspective, and what we now see is a total design or unifying structure in the narrative" (SS, 164). This appears to be very close to what Aristotle means by plot, though Frye himself often uses the word in the un-Aristotelian sense of a typical scenario (e.g., AC, 163).

Throughout Frye's analysis of the structure of the various *mythoi*, we can observe the familiar method of analogy at work. The action of comedy is like the action of a lawsuit; the action of romance like the cycle of nature; comedy like spring; romance, summer; and so on. The most consistently employed analogies, however, come from the dream-ritual opposition, derived in turn from psychoanalytic theory and anthropology. Thus we find Frye saying that the ternary action of comedy "is, ritually, like a contest of summer and winter in which winter occupies the middle action; psychologically, it is like the removal of a neurosis or blocking point and the restoration of an unbroken current of energy and memory" (AC, 171). Similarly, the quest romance, when translated into the terms of dreams, "is the search of the libido or desiring self for a fulfillment that will deliver it from the anxieties of reality but will still contain that reality." In ritual terms, it "is the victory of fertility over the waste land" (AC, 193). Insofar as the analogical method helps Frye to define a given *mythoi*, it does so by continually moving the frame of reference outward to a much larger context. The effect, as Frye recognizes, is to tell us not about an action in particular but about *mythoi* in general.[8]

Character Frye's second aim in this section of the Third Essay is to determine the typical character of each *mythos*. A typical character for Frye is a "stock type," though this expression is not meant to imply the antithesis of the lifelike character. All lifelike characters, he says, "owe their consistency to the appropriateness of the stock type which belongs to their dramatic function. That stock type is not the character but it is as necessary to the character as a skeleton is to the actor who plays it" (AC, 172). The framework for Frye's discussion of these types is a set of two pairs of categories, three of which (*alazon, eiron,* and *bomolochos*) derive from the previously mentioned *Tractatus.* To these Frye adds the "character whom Aristotle calls *agroikos,* [one we] may reasonably accept . . . as a fourth character type" (AC, 172). We are most familiar with these kinds of stock characters in comedy, yet in each of the other *mythoi* Frye locates types which correspond generally to the two basic oppositions: *alazon* (impostor) versus *eiron* (self-deprecator), *bomolochos* (buffoon) versus *agroikos* (churl, rustic).[9]

Characterization depends on function, Frye has said, and this principle underlies his differentiation of the four character types. An *alazon,* for example, is distinguished from an *eiron* on the basis of the separate roles they play in achieving a given narrative structure. However abstract the four general categories may appear, Frye's discussion of them, in most cases, involves a wide range of particular illustrations. Moreover, the reference of each category, contrary to what the Greek label might imply, is not singularly restricted to some unambiguous prototype: *alazon* and *eiron,* for example, come to mean much more than simply impostor and self-deprecator, respectively. In fact, Frye develops a number of subtypes within each category. To illustrate the procedure he uses in defining these types and their variations, we turn once again to his analysis of the comic and romantic *mythoi.*

Alazons, the humorous blocking characters of comedy, are impostors in the sense that either they are hypocrites of some sort or, what is more frequently the case, they lack self-knowledge. The classic form of the *alazon-eiron* contest is the scene "in which one character complacently soliloquizes while another makes sarcastic asides to the audience" (AC, 172). The *alazon* type includes such characters as the *senex iratus,* the obsessed pedant, the learned crank, and the *miles gloriosus.* And there are variations, even, on these types: "Occasionally a character may have the dramatic function of [a *senex*] without his characteristics," like Fielding's Squire Allworthy (AC, 172). At the other pole are the self-deprecating characters, the central type of which is the hero. The technical comic hero or heroine is frequently a rather undeveloped, neutral type, especially in those works where the ethical interest centers on the blocking characters. But there are other types of comic *eirons:* the tricky slave of Roman plays, the scheming valet and mischievous trickster of the Renaissance, the Spanish *gracioso,* Beaumarchais's Figaro, the amateur detective of modern fiction, and characters which embody the "spirit of comedy," like Shakespeare's Puck and Ariel. Frye calls the general type of comic *eiron* the "vice," somewhat ironic itself since the vice is usually benevolent.[10] A third variation is the retreating paternal figure, the old man who withdraws from the action at the beginning and returns at the end. Often this kind of character, as in

Jonson and Shakespeare, is the real *architectus,* the one who enables the comic ending to occur.

Characters in romance, to turn now to the second *mythos,* are seldom subtly drawn, since, in relation to the quest, they tend to be either for it or against it. "If they assist it," Frye says, "they are idealized as simply gallant or pure; if they obstruct it they are caricatured as simply villainous or cowardly" (AC, 195). Such characters therefore follow the dialectical pattern of the plot structure they serve. Frye likens this opposition to black and white chess pieces. The white correspond to the *eirons* of comedy, insofar as their function is to see the quest successfully completed, and it includes such types as the hero, the potential bride, and the "wise old man" or magician who watches over and often controls the action. The counterpart of the comic *alazon* is any character who seeks to avert the hero's goal. The blocking characters in this case are, of course, villains, and they assume such various forms as evil magicians, witches, traitors, monsters, and the like (AC, 195–96).

In a similar fashion Frye establishes a parallel between the buffoon of comedy and the Golux of romance. The former includes all those fools, clowns, pages, parasites, mad hosts, cooks, and masters of revelry whose function is to increase the mood of festivity (AC, 175). The romantic mood, on the other hand, is intensified by the Golux character (the term is borrowed from Thurber)—the various spirits and children of nature, such as nymphs, daughter figures, faithful giants, green men, and other sprites of mysterious origin.

The fourth archetypal character of comedy is the *agroikos,* one who functions in opposition to the festive buffoon, and in this category we find churls, rustics, and, in highly ironic comedy, plain dealers and malcontents—all refusers of festivity in one way or another. On the romantic side, and in opposition to the Golux and his kindred natural spirits, are the characters who "call attention to the realistic aspects of life, like fear in the presence of danger, which threaten the unity of the romantic mood" (AC, 197). The apotheosis of this character type is Sancho Panza, but it would include also figures like Spenser's dwarf, "the shrunken and wizened form of practical waking reality" (AC, 197).

Frye proceeds to identify the four poles of characterization in the tragic and ironic *mythoi* as well. For our immediate purpose, however, the review of the comic and romantic characters is sufficient to establish the procedure of Frye's argument. This method, as we have seen, depends on a series of dialectical oppositions. 'If we are told," Frye says in the introduction to his theory of *mythos,* "that what we are about to read is tragic or comic, we expect a certain kind of *structure* and *mood*" (AC, 162, italics added). These two concepts provide the basis for the most general opposition in the discussion of character. The first two types (*alazons* and *eirons* and their counterparts) are isolated according to the structural functions they perform, whereas the last two (*bomolochoi* and the *agroikoi*) derive ultimately from the roles they play in creating the narrative mood. Having established the opposition between structure and mood and used it to distinguish the two general types, Frye proceeds at the next level to set up another pair of oppositions based upon the dialectical pattern within each *mythos*. Characters must fall on one side or another of the conflict of comedy and of the quest of romance. Structure and mood, in other words, determine character; and since for Frye each of these is seen as dialectical, there must be a double bipolar distribution of character types. Although the *Tractatus* seems to figure importantly in Frye's discussion, his own schema does not necessarily derive from what the author of this brief treatise says about comic character. Frye simply takes the Greek terminology and adapts it to his own dialectical argument.[11] The various levels of opposing categories, then, constitute the primary methodological principle behind Frye's definitions here. Once the four main categories have been established, he relies chiefly upon the method of illustration, calling on a vast range of examples to define the various subtypes.

To define by illustration is one of Frye's preferred methods. Because of the easy style of the *Anatomy* and because it is not burdened by unnecessary scholarly paraphernalia, it is perhaps sometimes easy to overlook the extent of the allusive method. But the prodigious range of Frye's reading makes its way onto practically every page of the *Anatomy*; the result is extraordinarily demanding. To select one section at random—Frye's brief (twenty-two-page) treatment of comedy in the Third Essay—we discover no fewer than eighty references to specific literary works; a host of general allusions to such things as Restoration comedy, Renaissance drama, Gothic romances, Old and New Comedy, and the like, and casual allusion to a number of writers without reference to particular works.

Phases We turn now to the third major category in Frye's theory of *mythos*, recalling his argument that there are six phases to each of the pregeneric *mythoi* and also that the phases from adjacent *mythoi* tend to merge, or to blend "insensibly" into one another. This produces what Frye himself calls "a somewhat forbidding piece of symmetry" (AC, 177). He is referring to the fact that each of the phases of a given *mythos* is parallel to, but not coincident with, a phase in the adjacent *mythos*. To understand how he works out these relationships, we have to conceive of each *mythos* as containing two groupings of phases, three phases belonging to each group. The first three phases of one *mythos* are always related to the *first three* of an adjacent *mythos,* but the relation is seen as occurring only within *opposing halves* of the major dialectic, whereas the relation between the *last three* phases of any two *mythoi* occurs only within the *same half* of the innocence-experience dichotomy. This means, for example, that there can be no merging between the first three phases of comedy and tragedy, or the first three of romance and irony since they are opposite, not adjacent, *mythoi.* It also means that there can be no relation between (say) the first three phases of tragedy and irony because both of these *mythoi* lie within the "realistic" half of the cycle. These correspondences have been charted in Figure 11, in which the shaded areas represent all the relations, and only those, which Frye sees as occurring between different phases. The intricacy of the design will become clearer as we examine the details of Frye's argument.

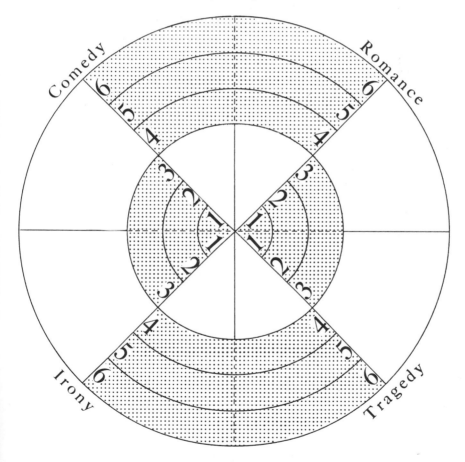

Figure 11. Parallel relations among the phases of the four *mythoi.*

The word "phase," as it is used in the Third Essay, refers to "one of six distinguishable stages of a mythos" (AC, 367). Since Frye's discussion is still at the pregeneric level, the word should not be misconstrued to mean literary species or subspecies, even though part of his discussion invites this identification.[12] Phases are more accurately seen in terms of Frye's assumption that, structurally, each *mythos* has a standard or typical pattern. From this perspective, a phase is a degree of variation in one of two directions from the norm, dissociating this last word from any implications of value it has. The degrees of variation, however, are determined by a number of criteria, which is why the term phase is difficult to define precisely. Sometimes Frye distinguishes the phases from each other in terms of the total plot pattern; at other times it is chiefly in terms of plot ending. Sometimes it is character; at other times, imagery. Increasing the complexity of the discussion, moreover, is the fact that Frye's model is cyclical as well as linear. These different procedures can be illustrated by comparing the criteria used to distinguish the phases within the comic and romantic *mythoi*.

As we have seen, the archetypal theme of comedy is *anagnorisis*: the comic structure leads toward the "recognition of a newborn society rising in triumph around a still somewhat mysterious hero and his bride" (AC, 192). Frye arranges the phases of comedy according to their place in the sequence which leads to this new society. In ironic comedy, or the first phase, society is furthest from its ultimate transformation. The emphasis here is on the blocking characters and the entertainers rather than the hero; the buffoons triumph over the plain dealers. The result is that the humorous society, rather than the one that should replace it, wins out; and the *eiron*—technically the comic hero—either fades into the background or joins forces, at the end, with the *alazons*. Frye calls this phase of comedy "ironic" not because of the *eiron*'s role, which is only nominally heroic, but because a sense of the demonic world keeps appearing in the background. Imminent catastrophes narrowly averted and potential tragedies never quite actualized—what Frye calls "the point of ritual death"—are a part of ironic comedy, and they suggest that such works still lie very much within the world of experience. "We notice too," says Frye, "how frequently the comic dramatist tries to bring his action as close to a catastrophic overthrow of the hero as he can get it, and then reverses the action as quickly as possible" (AC, 178). The imminent overthrow of the hero, then, is what makes such works ironic; the reversal of the action, coupled with the mood established by the *alazons* and buffoons, is what makes them comic.

In the second phase, or quixotic comedy, the hero runs away from the humorous society rather than transforming it; either this, or else the society constructed around the hero proves to be too weak to exist.

What we have then, as distinct from the first phase, is a separation of *eiron* and *alazon,* since neither of the forces they represent triumphs. There can be complex variations, however, on this simple pattern. The *eiron,* for example, may be partly an *alazon,* or "mental runaway," in which case "we have either a hero's illusion thwarted by a superior reality or a clash of two illusions" (AC, 180).

Third-phase comedy is the typical form. As we have seen in Frye's discussion of comic plot and character, the normal pattern shows the triumph of the *eiron* over the *senex iratus* or other blocking character, a victory which creates, in the *anagnorisis,* the beginnings of the new society. We can observe in passing that these first three stages of comedy—its ironic phases—correspond to the first three (or the satiric) phases of irony.

In the fourth phase, which might be called green-world or romantic comedy, we have moved out of the lower world of experience into the analogy of romance and innocence. This phase can be seen as operating on two social planes: one is realistic, which explains the proximity of this kind of comedy to the ironic phase; the other is idealistic, which explains why this stage is seen as romantic. Shakespeare's type of romantic comedy is Frye's typical example, "We may call it," he says, "the drama of the green world, its plot being assimilated to the ritual theme of the triumph of life and love over the waste land." Its action "begins in a world represented as a normal world, moves into the green world, goes into a metamorphosis there in which the comic resolution is achieved, and returns to the normal world" (AC, 182). The expression "green world" is meant to indicate the analogies which these comedies have to the world of ritual, like the rebirth of spring after winter, as well as to the world of dreamlike desire, as in the idealized but genuine "form of the world that human life tries to imitate" (AC, 184).

In fifth-phase comedy the ending is not so much a matter of the plot as it is the distanced perspective of the audience, who, looking down upon the action from a higher point of view, can distinguish the chaos of experience from the order of innocence. This phase, "less festive and more pensive" than fourth-phase comedy, can be called "Arcadian." In it, says Frye, "the reader or audience feels raised above the action." We look down on the plotting "as generic or typical human behavior: the action, or at least the tragic implication of the action, is presented as though it were a play within a play that we can see in all dimensions at once." And what is seen is not merely the movement from winter to spring, as in green-world comedy, but one from "a lower world of confusion to an upper world of order" (AC, 184).

Now in the first five phases, according to Frye, we see a progressive movement toward the redeemed society. His own recapitulation of this grand scheme is as follows:

Purely ironic comedy exhibits this society in its infancy, swaddled and smothered by the society it should replace. Quixotic comedy exhibits it in adolescence, still too ignorant of the ways of the world to impose itself. In the third phase it comes to maturity and triumphs; in the fourth it is already mature and established. In the fifth it is part of a settled order which has been there from the beginning, an order which takes on an increasingly religious cast and seems to be drawing away from human experience altogether. At this point the undisplaced *commedia,* the vision of Dante's *Paradiso,* moves out of our circle of *mythoi* into the apocalyptic or abstract mythical world above it. (AC, 185)

In the sixth stage we see that the total comic *mythos* has now come full circle. This is the *penseroso* phase, in which "the social units of comedy become small and esoteric, or even confined to a single individual" (AC, 185). The resulting mood is diametrically opposed to the festive spirit of ironic comedy, for the sixth phase presents a world of imaginative withdrawal, of the marvellous and the occult, of the Gothic romance and the ghost story.

Although a given comic phase may be understood in terms of cyclic pattern, as in the winter-spring cycle of fifth-phase comedy, the phases taken together constitute a linear movement. The total comic *mythos,* in other words, runs its course and dies. In the romantic *mythos,* however, the basic paradigm is overtly cyclical. And since the archetypal theme of romance is a series of marvelous adventures, our attention is focused not upon the social order, as in comedy, but upon the hero himself. The phases of romance, Frye says, "form a cyclical sequence in a romantic hero's life" (AC, 198). They begin with the myth of the birth of the hero in phase one, continue toward his mature exploits in phase three, and move finally to the level of purely contemplative adventure in phase six, where the cycle begins another revolution. The chief features in Frye's discussion of each of the six comic and romantic phases are indicated in Figure 12. Listed below the diagram are the parallel relationships between the comic and romantic phases and those of their adjacent *mythoi,* a matter we shall take up shortly.

Let us return now to the question of Frye's method of definition. In my commentary on the comic phases, I abstracted their major characteristics in order clearly to isolate his differentiating criteria. The major criterion is, of course, the new comic society, and the phases vary in relation to their distance, in either the ironic or romantic direction, from this norm.[13] Similarly, with regard to romance, the hero is established as the primary category, and each phase is seen therefore as a stage in the sequence of his life.

When Frye elaborates each of the phases, however, he characteristically focuses upon one of several sets of principles. Character, for example, is central to his distinction between the two ironic phases of comedy. Both character and plot figure importantly in his definition of the third comic phase. But these categories largely disappear in his analysis of the last three phases, where the social plane of comedy is less displaced. Some of the important norms here are imagery, as in the green-world analogies of the fourth phase; the attitude of the audience, as in the Arcadian fifth phase; and the underlying mood, as in the pensive sixth phase of individual detachment. A similar procedure is apparent in Frye's specific treatment of the romantic stages. References to the life of the hero, for example, all but disappear in his discussion of the last three phases, where theme and imagery emerge as the most important distinctions. A closer look at one of the phases will illustrate in more detail the kinds of criteria Frye appeals to.

In fourth-phase romance, he begins by noting, "the happier society

	COMEDY	ROMANCE
I	Ironic phase The infancy of the new society Example: *The Alchemist, Tartuffe*	The birth-of-the-hero phase Theme of mysterious origin, foundling Example: Moses story, Nativity story
II	Quixotic phase Adolescence of the new society Example: *The Wild Duck*	Pastoral innocence phase Youth of the hero Examples: Adam and Eve in Eden, Blake's *Thel, Kubla Khan*
III	Typical phase: the coming of age and the establishment of the new society Examples: Greek New Comedy, Plautus, Terence	Typical phase: the quest of the hero Example: St. George and Perseus
IV	Green-world phase The maturity and triumph of the new society Example: *A Midsummer Night's Dream*	Continuous innocence phase Theme: the maintenance of the innocent world Example: *Faerie Queene*, II & V
V	Arcadian phase New society as a part of the settled order Examples: *The Winter's Tale, Pericles*	Idyllic phase Theme: reflective, idyllic view of experience Examples: *Faerie Queene*, III; *Blithedale Romance*
VI	Gothic phase Collapse and disintegration of the new society Examples: Gothic thrillers, ghost stories, Huysman's *À Rebours*	*Penseroso* phase Theme: contemplative adventure Examples: Morris's *Earthly Paradise, The Decameron*

Figure 12. Phases of the comic and romantic *mythoi*. (Phases 1–3 of comedy are parallel to phases 1–3 of irony; phases 1–3 of romance are parallel to phases 1–3 of tragedy; phases 4–6 of comedy and romance are parallel to each other.)

	IRONY	TRAGEDY
I	Tragedy of dignity, based upon courage and innocence Central figure: the calumniated woman Example: *The Duchess of Malfi*	Satire of the low norm Typical figure: the flexibly pragmatic *eiron* Example: Erasmus's *Praise of Folly*
II	Tragedy of innocence Typical figure: young person Example: Ibsen's *Little Eyolf*	Quixotic satire Typical figure: successful rogue Example: picaresque novel
III	Tragedy of the hero's achievement Typical figure: prototype of Christ Example: *Samson Agonistes*	Satire of the high norm Typical figure: the giant killer Example: Rabelais, Petronius
IV	Typical phase: Tragedy of the fall of the hero Central figure: character of hybris and hamartia Example: most Greek and Shakespearean tragedy	Irony of explicit realism Typical figure: the all-too-human hero Example: Tolstoy's novels, Conrad's *Lord Jim*
V	Tragedy of lost direction, lack of knowledge, or meager heroism Typical figure: in lower state of freedom than audience Examples: *Timon of Athens, Oedipus Rex*	Irony of fatalism Typical figure: caught on wheel of fortune Example: *The Dynasts*
VI	Tragedy of shock and horror Typical figure: humiliated or agonized hero Examples: *Prometheus Bound, Titus Andronicus*	Irony of unrelieved bondage Typical figure: victim of misery, madness, or social tyranny Examples: *1984, The Penal Colony*

Figure 13. Phases of the tragic and ironic *mythoi*. (Phases 1–3 of tragedy are parallel to phases 1–3 of romance; phases 1–3 of irony are parallel to phases 1–3 of comedy; phases 4–6 of tragedy and irony are parallel to each other.)

is more or less visible throughout the action instead of emerging only in the last few moments" (AC, 200–201). This observation permits Frye to establish the parallel to fourth-phase comedy, about which he has made a similar claim (AC, 182). Next he isolates the central theme of this phase, "that of the maintaining of the integrity of the innocent world against the assault of experience" (AC, 201). This is not an unexpected observation, given the two-storied universe within which the cycle of *mythoi* revolve: in the fourth phase we cross over the boundary where romance and tragedy merge into the upper level of innocence. What forms, then, might such a theme take? Frye's answer is that sometimes it shows itself as moral allegory, as "in Milton's *Comus,* Bunyan's *Holy War,* and many morality plays, including *The Castell of Perseveraunce.*" At other times the form is a simpler scheme, intended merely to preserve the festive mood, as in the *Canterbury Tales* (AC, 201).

Having identified the fourth-phase theme as "the integrity of the innocent world," Frye then turns to specify its social and individual characteristics. In other words, his question now becomes: What is the nature of this integrated world which must be defended against the assaults of experience? Frye's answers come by way of *The Faerie Queene,* which serves him throughout as the classic example of the quest romance in English literature. The individual aspect of the innocent world, Frye says, is the allegory of temperance, based upon continence, in Book II of Spenser's poem; its social aspect is the legend of justice, based upon power, in Book V. He concludes his discussion by calling attention to several of the primary fourth-phase images: the beleaguered castle, the monster tamed by the virgin, the Gorgon's head on Athene's shield, among others.

What we observe in this brief review of Frye's fourth-phase romance is a definition based upon several principles. Little is said about this phase as a stage in the cyclical sequence of the hero's life. The hero, in fact, enters the discussion only obliquely in Frye's comments about heroic innocence (AC, 201). His chief categories are much broader: the happier society, the world of innocence, and the individual and social aspects of fourth-phase allegory. The definition depends finally upon statements about theme and imagery in the context of these broad categories.

In summary, Frye differentiates the phases by appealing to the same categories he used to define the pregeneric *mythoi* in the first place: imagery, theme, plot structure, character, and mood. There are, of course, other principles, like the perspectives of the audience, which are introduced from time to time (see, e.g., AC, 184, 237), and we are always aware of the vertical dialectic which lies behind the phases of each *mythos.* The phases, that is, vary in relation to their distance from two poles. Those of comedy lie between the poles of irony and romance; those of romance, between tragedy and comedy; of tragedy, between romance and irony; and of irony, between comedy and tragedy (see Figure 11). But whatever combination of criteria Frye appeals to, it is clear that when he defines "phase" as a stage of a *mythos,* he is not referring to literary kinds, a topic reserved for the Fourth Essay. He is speaking rather of broad narrative movements which extend beyond, as well as cut across, individual literary works. A phase may be an isolable part of a whole work, like one book of *The Faerie Queene* or Dante's vision at the end of the *Paradiso,* or it may encompass a group of writings by a single author, like Shakespeare's romantic comedies (*A Midsummer Night's Dream, As You Like It, The Merry Wives of Windsor, The Winter's Tale*). A phase may include works whose common feature is a particular rhetorical convention, like the symposium device (AC, 202–3); or its definition may largely depend on the perspective of the audience, as in fifth-phase comedy.

As already indicated, Frye conceives of each phase of a given *mythos* as parallel to a phase in the adjacent *mythos*. To pose the issue as a question: What are the similarities between comic romance and romantic comedy, between tragic irony and ironic tragedy, between ironic comedy and comic irony, and between tragic romance and romantic tragedy? The distinction between any pair of these categories, Frye says, "is tenuous, but not quite a distinction without a difference" (AC, 177). Figures 11, 12, and 13, the last two of which outline the twenty-four phases, can serve as our framework for considering their parallels. Whereas Frye explicitly calls attention to some of the correspondences, others exist only by implication. Our concern is to determine the principles which underlie their similarity.

As indicated in Figure 12, phases four through six of comedy and romance correspond to each other. Frye establishes the correspondence by isolating one or more characteristics of each of the three comic phases and by showing how they also appear in the romantic ones. The thing which fourth-phase comedy and romance have in common is the fact that in both "the happier society is more or less visible throughout the action instead of emerging only in the last few moments" (AC, 200–201). We have already noticed how, in fourth-phase comedy, the vision of innocence represented by green-world imagery appears long before the ending, say, of a Shakespearean play and establishes itself as the norm by which to judge the comic resolution. A similar vision of the innocent world, as we have also seen, underlies fourth-phase romance, its thematic aim being to maintain the integrity of this vision against the encroachments of the world of experience.

The common factor embodied in fifth-phase comedy and romance is their tendency both to give prominence to the natural cycle and to take a reflective, detached, and idyllic view of experience (AC, 184, 202). In the sixth, or *penseroso*, phase of the two *mythoi*, the similarity is in the nature of the comic society; in both phases, society is shown as having broken up into small, occult units, the smallest of which is the contemplative individual himself (AC, 185–86, 202).

Let us consider one more example in which we can observe still different criteria being used to establish the parallels. The similarity between second-phase romance and tragedy, Frye argues, is that both represent the innocent youth of the hero. In romance this phase is "most familiar to us from the story of Adam and Eve in Eden before the Fall. [It] presents a pastoral and Arcadian world. . . . Its heraldic colors are green and gold, traditionally the colors of vanishing youth. . . . it tends to center on a youthful hero . . . [and] in later phases

it is often recalled as a lost happy time or Golden Age" (AC, 199–200).
The parallel phase of tragedy

> corresponds to the youth of the romantic hero, and is in one way
> or another the tragedy of innocence in the sense of inexperi-
> ence, usually involving young people. . . . The phase is domi-
> nated by the archetypal tragedy of the green and golden world,
> the loss of the innocence of Adam and Eve, who, no matter how
> heavy a doctrinal load they have to carry, will always remain
> dramatically in the position of children baffled by their first
> contact with an adult situation. (AC, 220)

Here the affinity is based on several distinctions. The stage in the life
of the hero, the archetype of Adam and Eve, the vision of innocence or
inexperience, the green- and golden-world imagery are all characteristics common to both second-phase tragedy and romance. Frye can thus
establish the parallel relations between the phases by appealing either
to a single criterion, like the size of the social unit in sixth-phase comedy and romance, or to a wide range of criteria like those just mentioned. The criteria can extend, moreover, from something as particular as imagery or the age of the hero to something as general as the
vision of society embodied in a literary work.

Terminologically, many of the categories we have been examining
are, even though borrowed, peculiarly Frye's. Conceptually, however,
the Third Essay treats principles long familiar in the history of criticism—principles such as imagery, plot and its various parts, character,
theme, and mood. What *is* unique about the theory of myths is the
ordered and schematic structure of its presentation. In his comments
on the *Anatomy* in recent years, Frye keeps returning to this point.
Reflecting on the book ten years after, he says he sees it primarily not
as systematic but as schematic. "The reason why it is schematic is that
poetic thinking is schematic. . . . The *Anatomy*, especially in its third
essay, attempts to provide an outline of a schema which . . . 1 hoped
would serve as a guide to practical criticism."[14] The same note is
sounded almost twenty years after:

> *Anatomy of Criticism* presents a vision of literature as forming a
> total schematic order, interconnected by recurring or conven-
> tional myths and metaphors, which I call archetypes. The vision
> has an objective pole: it is based on a study of literary genres and
> conventions, and on certain elements in Western cultural his-
> tory. The order of words is there. . . . The fact that literature is
> based on unifying principles as schematic as those of music is

concealed by many things, most of them psychological blocks, but the unity exists and can be shown and taught to others. (SM, 118)

The analogy to music carries us back to the point where our analysis of Frye's theory of myths began. It is reminiscent of another mythographer who relies upon analogies from music to articulate his arguments, Claude Lévi-Strauss. There are, in fact, some striking similarities between the framework Frye uses to analyze archetypal forms and the one Lévi-Strauss has developed for the study of myth.[15] These similarities also take us back to beginnings—to the principles of *mythos* and *dianoia*.

To initiate his discussion of imagery, we recall, Frye engages in an abstract account of spatial and temporal form. The form of a poem can be seen either "as stationary or as moving through the work from beginning to end." Whichever perspective we choose, the form remains the same, "just as a musical composition has the same form when we study the score as it has when we listen to the performance" (AC, 83). When Frye relates these principles to pattern and rhythm, he turns once again to music: "The average audience at a symphony knows very little about sonata form, and misses practically all the subtleties detected by an analysis of the score; yet those subtleties are really there, and as the audience can hear everything that is being played, it gets them all as part of a linear experience; the awareness is less conscious, but not less real. The same is true of the response to the imagery of a highly concentrated poetic drama" (AC, 85–86).

The logical framework of Lévi-Strauss's system is, like Frye's, based on a series of opposing yet related categories, most of which derive from his study of structural linguistics and semiology. We know from what the brain can do with patterns of sound, according to Lévi-Strauss, that it can manipulate pairs of relations and make plus-minus distinctions as in matrix algebra. He believes that other elements of culture form similar sign languages which the brain uses to apprehend their forms. Corresponding to Frye's idea of narrative, or *mythos* as movement, is Lévi-Strauss's conception of the syntagmatic nature of myths: they consist of a series of details linked together in a chain, diachronically. In order to tell the myth we simply follow the temporal sequence of the story. But myths also have what he calls paradigmatic relations, entire units of meaning which have been superimposed on each other to form a synchronic pattern. To understand a myth, he argues, we have to disregard the diachronic dimension altogether and consider only the pattern formed by each unit. Something similar, he points out, occurs in music. Because patterns of musical notes recur at intervals, an orchestra score must be read diachronically along one axis if it is to make melodic sense. But it also must be read synchronically, or vertically along the other axis, if it is to make harmonic sense. There is a close parallel, then, between Frye's spatial-temporal and stasis-movement axes, on the one hand, and Lévi-Strauss's synchronic-diachronic categories on the other. Once again we return to beginnings, for these universal axes form the ground plan upon which Frye erects the imposing and schematically intricate edifice of his Third Essay.[16]

4

Theory of Genres

Rhetorical Criticism

"The problem of convention," Frye says in the Second Essay, "is the problem of how art can be communicable. . . . As the archetype is the communicable symbol, archetypal criticism is primarily concerned with literature as a social fact and as a mode of communication. By the study of conventions and genres, it attempts to fit poems into the body of poetry as a whole" (AC, 99). Frye's description of these conventional and generic modes of communication is found in the Third and Fourth Essays, the latter of which is entitled "Rhetorical Criticism." Rhetorical issues are raised throughout the First Essay. In the sense, then, that modes of communication have traditionally been located in the province of rhetoric, each of the first three essays is concerned to some degree with the anatomy of rhetorical conventions. When we come to the Fourth Essay, however, this highly general observation must give way to the more restricted issues of what is specifically called "rhetorical criticism" and of its relation to Frye's theory of genres. In pursuing these topics we have the advantage of the framework Frye sketches at the beginning of the Fourth Essay. It indicates the place of rhetoric in his system as a whole and outlines his distinction between persuasive and ornamental rhetoric, the latter of which is his chief concern.

The far-ranging framework, which recapitulates the view of art proposed in the *Anatomy,* is based upon the age-old division of reality into three categories, described variously as thought, action, and passion, or truth, goodness, and beauty. In this division, Frye says,

> the world of art, beauty, feeling, and taste is the central one, and is flanked by two other worlds. One is the world of social action and events, the other the world of individual thought and ideas. Reading from left to right, this threefold structure divides human faculties into will, feeling, and reason. It divides the mental constructs which these faculties produce into history, art, and science and philosophy. It divides the ideals which form compul-

sions or obligations on these faculties into law, beauty, and truth. (AC, 243)

What Frye calls the "diagrammatic framework" of these triads is presented in Figure 14. A glance at the chart will indicate how the special terminology Frye has employed up to this point falls neatly into the triadic schema: using the method of analogy, he can conveniently fit *mythos, ethos,* and *dianoia* into the diagram. *Ethos,* as Frye has defined the term, stands at the center, flanked on one side by the verbal imitation of action (*mythos*) and on the other by the verbal imitation of thought (*dianoia*). Similarly, the poetic symbol finds its place in the framework midway between event and idea, example and precept, ritual and dream—all of which were used in the Second Essay to define the phases of symbolism.

But Frye also recognizes a second aspect of the same triadic scheme, corresponding to the last three qualitative parts of Aristotle's analysis of tragedy: music, diction, and spectacle. He develops this threefold division in another series of analogies:

> The world of social action and event, the world of time and process, has a particularly close association with the ear. The ear listens, and the ear translates what it hears into practical conduct. The world of individual thought and idea has a correspondingly close association with the eye, and nearly all our expressions for thought, from the Greek *theoria* down, are connected with visual metaphors. Further, not only does art as a whole seem to be central to events and ideas, but literature seems in a way to be central to the arts. It appeals to the ear, and so partakes of the nature of music, but music is a much more concentrated art of the ear and of the imaginative perception of time. Literature appeals to at least the inner eye, and so partakes of the nature of the plastic arts, but the plastic arts, especially painting, are much more concentrated on the eye and on the spatial world. . . . Considered as a verbal structure, literature presents a *lexis* which combines two other elements: *melos,* an element analogous to or otherwise connected with music, and *opsis,* which has a similar connection with the plastic arts. (AC, 243–44)

This second series of triads comprises what Frye sees as the rhetorical aspect of literature, one which "returns us to the 'literal' level of narrative and meaning" (AC, 244). We recall not only that Frye frequently equates rhetorical criticism with the procedures of the New Critics but also that he establishes, in the Second Essay, a correspondence between these procedures and the literal phase of symbolism.[1]

Three Worlds of "Good" in *Anatomy of Criticism*	Social Action and Events	Art, Beauty, Feeling, Taste	Individual Thoughts and Ideas
Human Faculties	Will	Feeling	Reason
Mental Constructs	History	Art	Philosophy, Science
Ideals	Law	Beauty	Truth
Poe's Schema	Moral Sense	Taste	Pure Intellect

First Three Aristotelian Elements	*MYTHOS:* Verbal Imitation of an Action	*ETHOS:* Human Nature and Human Situation	*DIANOIA:* Verbal Imitation of Thought
Categories of the Second Essay	Event	Poetic Symbol	Idea
	Example		Precept
	Ritual		Dream

Second Three Aristotelian Elements	*Melos* The Musical	*Lexis* as Diction *Lexis* as Imagery	*Opsis* The Pictorial
Pound's Schema	*Melopoeia*	*Logopoeia*	*Phanopoeia*
The "Trivium"	Grammar: Narrative or Right Order	Rhetoric	Logic: Produced Sense

Figure 14. Triadic framework of *Anatomy of Criticism*.

Frye also defines rhetoric by means of the traditional "trivium," locating it midway between grammar and logic. The definition arises from an analogy between *mythos* and grammar on the one hand and between *dianoia* and logic on the other. "As grammar may be called the art of ordering words," Frye observes, "there is a sense—a literal sense—in which grammar and narrative are the same thing; as logic may be called the art of producing meaning, there is a sense in which logic and meaning are the same thing" (AC, 244). In this view, grammar is "understood primarily as syntax or getting words in the right (narrative) order," whereas logic is "understood primarily as words arranged in a pattern with significance" (AC, 244–45). Rhetoric, because of its central position in this framework, synthesizes grammar and logic, just as *lexis* performs the same function in relation to *melos* and *opsis*. Frye translates *lexis* as " 'diction' when we are thinking of it as a narrative sequence of sounds caught by the ear, and as 'imagery' when we are thinking of it as forming a simultaneous pattern of meaning apprehended in an act of mental 'vision' " (AC, 244). *Lexis,* in fact, *is* rhetoric, or rather ornamental as distinct from persuasive rhetoric. Similarly, if we consider grammar as the art of ordering words and logic as the art of producing meaning, then literature "may be described as the rhetorical organization of grammar and logic" (AC, 245). The affinity between diction as a narrative sequence and *mythos,* on the one hand, and imagery as a pattern of meaning and *dianoia,* on the other, should not go unnoticed.

These definitions of rhetoric are quite inclusive and operate at a high level of generality. But the broad distinctions, especially the relationship of verbal pattern to music and spectacle, figure importantly in the theory of genres, serving to differentiate, for example, among the four kinds of literary rhythm (about which more later). Before turning to the organization of Frye's theory of genres, I want to make explicit his distinction between ornamental and persuasive rhetoric. "These two things," he says, "seem psychologically opposed to each other, as the desire to ornament is essentially disinterested, and the desire to persuade is essentially the reverse" (AC, 245). This is a distinction of ends, or a difference between final and instrumental value. Thus the movement of ornamental rhetoric is seen as centripetal, acting upon its hearers statically and producing the admiration of beauty and wit for its own sake, whereas the movement of persuasive rhetoric is centrifugal, leading the audience "kinetically toward a course of action." The former "articulates emotion; the other manipulates it" (AC, 245). Frye's concern is chiefly, though by no means exclusively, with ornamental rhetoric, which he equates, as already noted, both with the *lexis* of poetry and finally with the hypothetical structure of literature itself.

The basic organization of the Fourth Essay derives from what Frye, following Coleridge, calls "initiative," or the "controlling and coordinating power" which "assimilates every thing to itself, and finally reveals itself to be the containing form of the work."[2] The initiative is comprised of four separate categories: the theme; the unity of mood which determines imagery; the meter, or integrating rhythm; and the genre. This complex of factors, Frye asserts, governs the process of poetic composition. He has treated the first two initiatives in his discussion of archetypal images and narratives in the Third Essay. The remaining two, rhythm and genre, are the controlling ideas of the Fourth.

Although within the larger diagrammatic framework Frye's definition of rhetoric is general, it has a more specialized and traditional reference as it relates to the fourth factor of a writer's initiative (the genre). "The basis of generic criticism," he says, "is rhetorical, in the sense that the genre is determined by the conditions established between the poet and his public" (AC, 247). Frye calls this rhetorical element the *radical of presentation,* by which he means the fundamental, original, or ideal way in which a literary work is presented. The radical of presentation of fiction, for example, is the book or printed page; for drama, it is enactment by hypothetical characters.[3] In the last section of his "Introduction" to the Fourth Essay, Frye sketches the relationship among the author, the audience, and the radical of presentation for each of his four generic categories—drama, *epos,* fiction, and lyric. He also specifies for each genre both a predominant rhythm and a mimetic form. These relationships are summarized in Figure 15.

"Radical of presentation," "predominant rhythm," and "mimetic form" are, therefore, the three primary categories used to distinguish the four genres. Only one of these concepts, however, is extensively used in the remainder of the Fourth Essay. It seems clear that Frye wants to establish a relationship, on the one hand, between rhythm and the organization of *melos-lexis-opsis,* and on the other hand, between the radical of presentation and the mimetic form of each genre. The first

		DRAMA	EPOS	FICTION	LYRIC
RADICAL OF PRESENTATION		Enactment by hypothetical characters	Oral address	Book or printed page	Hypothetical form of I-thou relationship
AUTHOR OR POET		Poet concealed from audience	Speaking poet	Poet as person disappears	Poet speaking to himself, God, muse, etc.
	AUDIENCE	Observers-listeners as group	Listeners as group	Reader as individual	Poet has his back to audience, which overhears
MIMETIC FORM		External mimesis (outward representation of sound & imagery)	Mimesis of direct address	Mimesis of assertion	Internal mimesis (inward representation of sound & imagery)
	RHYTHM	Rhythm of decorum: appropriateness	Metrical rhythm: recurrence	Semantic rhythm: continuity	Oracular rhythm: association

Figure 15. The generic differentiae.

of these relationships is clearly developed: in what is perhaps Frye's most original contribution in the entire essay, he shows that the rhythm of each genre has its characteristic *melos* and *opsis*. The second relationship, however, after it has been used to differentiate the four genres, almost completely disappears in the discussion of generic forms, as we shall see when we look at the principles Frye uses to distinguish the *specific forms* of each genre.

To summarize the several conclusions which can be drawn from Frye's initial framework of categories: first, "rhetoric" is used in two distinct senses, closely paralleling the two rhetorical concerns in the First Essay. Ornamental rhetoric, the *lexis* of poetry, is an internal, centripetal category, similar to the rhetorical principle underlying the concept of "fictional modes." But rhetoric in the second sense, defined as the radical of presentation, is analogous to the ethical relationship between poet and audience which Frye has used to define "thematic modes."

Second, the main function which the second rhetorical category serves is to *define* the four genres: rhythm, form, and the radical of presentation provide the generic differentiae. And the main function served by the first rhetorical category (the organization of *melos, lexis,* and *opsis*) is to provide principles for an ingenious discussion of generic rhythm. This first category has the additional function of helping to differentiate the various rhythms; the rhythm of *epos,* for example, is distinguished not only by the comparatively regular meter of recurrence but also by the peculiar rhetorical manifestations of *melos* and *opsis,* such as onomatopoeia.

Third, rhetoric in the second sense is essentially a matter of style. Frye is not primarily a stylistic critic. But his discussion of rhythm is the one place in the *Anatomy* where he does turn to what Angus Fletcher calls the microstructure of literature, the effects of individual lines and phrase units.[4]

We should hardly expect, in reading an essay on rhetorical criticism, to encounter the unlikely combination of so particular a topic as prosody with so general a one as genre. But to turn from a discussion of poetic phrase units to a topic like the specific continuous forms of prose fiction is characteristic of Frye's ingenuity. It is because he sees all literature in its relation to other literature that he can move from the microscopic to the macroscopic levels without so much as casting a glance at the countless rhetorical concerns that lie somewhere in between. The point to be made is that Frye is writing a theory of criticism rather than a manual of style; thus his aim is to show how the concerns of stylistic criticism can fit within his synoptic view. Moreover, he sees the New Criticism as having adequately treated the texture of literary rhetoric. Perhaps the more important conclusion is that, by using the radical concept of rhythm in its smallest and largest senses, Frye forces us to see the integral relationship between two very different literary phenomena, both of which call for a social response. Frye's theory of rhetoric, finally, is one which unites style and genre—a point I intend to illustrate now by turning to an analysis of the four genres.

Frye's definitions of the genres should not be understood as absolute or mutually exclusive categories into which any work can be neatly fitted. The purpose of generic criticism, he argues, is not so much to classify as it is to clarify "traditions and affinities, thereby bringing out a large number of literary relationships that would not be noticed as long as there were no context established for them" (AC, 247–48). One of the main contexts is the radical of presentation. But since this expression refers only to the way in which works of literature were originally or ideally presented, we can expect many works to fit into more than one category. It is less important, Frye says, to worry about how to classify, say, a Conrad novel, where the narrative technique involves both the written and spoken word, than it is to recognize that this novel embodies two different radicals of presentation (AC, 247). Similarly, "the novels of Dickens are, as books, fiction; as serial publications in a magazine designed for family reading, they are still fundamentally fiction, though closer to *epos.* But when Dickens began to give readings from his own works, the genre changed wholly to *epos;* the emphasis was then thrown on immediacy of effect before a visible audience" (AC, 249). The point is that genres are based on conventions; and while it is convenient for Frye's argument to isolate four possible relations by which writers can communicate to their audiences, the history of literature, with its novels and closet dramas, shows that a given work does not always rely upon a single generic convention.

Characteristic rhythm and predominant form are the two principles underlying the arrangement of the Fourth Essay. Frye first explains the typical pattern of movement characteristic of the genres and then isolates their specific forms. My aim at this point is to uncover the argument behind the abstract rhetorical terminology just outlined.

Generic Rhythm

Epos   The characteristic rhythm of *epos,* defined as that genre where the radical of presentation is oral address (or the *mimesis* of direct address), is a comparatively regular meter (AC, 250). Frye's treatment of this kind of rhythm is essentially a commentary on English prosody. This observation should be qualified, however, by saying that he is not so much interested in the linguistic or literary details of prosody as he is in the broader theoretical similarities between the rhythm and pattern of *epos,* on the one hand, and *melos* and *opsis,* on the other. His argument begins with a series of metrical illustrations, used to support his thesis that the four-stress line "seems to be inherent in the structure of the English language" (AC, 251). By isolating stress as the primary constitutive principle of poetic rhythm, Frye throws the emphasis upon intensity and duration, the quantitative aspects of sound. There are several ways, however, of accounting for these two factors in the study of versification. That is, rhythm can be defined by counting the number of syllables to a line, or the number of accents, or by noting the specific temporal measure of a line. But Frye, as his illustrations indicate, relies primarily on stress, his concern being to show the number and disposition of accents within a line. This leads to the crux of his argument: the analogy between music and poetry. In those kinds of music which have been contemporary with all stages of modern English poetry (i.e., anything after Middle English), "we have had almost uniformly a stress accent, the stresses marking rhythmical units (measures) within which a variable number of notes is permitted" (AC, 255). Therefore, when stress accent predominates in poetry, it is "musical" poetry, in the sense that its structure resembles the music contemporary with it. "This technical use of the word musical," Frye adds,

> is very different from the sentimental fashion of calling any poetry musical if it sounds nice. In practice the technical and sentimental uses are often directly opposed, as the sentimental term would be applied to, for example, Tennyson, and withdrawn from, for example, Browning. Yet if we ask the external but relevant question: Which of these two poets knew more about music, and was *a priori* more likely to be influenced by it? the answer is certainly not Tennyson. (AC, 255)

Frye thus concludes that the word "musical"—Aristotle's *melos*—is more properly used as a critical term to describe the "cumulative rhythm" (AC, 256, 258) produced by a variable number of syllables between sharp stresses. Cumulative rhythm yields the "harsh, rugged, dissonant poem" (AC, 256). "When we find sharp barking accents, crabbed and obscure language, mouthfuls of consonants, and long lumbering polysyllables, we are probably dealing," Frye says, "with *melos,* or poetry which shows an analogy to music, if not an actual influence from it" (AC, 256). In addition to Browning, Frye includes Burns, Smart, Crashaw, Cowley, Skelton, Wyatt, and Dunbar among the musical poets. On the other hand, poets of the "metronome beat" (AC, 256), those who strive to achieve slow movement, balanced sounds, regular meter, and resonant rhythms, are unmusical poets, or they are musical only in the sentimental sense. Frye's examples of this type, in addition to Tennyson, include Pope, Keats, Spenser, Surrey, Gray's Pindarics, Arnold's *Thyrsis,* and Herbert's stanzaic poems (AC, 257).

Recounting the stages of Frye's argument, we see that he begins by defining *epos* as that genre in which the poet speaks to his listeners as a group by means of a form imitative of direct address. He then argues that poetry, conceived of as *lexis,* is a combination of two elements, one (*melos*) analogous to music, the other (*opsis*) to the plastic arts. The same concept may be expressed, Frye says, by translating *lexis* as "diction" when we are thinking of the musical element, and as "imagery" when we are thinking of it visually. Third, Frye maintains that each of the genres has a predominant rhythm. What he has done, then, in his discussion of *epos,* is to locate its rhythm in the principle of recurrence, defined as the quantitative relation between accent and meter.[5] Since poetic meter is analogous to the metrics of music, Frye refines his definition of quantitative recurrence by using the principle of *melos.* The result, as we have seen, is the distinction between technical and sentimental forms of *epos.*

What remains is for Frye to discover the element of *epos* analogous to *opsis.* This he finds in imitative harmony or onomatopoeia. But since this technical device depends essentially on sound, it is not immediately obvious why Frye correlates it to *opsis,* rather than to *melos* where it would seem more naturally to belong. The explanation is that he does not use onomatopoeia in the strict sense of words which imitate sound; rather, he uses it to mean all of those *combinations* of words in which any correspondence between sound and sense results. Sometimes the sense produced by the sound is visual, in which case it is appropriate to speak of verbal *opsis.* At other times, however, as Frye's illustrations indicate, onomatopoetic devices perform a different function, one that can be described as qualitative, like the suggestion of a mood. In these cases, no particular visual element need necessarily be present. Thus the analogy between imitative harmony and *opsis* loses some of its force, which may be one of the reasons why Frye himself speaks of the relations between *epos* and the pictorial arts as perhaps somewhat "far-fetched" (AC, 258). That it does make sense, however, to speak of visual onomatopoeia can be illustrated by this passage:

> The most remarkably sustained mastery of verbal *opsis* in English, perhaps, is exhibited in *The Faerie Queene,* which we have to read with a special kind of attention, an ability of catch visualization through sound. Thus in
> >   The Eugh obedient to the bender's will,
> the line has a number of weak syllables in the middle that makes

it sag out like a bow shape. When Una goes astray the rhythm
goes astray with her:
> And Una wandring farre in woods and forrests. . . .

(AC, 259–60)

Neither of Frye's examples is strictly onomatopoetic in the sense that it
employs words imitative of sounds. But in both lines the combination
of sounds does reinforce the sense by creating an image; thus Frye's
use of the expression "verbal *opsis.*"

Imitative harmony, of course, is not restricted to *epos.* But Frye
sees it as a continuous device in this genre, especially in the verse
forms,[6] whereas in drama, fiction, and lyric it appears only occasionally
(AC, 261–62). "We have stressed imitative harmony," he says, "because
it illustrates the principle that while in Classical poetry sound-pattern
or quantity, being an element of recurrence, is part of the *melos* of
poetry, it is part of the *opsis* in ours" (AC, 262). The breadth of reference of the terms in this sentence results not only from the fact that a
word like *opsis* is itself analogical, indicating a literary connection with
the pictorial arts, but also from the fact that in the expression "imitative
harmony" we have an analogy to *opsis.* In other words, onomatopoeia is
analogous to verbal *opsis,* which is in turn analogous to the pictorial
arts. This kind of argument illustrates Frye's analogical method at its
most complex level.

Although Frye seems to suffer some difficulty in making explicit
the influence of *opsis* on his first genre, we should not let this obscure
his main point: that in verse *epos* a complex of factors (stress, meter,
quantitative sound patterns) produces a rhythm of recurrence. This is
what distinguishes *epos* from the other genres, along with its different
radical of presentation.[7]

Prose Fiction   The radical of prose forms, Frye's second genre, is the
book or printed page. Together with *epos,* these forms, most notably
prose fiction, constitute "the central area of literature" (AC, 250). Historically, however, the radicals of *epos* and fiction constitute a kind of
dialectical tension: "*Epos* and fiction first take the form of scripture and
myth, then of traditional tales, then of narrative and didactic poetry,
including the epic proper, and of oratorical prose, then of novels and
other written forms" (AC, 250). Implicit here is the sequence of modes
developed in the First Essay. As we move along this sequence, according to Frye, "fiction increasingly overshadows *epos,* and as it does, the
mimesis of direct address changes to a mimesis of assertive writing.
This in its turn, with the extremes of documentary or didactic prose,
becomes actual assertion, and so passes out of literature" (AC, 250).

Just as Frye uses the dialectic of assertion versus direct address to differentiate the mimetic forms of fiction and *epos,* so he establishes two other poles to account for their different rhythms. In every work of literature, "we can hear at least two distinct rhythms. One is the recurring rhythm. . . . The other is the semantic rhythm of sense, or what is usually felt to be the prose rhythm. . . . We have verse *epos* when the recurrent rhythm is the primary or organizing one, and prose when the semantic rhythm is primary" (AC, 263). Although prose rhythm is continuous, rather than recurrent, it does exhibit a number of metrical influences. These are especially apparent in pre-seventeenth-century prose forms, like euphuism. By the time of Dryden, however, prose has moved quite a distance from *epos;* hence its "distinctive rhythm . . . emerges more clearly" (AC, 265).

Frye characterizes this rhythm by pointing to the affinities between literary prose and, once again, *melos* and *opsis.* Among the signs of prose *melos* is the "tendency to long sentences made up of short phrases and coordinate clauses, to emphatic repetition combined with a driving linear rhythm, to invective, to exhaustive catalogues, and to expressing the process or movement of thought instead of the logical word order of achieved thought" (AC, 266). The *opsis* of prose, on the other hand, includes the "tendency to elaborate pictorial description and long decorative similes," as well as the Jamesian "containing sentence" in which every element of syntax forms a pattern to be comprehended simultaneously (AC, 267).

Whether or not this last characteristic can legitimately be called a manifestation of rhythm depends, of course, on the definition of rhythm one starts with. Frye never explicitly defines rhythm. It is clear that his use of the word is not confined to its stricter sense of a sequence of approximately equal linguistic units. It is no less clear that he understands rhythm as something more than its etymological sense of a pleasing flow of sounds. Because Frye's use of the term *opsis* (introduced to help define prose rhythm) is related to the static, imagistic, and conceptual aspects of literature, it appears to violate the conventional meanings of the word rhythm. In fact, in most of the instances where Frye uses *opsis* he is commenting not on rhythm in particular but on style in general.

As we have observed, Frye conceives of *epos* and fiction as constituting the center of literature. On one side lies drama, its radical of presentation being enactment, and its mimetic form, the external representation of sound and imagery. On the other side lies lyric, its radical being indirect address, or the poet talking to himself, so to speak; and since, as Frye says, the lyric poet "turns his back on his listeners," its mimetic form is the internal representation of sound and imagery (AC, 249–50).

Drama Frye's treatment of the rhythm of drama is brief for two reasons. First, the *melos* and *opsis* of drama are obvious: actual music and spectacle. Second, although Frye labels the rhythm of drama "decorum," the genre itself actually has no controlling rhythm (AC, 250). Consequently, even though he retains the term, his discussion remains largely a matter of style. The argument is this: Style is mainly a function of the writer's distinctive voice (*le style c'est l'homme*); in drama this cannot be rendered directly since the writer must work through the dialogue of his characters; therefore, he has to adapt his own style to what his play demands. Such adaptation is decorum, or making the style appropriate to the content. "Decorum is in general," Frye says, "the poet's *ethical* voice, the modification of his own voice to the voice of a character or to the vocal tone demanded by subject or mood. And as style is at its purest in discursive prose, so decorum is obviously at its purest in drama, where the poet does not appear in person" (AC, 269). The rhythm of drama must finally be seen in terms of the rhythms of *epos* and prose. This is because drama tends to gravitate toward one or the other pole: dramatic *epos* or dramatic prose (AC, 269).

Frye claims that *epos* and fiction tend to manifest themselves respectively as myth and realism, but the correlation among the modes of the First Essay and the genres of the Fourth is even more explicit than this. "In the historical sequence of modes," he says, "each genre in turn seems to rise to some degree of ascendancy" (AC, 270). *Epos* is more prominent in the mode of myth and romance; drama, in the high-mimetic mode of the Renaissance; fiction, other forms of prose, and verse, in the low-mimetic mode.[8] We should expect, then, that Frye would seek to correlate the remaining genre—lyric—with the most recent forms in the historical sequence of modes, which is precisely what he does, saying that "it looks as though the lyric genre has some peculiarly close connection with the ironic mode and the literal level of meaning" (AC, 271).

Lyric The typical rhythm of lyric is "oracular, meditative, irregular, unpredictable, and essentially discontinuous, . . . emerging from the coincidences of the sound-pattern" (AC, 271). It differs from prose rhythm in being less conscious and deliberative. It differs from the rhythm of *epos* in being less habitual and less regularly metrical. And it differs from dramatic rhythm in not having to adapt to the demands of decorum. Frye labels the rhythm of lyric "association," the reason being that the creative process for this genre is typically "an associative rhetorical process, most of it below the threshold of consciousness, a chaos of paronomasia, sound-links, ambiguous sense-links, and memory-links very like that of the dream" (AC, 271–72).

Frye develops the relationship of the verbal pattern of lyric to music and spectacle with a host of analogues and illustrations. His method for further refining his definition of the rhythm of association is itself associative. The *melos* aspect of lyric is likened to cantillation—or to the fact that the words of poetry often yield themselves easily to the chant. The pictorial aspect, on the other hand, is associated with such things as typography and stanzaic arrangement at one extreme and visual imagery at the other (AC, 273–74).

Frye also sees an analogy between lyrical *melos* and *opsis* and "two elements of subconscious association," which he calls, "if the terms are thought dignified enough, babble and doodle" (AC, 275). Babble is the *Urform* which sound associations take in naive lyrics, like nursery rhymes and work songs, "where rhythm is a physical pulsation close to the dance, and is often filled up with nonsense words" (AC, 276). Incantation, uncontrolled physical response, magic, and pounding movement are several of the manifestations of babble. And since these elements can be characteristics of more sophisticated forms, Frye finds a more sophisticated term for this musical quality of the lyric. "The radical of *melos*," he says, "is *charm*" (AC, 278). Doodle, on the other hand, is the unconscious *Urform* of verbal design, the kind of thing that might be "scribbled in notebooks to be used later; a first stanza may suddenly 'come' and then other stanzas of the same shape have to be designed to go with it, and all the ingenuity that Freud has traced in the dream has to be employed in putting words into patterns" (AC, 278). Frye later dignifies the lyrical doodle by relabeling it also: "The radical of *opsis* in the lyric is *riddle*, which is characteristically a fusion of sensation and reflection, the use of an object of sense experience to stimulate a mental activity in connection with it."[9]

Style

The different rhythms which make up Frye's manual of style are in effect three, rather than four, drama possessing no rhythm peculiar to itself. These three rhythms taken together constitute what turns out to be a subtle theory of language, based on the expressive functions of prose, verse, and associative processes. Frye returns to the question of language and style in *The Well-Tempered Critic*, the second chapter of which is an attempt, as he says, "to reshape, in a slightly simpler form, some of the distinctions made in the fourth essay" of the *Anatomy*.[10] If it is simpler, however, it is also more analytical, more technical, and in some respects more schematic than the first part of the Fourth Essay. Because of this, and because the reshaping helps both to clarify and to expand the earlier ideas, we need to look briefly at the later argument.

Among Frye's several aims in *The Well-Tempered Critic* is to reformulate the traditional notion of three levels of style by placing them into a more literary and less social frame of reference; to do this he posits the principle of "three primary verbal rhythms" distinguishable in ordinary speech. These are verse rhythm, dominated by "a regularly repeated pattern of accent or meter, often accompanied by other recurring features, like rhyme or alliteration"; prose rhythm, dominated by "the sentence with its subject-predicate relation"; and associative rhythm, dominated by the short, irregular phrase and by "primitive syntax" (WTC, 18–24, 55). Although these rhythms are said to characterize "ordinary speech," it is obvious that they are similar to the rhythms of recurrence, continuity, and association—the categories Frye uses in the *Anatomy* to define, respectively, *epos,* fiction, and lyric. In *The Well-Tempered Critic,* however, the approach is somewhat different, for Frye sees the three kinds of rhythm as combining with each other in such a way as to produce six possible matrices: verse influenced by prose and associative rhythm; prose influenced by associative rhythm and verse; and associative rhythm influenced by verse and prose. Each of the primary rhythms, in other words, can be said to move in the direction of each of the other two. In the course of this movement, Frye is able to identify, in addition to the primary form of each rhythm, two additional stages: secondary or mixed forms, and tertiary or experimental ones. If prose, for example, with its continuous, syntactical, and expository rhythm, is taken as one primary form, it can be seen as passing through two isolable stages as it moves toward verse: rhetorical oratory and euphuism. Similarly, the influence of associative rhythm on normal prose can result in discontinuous aphorism (the secondary form) and oracular prose (the tertiary form). A little reflection shows that two types of rhythm for each matrix will yield twelve possible combinations, or, when the primary forms are added, fifteen categories altogether. In order for us to follow the course of Frye's argument, I have represented this elaborate design graphically in Figures 16, 17, and 18.

A study of the interlocking classes of these charts (which represent but a small part of Frye's brilliantly conceived lectures) will reveal the way in which the various literary styles in particular derive ultimately from the rhythms of language in general. It is this part of his argument which shows an especially close parallel to the Fourth Essay of the *Anatomy.* As in all our attempts, however, to represent Frye's thought schematically, these diagrams suggest a sharper disjunction between stylistic forms than he would want ultimately to make. He does not intend to develop a mechanical means for fitting any work into its appropriate slot without remainder. Rather, the fifteen categories should be seen as relative positions on a sliding scale of stylistic rhythms.[11]

	FORMS INFLUENCED BY PROSE	FORMS INFLUENCED BY ASSO-CIATIVE RHYTHM
Primary	Normal: the familiar territory of continuous verse, equidistant from prose and associative rhythm Example: Pope's heroic couplets	
Secondary	Conversational (mixed): combination of iambic pentameter and semantic prose rhythm; absence of rhyme Examples: blank verse of Milton, Keats, Tennyson, Browning, Wordsworth	Lyric: more strongly influenced by associative rhythm than continuous verse; discontinuous features such as alliteration, patterns of repetition, complex verse rhyme, etc. Example: *The Faerie Queene*
Tertiary	*Knittelvers* (intentional doggerel): prose element in diction and syntax so strong that remaining features of verse appear as continuous parody; either disappearing or unobtrusive rhyme; tendency toward satire, discontinuity, and paradox Examples: Donne's "Fourth Satire," Butler's *Hudibras*, Byron's *Don Juan*, Browning, Gilbert, Ogden Nash	Echolalic: extreme use of rhetorical sound patterns (identical rhymes, intensified sound patterns); tendency toward discontinuity and verbal wit Examples: poems of dream, reverie, and charm; parts of Spenser; Poe; Swinburne ("verbal blues and pensive jazz" together)

Figure 16. Influence of prose and associative rhythm on *verse.*

	FORMS INFLUENCED BY VERSE	FORMS INFLUENCED BY PROSE
Primary	Normal: as a rhythm itself, subliterary. Simple patterns of repetition, as in communal chants, ballad refrains, nursery rhymes.	
Secondary	Free verse: series of phrases, with no fixed metrical pattern, rhythmically separated; tendency toward the catalogue Examples: Ossian, Whitman	"Free prose": associative rhythm influenced, but not organized, by the sentence; the associative monologue; congenial to prose satire; uninhibited punctuation Examples: personal letters, diaries (e.g., Samuel Sewall's), Swift's *Journal to Stella*, Burton's *Anatomy of Melancholy*, Sterne's *Tristram Shandy*
Tertiary	Imagistic: associative writing as close to verse as possible without becoming verse; catalogue poetry; hypnotic chant based on devices of repetition Examples: Amy Lowell's imagism, John Gould Fletcher's "color symphonies"	Stream-of-consciousness: the mingling of associative and prose rhythms in extreme form; echolalia; repetition of sound and thematic words Examples: Joyce; certain forms of prayer, as in Donne's *Meditations*

Figure 17. Influence of verse and prose on *associative rhythm.*

	FORMS INFLUENCED BY VERSE	FORMS INFLUENCED BY ASSO-CIATIVE RHYTHM
Primary	Normal: the language of exposition and description; consistent with sentence rhythm; features of associative rhythm are purely "accidental"; continuous forms Example: Darwin's *Origin of the Species*	
Secondary	Rhetorical (oratorical): expository language, but with unmistakable metrical qualities, deliberately employed; meditative element appeals to imagination or emotions Examples: Gibbon's *Decline and Fall,* Churchill's 1940 speeches, Gettysburg Address, Johnson's letter to Chesterfield, Browne's *Urn Burial,* Taylor's *Holy Dying*	Discontinuous (aphoristic): tone of ordinary conversation; easy use of parenthesis, unforced repetition of certain words and ideas; produces clichés, accepted ideas, proverbs, epigrams, and parodies of these Examples: Shaw's prose, Blake's proverbs, philosophical *sententiae,* proverbial religious wisdom
Tertiary	Euphuistic: ornamenting of prose rhythm by rhetorical devices of verse (rhyme, alliteration, assonance, metrical balance, etc.); discontinuous and paradoxical Examples: Greene's *Card of Fancy*; Lyly; Thomas's *Under Milk Wood*	Oracular: rhythmically based prose with elusive and paradoxical qualities; extreme forms tend toward parody by aiming to break through entire process of verbal articulation Examples: Rimbaud's *Season in Hell,* Nietzsche's *Thus Spake Zarathustra,* René Char, St. John Perse, Paul Fort

Figure 18. Influence of verse and associative rhythm on *prose.*

Having distinguished the primary rhythms of ordinary speech and shown how they influence and interact with each other, Frye turns back to the question of three levels of style, seeking to relate the traditional division of low, middle, and high styles not merely to verbal rhythms themselves but to kinds of poetic diction as well. This part of *The Well-Tempered Critic* represents an extension of the ideas developed in *Anatomy of Criticism.* It is based on another set of dialectical pairs, two tendencies in literature which Frye calls the hieratic and the demotic:

> The hieratic tendency seeks out formal elaborations of verse and prose. The hieratic poet finds, with Valéry, that the kind of poetry he wants to write depends, like chess, on complex and arbitrary rules, and he experiments with patterns of rhythm, rhyme and assonance, as well as with mythological and other forms of specifically poetic imagery. The demotic tendency is to minimize the difference between literature and speech, to seek out the associative or prose rhythms that are used in speech and reproduce them in literature. (WTC, 94)

This pair of terms, together with the three rhetorical levels, produces yet another matrix of classes: high, middle, and low hieratic; high, middle, and low demotic. It is convenient to represent this framework by means of a chart also (Figure 19). As is the case with all of Frye's

	DEMOTIC	HIERATIC
LOW	Literary use of colloquial and familiar speech (the theoretical view expressed in Coleridge's criticism of Wordsworth's *Preface*) Examples: the vulgar idiom in fictional and dramatic dialogue; colloquialisms used to provide lower tone, as in Whitman; intentional doggerel as in *Hudibras* and *Sweeney Agonistes;* neurotic, compulsive babble of the ego, as in Dostoevsky's *Notes from Underground* and in Beckett.	Words in process; language which bypasses conventionally articulate communication; influenced by associative rhythm; the area of creative association which suspends conventional rules Examples: deliberate wit; experimental, tertiary forms (euphuism, echolalia); free verse and "free prose"; Sterne; Smart's *Jubilate Agno; Finnegans Wake*
MIDDLE	Ordinary language of communication, at once plain and cultivated Examples: expository prose and narrative; didactic verse	Formal language of poetic expression; what Hopkins calls "Parnassian" style; literature as art of conventional communication Examples: deliberately rhetorical prose, as in Gibbon; the formulaic epic
HIGH	Sent01entious and aphoristic use of language; deals with the traditional and familiar, elevated to level of sublime; essentially discontinuous; the social apotheosis of proverb Examples: sacred writings throughout; literary forms of religious revelation	Language used to express the intense momentary vision or the epiphany; individual rather than social vision Examples: the discontinuous, oracular lyric, as in Eliot, Pound, Rilke, Valéry; lyrical portions of *Vita Nuova* (Dante) and *The Dark Night of the Soul* (St. John of the Cross)

Figure 19. Levels of style.

schemata, however, more is required to define a given class than simply a combination of the categories on his vertical and horizontal axes.

This can be illustrated by observing the kinds of criteria Frye uses to define, say, the high demotic and hieratic styles. The high demotic style is "essentially aphoristic" and sentential; it deals "with the traditional and familiar," elevated to the level of the sublime; it manifests itself chiefly in discontinuous forms; it represents the social apotheosis of the proverb (WTC, 101–3). The hieratic style, on the other hand, is, at its highest level, more a matter of intensity than sublimity; it is language used to express the momentary vision, or epiphany; it manifests itself in the discontinuous, oracular lyric (WTC, 103–4). These principles are similar to those Frye has used to distinguish the rhythmical forms (Figures 16–18), but with this difference: his categories now are much more a function of the reader's response, recognition, and acceptance. The high demotic style deals, Frye says,

> with those moments of response to what we feel most deeply in ourselves, whether love, loyalty or reverence. . . . Such points of concentration do not differ in kind from middle or low style, and hence do not violate the context from which they emerge. They are of relatively short duration, as they do not depend on

sequence or connection. What they do depend on is the active participation of the reader or hearer: they are points which the reader recognizes as appropriate for the focusing of his own consciousness. (WTC, 102)

This passage, seen in relation to Frye's disjunction between knowledge and experience, is clearly on the experiential side and thus moves away from those kinds of norms which, more often than not, he seeks to establish. The question of style, therefore, at its "highest" levels at least, is partially a matter of subjective intuition, not unlike the Arnoldian "touchstones."[12]

The context of subjective response provides the occasion for Frye to move out into an even broader series of contexts.

> Our present argument seems to indicate the existence of two kinds of "high" literary experience, . . . one in general verbal practice and one more strictly confined to literature; one a recognition of something like verbal truth and the other a recognition of something like verbal beauty. High style in demotic writing depends largely on social acceptance: it is the apotheosis of the proverb, the axioms that a society takes to its business and bosom. Hieratic writing is more dependent on canons of taste and esthetic judgment, admittedly more flexible and more elusive than counsels of behavior. (WTC, 105–6)

Acceptance and taste, truth and beauty—these criteria form one of the contexts for determining high style and must therefore be set beside the other, less expansive norms (rhythm, form, diction, etc.) that Frye employs to classify the literary uses of language.

We observed at the beginning of this chapter that both aspects of Frye's rhetorical criticism—the stylistic and the generic—call for a social response. His theory of rhythm and, as an extension, his theory of style illustrate this well, for his argument gradually expands from a concern with particular and more or less objectively identifiable elements of style, like poetic meter, to a concern with the broader stylistic contexts, defined in relation to community acceptance and social taste. When he defines high style as the "recognition of truth and beauty in verbal form" (WTC, 108), we can see more clearly the place of rhetoric in the triadic framework outlined at the beginning of the Fourth Essay. The theories of rhythm and style, however, form but half of Frye's theory of rhetoric, and we must turn now to examine his taxonomy of specific forms.

Generic Forms

Anatomy of Criticism dissects not simply the obvious features of the body of literature but the obscure ones as well. Nowhere is this more evident than in the last half of the theory of genres, where we discover such specific forms as *auto,* symposium, archetypal masque, and even one called "anatomy" itself. Frye's use of the word "specific" should not be understood to mean that he is proposing neatly to classify all the species of a given genre (e.g., drama). His "specific forms" approximate only roughly what are commonly thought of as literary species (e.g., tragic drama).

Several of the fundamental assumptions we have encountered thus far appear also in this section. The dichotomy between fictional and thematic, which made its first appearance in the theory of modes, reappears here as one of the organizing principles of Frye's discussion, illustrating, incidentally, that the *Anatomy* has something of a cyclic design itself, the categories of the Fourth Essay turning back to those of the First. Fictional and thematic serve to separate the four genres into two distinct groups. Under the first category Frye locates drama and prose fiction; and under the second, *epos* and lyric. Prose forms which are more thematic than fictional, like oratorical prose, and verse forms which are more fictional than thematic, like the purely narrative poem, take their respective places in the dichotomy (AC, 243). Since the genres tend toward one or the other of the modal categories, we can expect to find the cyclical paradigm at work here also. Other important principles recurring throughout Frye's treatment of the specific forms are the innocence-experience dichotomy, the conception of art as lying midway between history (event) and philosophy (idea), and the analogy of literature to *melos* and *opsis* which we have examined above. These principles guide Frye's discussion of the specific forms.

Specific Forms of Drama   The traditional division of drama into tragedies and comedies is, according to Frye, "a conception based entirely on verbal drama, and does not include or account for types of drama, such as the opera or masque, in which music and scenery have a more organic place" (AC, 282). He attempts to modify the traditional view by means of yet another elaborate paradigm, this one a combination of his familiar cyclical and dialectical models. The first *dialectical* principle underlying his argument is the division of dramatic kinds into two large categories, spectacular and mimetic. A related pair of categories, epiphany (or pure vision) and mime (or pure image), constitutes what might be conceived of as the extreme dramatic points of an imaginary vertical axis. At the horizontal poles of this figure lie two other dramatic forms, what Frye calls the "history-play" (or act-play) with its emphasis on pure event and the "philosophy-play" (scene-play or symposium) with its emphasis on pure idea. Now if we were to connect these points with four arcs we approximate the kind of circular model Frye has in mind, around the perimeter of which he locates the various specific forms. Figure 20 represents a simplified version of this diagram. A glance at the figure will indicate the central defining role which such dialectical pairs as event and idea, and myth and irony assume in the overall design.

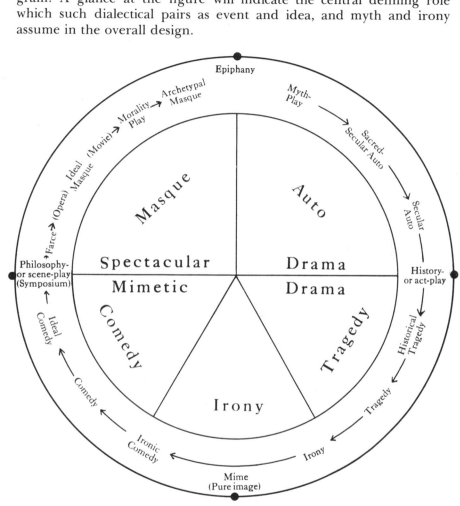

Figure 20. Specific forms of drama.

The upper-right-hand quadrant of the diagram represents what Frye provisionally calls the "myth-play," later relabeled the *auto* (the name is taken from Calderon's *Autos Sacramentales*) because of the ambiguities attendant on the word "myth." His method of defining this form is a complex one, drawing as it does upon a number of criteria. In the first place, the *auto* is spectacular drama, which means that music and scenery have just as organic a role in determining its form as language itself: its material cause is not exclusively verbal. Frye sees a number of variations on the basic form. In its most restricted sense *auto* means "a form of drama in which the main subject is sacred or sacrosanct legend, such as miracle plays, solemn and processional in form but not strictly tragic" (AC, 365). Using this definition as a starting point, he outlines, in a kind of quasi-historical way, the movement from pure or sacred *auto* to forms which are at once sacred and secular (e.g., the Japanese No drama) and then to forms in which the sacred element is completely displaced. This latter would be a purely secular *auto,* or what could also be called, as Frye's examples indicate, a heroic romance (e.g., Marlowe's *Tamburlaine*). Other examples of the *auto* include Aeschylus' *The Suppliants,* its "predominantly musical structure" comparable to the modern oratorio, and Wagner's operas, which expand "the heroic form all the way back to the sacramental drama of the gods" (AC, 283). Throughout Frye's discussion of the *auto* he relies not only on concepts related to the means of imitation (spectacular) and the dramatic subject (either pure or displaced sacred legend) but also upon such criteria as the characteristic mood and resolution, the symbolic emphasis, the type of hero, the source of the dramatic catastrophe, and the kind of audience appeal. Here, for example, are some excerpts from the discussion of pure or sacred *auto:* "The characteristic mood and resolution of the myth-play are pensive.... The myth-play emphasizes dramatically the symbol of spiritual and corporeal communion.... The appeal of the myth-play is a curious mixture of the popular and esoteric" (AC, 282). The method of definition, in short, is not a simple one, relying upon at least a half-dozen important distinctions.

The same is true of Frye's discussion of those forms which occupy the other quadrant of his "spectacular" semicircle and to which he attaches the label "masque." (We pass over his treatment of dramatic tragedy, irony, and comedy, where the method consists chiefly of placing distinctions we have previously encountered—in the theory of modes and the theory of *mythoi*—into a dramatic context.) When Frye comes to the fourth quadrant, having concluded his discussion of comic dramatic forms, he remarks: "We are strongly tempted to call our fourth area 'miscellaneous' and let it go; but it is precisely here that new generic criticism is needed" (AC, 287). Thus he devotes more space to analyzing the various forms of the masque than to all of the other dramatic forms combined.

The masque, according to the definition of Frye's glossary, is "a species of drama in which music and spectacle play an important role and in which the characters tend to be or become aspects of human personality rather than independent characters" (AC, 366). Spectacular drama, with its emphasis on both *melos* and *opsis,* is, so to speak, the genus of both masque and *auto*. The two forms, however, are similar in one other respect: the structure of both is not parabolic, as in mimetic drama, but linear. In other words, whereas typical five-act tragedies and comedies work toward an end which illuminates the beginning, spectacular drama "is by nature processional, and tends to episodic and piecemeal discovery, as we can see in all forms of pure spectacle, from the circus parade to the revue" (AC, 289). Thus what differentiates masque and *auto* from mimetic drama is both their spectacular basis and their processional structure. On the other hand, what distinguishes masque from *auto* as separate species of spectacular drama is a question best approached by considering Frye's elaboration of the major subspecies within the former category.

He conceives of these subspecies as located on a continuum, running from the ideal masque at one end to the archetypal masque at the other. The difference between these two extremes is largely a matter of the different conceptions of the audience they assume. The ideal masque, Frye says, is "usually a compliment to the audience, or an important member of it, and leads up to an idealization of the society represented by that audience" (AC, 287), whereas the archetypal masque "tends to individualize its audience by pointing to the central member of it" (AC, 290). The conception of the audience, moreover, is one of the things which distinguishes masque from both the *auto* and the mimetic forms. "The essential feature of the ideal masque," Frye says,

> is the exaltation of the audience, who form the goal of its procession. In the *auto,* drama is at its most objective; the audience's part is to accept the story without judgement. In tragedy, there is judgement, but the source of the tragic discovery is on the other side of the stage; and whatever it is, it is stronger than the audience. In the ironic play, audience and drama confront each other directly; in the comedy the source of the discovery has moved across to the audience itself. The ideal masque places the audience in a position of superiority to discovery. The verbal action of *Figaro* is comic and that of *Don Giovanni* tragic; but in both cases the audience is exalted by the music above the reach of tragedy and comedy, and, though as profoundly moved as ever, is not emotionally involved with the discovery of plot or characters. It looks at the downfall of Don Juan as spectacular entertainment. (AC, 289)

There are yet other important criteria in Frye's definition of the ideal masque. It draws, he says, upon "fairly stock" narratives and characters (AC, 287), its emphasis is on the ideal, its settings are Arcadian—characteristics which explain its proximate relation to comedy as well as suggesting one of the reasons for the audience's exaltation. As drama moves away from comedy and toward the apex of Frye's cycle, it enters the area of the archetypal masque, a species which not only individualizes its audience, as we have seen, but becomes more serious in the process. Like all forms of spectacular drama its settings are detached from time and space, "but instead of the Arcadias of ideal masque, we find ourselves frequently in a sinister limbo, like the threshold of death in *Everyman,* the sealed underworld crypts of Maeterlinck, or the nightmares of the future in expressionist plays" (AC, 290). The archetypal masque, in short, is the prevailing species we encounter in most contemporary "highbrow drama," especially European forms, and in "experimental operas and unpopular movies" (AC, 290). The word "archetypal" here is explicitly Jungian and has little relation to its ordinary meaning for Frye as the conventional, recurring symbol. We should remember that in his definition of the masque proper, *ethos* means "aspects of personality rather than independent characters." In the ideal masque, *ethos* becomes the stock or type character. In the archetypal masque, with its sinister setting, it becomes the "interior of the human mind" as characterization breaks down "into elements and fragments of personality" (AC, 291); thus the appropriateness of the Jungian terminology. "This is why," Frye says, "I call the form the archetypal masque, the word archetype being in this context used in Jung's sense of an aspect of the personality capable of dramatic projection. Jung's persona and anima and counsellor and shadow throw a great deal of light on the characterization of modern allegorical, psychic, and expressionist dramas, with their circus barkers and wraith-like females and inscrutable sages and obsessed demons" (AC, 291).

The ideal and archetypal forms of the masque are but two of the many species that Frye locates along the arc of his fourth quadrant. The opera, or "musically organized drama," flanks the masque on one side; and the movie, or "scenically organized drama," on the other. Other dramatic species with affinities toward one or the other, or both, of these forms are puppet plays, Chinese romances, commedia dell'arte, ballet, and pantomime (AC, 288). Two other forms that Frye mentions are farce and morality plays: the former lies close to the ideal masque, and the latter, with their type characters representing good and evil in open conflict, approach the area of the archetypal masque (AC, 290). Finally, at the extreme right of the archetypal masque, which brings us to the beginning of the *auto,* we reach the point of the epiphany, "the dramatic apocalypse or separation of the divine and the demonic, a point directly opposite the mime, which presents the simply human mixture" (AC, 292). This is the area Nietzsche had in mind when he spoke of the birth of tragedy as the Dionysian revel of satyrs being brought into line with the mandates of an Apollonian god (AC, 292), the two opposites representing in a general way Frye's own masque and *auto.*

Standing back from Frye's treatment of the specific forms of drama, we observe, by way of summary, that he begins his argument at the level of Aristotle's efficient cause: the manner of imitation, or in Frye's own terms, "the radical of presentation." This permits him to distinguish drama—those works enacted by hypothetical characters— from the other genres. He then moves to the level of what Aristotle would call the material cause, the means of imitation. His assumption at this point is that a concentration on the *lexis* of drama cannot properly account for those species in which *melos* and *opsis* play an important, if not a dominant role. Thus, to provide a more synoptic view, Frye uses the concept "spectacular" to describe those forms where music, dance, and scenic or sensational means are directed toward an end that ordinarily excludes the dramatic tensions peculiar to the parabolic structure of comedy and tragedy. His division between spectacular and mimetic (or verbal) drama, therefore, is chiefly a distinction based on the different means of imitation. At this point our Aristotelian parallel breaks down; for when Frye comes to differentiate *auto* from masque or to distinguish among the various subtypes of a given species, he relies on a wide variety of criteria: mood, resolution, theme, character, setting, symbolic emphasis, nature of the audience—all of these plus a host of specific works used as illustrations. It would be possible to draw a general analogy between some of these principles and Aristotle's formal and final causes, since Frye does speak at times about *what* is being represented and the peculiar effect the representation achieves; but this would be to distort his argument since these principles are not employed consciously or consistently. More to the point is the fact that the kinds of criteria Frye uses, once he has passed beyond the spectacular-mimetic distinction, are the same as those employed to distinguish the *mythoi* in his theory of archetypes. This is why his survey of the specific forms is more an analysis of the kinds of dramatic fictions than a neat classification of dramatic species.[13] This is especially true of the subtypes where, for example, ideal comedy and ideal masque, or archetypal masque and morality play tend to merge almost indistinguishably into one another. The differentiating criteria, however, do provide for a synoptic account of significant variations within the genre of drama, which is Frye's aim; and the entire effort must be judged as a meaningful expansion of the traditional perspective. A somewhat different set of criteria, however, underlies Frye's analysis of the specific forms of prose fiction, a topic to which we now turn.

Specific Continuous Forms: Prose Fiction Frye's treatment of prose fiction, if not one of the most influential aspects of his theory, is at least one of the best-known and most frequently anthologized parts of the *Anatomy*.[14] By the expression "continuous forms" Frye means those literary works in which the predominant rhythm is that of semantic continuity. He includes "prose fiction" in the title of this section for the obvious reason that there are some continuous forms which are neither prose nor fiction: thematic epics, didactic poetry and prose, compilations of myth— any form, in short, where the poet "communicates as a professional man with a social function" (AC, 55). This quotation comes from the First Essay where Frye makes the distinction between episodic and encyclopaedic works, arguing that the latter are continuous in the sense of forming more extended patterns. Therefore "continuous," as it applies to prose fiction in the Fourth Essay, refers not only to the continuity of semantic rhythm but also to the relative length of the fictional work.

The organization of this section derives from a distinction among four major types of prose fiction, represented in Figure 21. The two pairs of categories here are based upon different principles. "Personal" refers to *ethos* or characterization and "intellectualized" to *dianoia* or content, whereas the extroverted-introverted dichotomy is essentially a matter of rhetorical technique, the latter terms describing whether a writer's manner of representation tends more toward objectivity or subjectivity. These are not the only categories, however, which Frye uses to define his fictional forms. The bulk of his argument consists of drawing certain distinctions between the two forms of "personal" fiction (novel and romance) and between the two "intellectualized" forms (confession and anatomy).

	extroverted	introverted
ETHOS: personal	Novel	Romance
DIANOIA: intellectualized	Anatomy	Confession

Figure 21. Specific continuous forms of prose fiction.

"The essential difference between novel and romance," says Frye, "lies in the conception of characterization" (AC, 304). He illustrates this by setting down a series of opposing qualities which are said respectively to characterize the two forms:

The romancer does not attempt to create "real people" so much as stylized figures which expand into psychological archetypes. It is in the romance that we find Jung's libido, anima, and shadow reflected in the hero, heroine, and villain respectively. That is why romance so often radiates a glow of subjective intensity that the novel lacks, and why a suggestion of allegory is constantly creeping in around its fringes. Certain elements of character are released in the romance which make it naturally a more revolutionary form than the novel. The novelist deals with personality, with characters wearing their *personae* or social masks. He needs the framework of a stable society, and many of our best novelists have been conventional to the verge of fussiness. The romancer deals with individuality, with characters *in vacuo* idealized by revery, and, however conservative he may be, something nihilistic and untamable is likely to keep breaking out of his pages. (AC, 304–5)

The ultimate reference for each pair of terms in this dialectic of opposites is *ethos*. In other words, determining whether a work of prose fiction is realistic or allegorical, conservative or revolutionary, stable or untamable, calm or intense, social or individual, and thus whether it is a novel or a romance, requires that our attention be focused essentially not upon *mythos* or *dianoia* but upon characterization. I say "essentially" because there are other, although less important, considerations. Frye observes, for example, that the plot and dialogue of the novel have an affinity with the conventions of the comedy of manners, whereas the conventions of romance are linked more closely with the tale and the ballad (AC, 304). Moreover, Frye outlines a difference in the approaches of the novelist and the romancer to historical material. The novelist, dealing creatively with history, "usually prefers his material in a plastic, or roughly contemporary state, and feels cramped by a fixed historical pattern" (AC, 306). In the romance, on the other hand, the historical pattern is usually less fluid and contemporary, most romances being set in the past. Frye sees some relation between this last tendency and his theory of modes: the romance as a mode lying between myth and realism is obviously, in the sequence outlined in the First Essay, further removed chronologically from the mimetic and ironic tendencies appropriate to the novel. It is no accident, Frye observes, that "most" 'historical novels' are romances" (AC, 307).

As a concept for defining the confession and the anatomy, *ethos* plays a secondary role. The confession, a specialized form of autobiography, presents a writer's life in such a way as "to build up an integrated pattern" (AC, 307). But even though the subject is ostensibly the author himself, "some theoretical or intellectual interest" nearly always plays a dominant role. This is what distinguishes the confession from the novel proper, where the theoretical interest is always subordinated to the technical problem of "personal relationships" (AC, 308). The anatomy is also an "intellectualized" form, similar to the confession in its ability to represent theoretical statements and abstract ideas. It differs in being one step further removed from a concern with *ethos*. Its characters are more stylized than realistic, not so important in themselves as in the mental attitudes they express. In Frye's words, the anatomy "presents people as mouthpieces of the ideas they represent" (AC, 309). It is a "loose-jointed narrative form" (AC, 309), embracing a wide variety of subtypes which range from pure fantasy at one extreme to pure morality at the other. It differs from the romance in that it "is not primarily concerned with the exploits of heroes, but relies on the free play of intellectual fancy and the kind of humorous observation that produces caricature" (AC, 309–10); thus the tendency of the anatomy toward various kinds of satire.

Once Frye has distinguished the four types, he is quick to note that very few exist in "pure" form. "There is hardly any modern romance," he says, "that could not be made out to be a novel, and vice versa. The forms of prose fiction are mixed, like racial strains in human beings, not separable like the sexes" (AC, 305). Similarly, we find Frye making such statements as these: the confession "merges with the novel by a series of insensible gradations"; or, "the anatomy, of course, eventually begins to merge with the novel, producing various hybrids" (AC, 307, 312). Thus Frye's specific forms are more like "strands," to use his own word, combined in various ways in a given work of prose fiction.

Despite the fact that the four principal strands cannot, on the whole, be found as pure species, Frye nonetheless gives a number of examples of the kinds of works and writers he would place in each category. Some of these, including typical "short" forms, are represented in the following outline, which also lists his examples for the eleven possible combinations among the four categories.

1. Novel
   Fielding, *Tom Jones*   Jane Austen's works
   Dickens, *Little Dorrit*   Defoe
   Butler, *The Way of All Flesh*   James
   Huxley, *Point Counterpoint*
   Short form: Short stories (e.g., Chekhov, Mansfield)

2. Romance
    Brontë, *Wuthering Heights*   William Morris
    Bunyan, *The Pilgrim's Progress*   Hawthorne
    Maturin, *Melmoth the Wanderer*   Scott
    Short form: Poe's tales; Boccaccio, *Decameron*

3. Confession
    Augustine, *Confessions*   Bunyan, *Grace Abounding*
    Rousseau, *Confessions*   Newman, *Apologia*
    Browne, *Religio Medici*   Hogg, *Confessions of a Justified
                                         Sinner*
    Short form: the familiar essay; Montaigne's *livre de bonne foy*

4. Anatomy
    Athenaeus, *Deipnosophists*   Kingsley, *Water Babies*
    Macrobius, *Saturnalia*   Boethius, *Consolation of
    Southey, *The Doctor*   Philosophy*
    Burton, *Anatomy of Melancholy*   Amory, *John Buncle*
    Landor, *Imaginary Conversations* Voltaire, *Candide*
    Flaubert, *Bouvard et Pecuchet*   Walton, *The Compleat Angler*
    Butler, *Erewhon; Erewhon Revisited* Wilson et al., *Noctes Ambrosianae*
    Huxley, *Brave New World*   Petronius, Lucian, Varro,
    Carroll, *Alice in Wonderland*   Rabelais, Erasmus, Peacock
    Swift, *Gulliver's Travels*
    Short form: dialogue or colloquy, as in Erasmus, Voltaire; *cena* or
    symposium

5. Novel-Romance
    George Eliot's early novels   Austen, *Northanger Abbey*
    Hawthorne, *The Scarlet Letter*   Flaubert, *Madame Bovary*
    Conrad, *Lord Jim*

6. Novel-Confession
    Defoe, *Moll Flanders*   Joyce, *A Portrait of the Artist* . . .

7. Novel-Anatomy
    Sterne, *Tristram Shandy*   George Eliot's later novels
    Proletarian novels of the 1930s

8. Romance-Confession
    De Quincey, *Confessions of an*   Borrow, *Lavengro* and *The
      English Opium Eater*   Romany Rye*

9. Romance-Anatomy
    Melville, *Moby Dick*   Rabelais

10. Confession-Anatomy
    Carlyle, *Sartor Resartus*   Kierkegaard, *Either/Or*

11. Novel-Romance-Confession
    Richardson, *Pamela*

12. Novel-Romance-Anatomy
    Cervantes, *Don Quixote*

13. Novel-Confession-Anatomy
    Proust

14. Romance-Confession-Anatomy
    Apuleius

15. Novel-Romance-Confession-Anatomy
    Joyce, *Ulysses*

All of this is highly schematic. Frye makes it that way deliberately, for he wants first to analyze the forms of prose fiction (the first four categories) and then synthesize them (the last eleven) "in order to suggest the advantage of having a simple and logical explanation for the form of, say, *Moby Dick* or *Tristram Shandy*" (AC, 313). Whether or not Frye's approach is in fact simple and logical is perhaps a matter for debate, though the issue cannot be decided except in terms of the criteria he himself has chosen for his distinctions. The more significant point seems to be that Frye is offering an "explanation" for the specific forms, not a taxonomy for its own sake.

The claims that Frye makes for generic criticism of the variety just outlined are more directly stated in this section than in the one on drama. He himself asks what function is served by the distinction, say, between novel and romance, especially when, as he has argued, there are few "pure" forms of either. His answer is that a writer "should be examined in terms of the conventions he chose" (AC, 305), an answer directed especially toward the novel-centered view of prose fiction. Frye makes this point several times; perhaps it is best expressed in the following passage:

> William Morris should not be left on the side lines of prose fiction merely because the critic has not learned to take the romance form seriously. Nor, in view of what has been said about the revolutionary nature of the romance, should his choice of that form be regarded as an "escape" from his social attitude. If Scott has any claims to be a romancer, it is not good criticism to deal only with his defects as a novelist. The romantic qualities of *The Pilgrim's Progress,* too, its archetypal characterization and its

revolutionary approach to religious experience, make it a well-rounded example of a literary form: it is not merely a book swallowed by English literature to get some religious bulk in its diet. Finally, when Hawthorne, in the preface to *The House of the Seven Gables,* insists that his story be read as romance and not as novel, it is possible that he meant what he said, even though he indicates that the prestige of the rival form has induced the romancer to apologize for not using it. (AC, 305–6)

The plea here, in part, is for a less provincial attitude, for an ecumenical perspective which does not relegate some forms of prose, like the confession, to that "vague limbo of books which are not quite literature because they are 'thought,' and not quite religion or philosophy because they are Examples of Prose Style" (AC, 307).

Frye believes that critics have been especially remiss in not taking account of the anatomy. Although this tradition contains a rather curious assortment of works, he attempts to show that it is more than simply a miscellaneous catch-all for types of prose which the other categories do not adequately describe. It is difficult not to conclude, given the criteria of Frye's discussion, that his "anatomy" is any less unified and conventional a form than the other three. Recognizing that it does appear both as a pure form (Boethius' *Consolation,* Burton's *Anatomy,* Walton's *Compleat Angler*) and in combination with other forms should, Frye argues, "make a good many elements in the history of literature come into focus" (AC, 312). Philip Stevick, for one, has shown the anatomy to be a useful distinction.[15]

Frye almost invites us to consider the similarity between the anatomy as a prose form and his own *Anatomy*: some of the phrases he uses to describe the former are, *mutatis mutandis,* apt characterizations of his own work. Consider, for example, the following: The anatomy "relies on the free play of intellectual fancy." It "presents us with a vision of the world in terms of a single intellectual pattern" (AC, 310). "The word 'anatomy' in Burton's title [*Anatomy of Melancholy*] means a dissection or analysis, and expresses very well the intellectualized approach of this form" (AC, 311). And finally, the anatomist, "dealing with intellectual themes and attitudes, shows his exuberance in intellectual ways, piling up an enormous mass of erudition about his theme" (AC, 311). If the analogy is intentional on Frye's part, and it seems to be, his own title is not without that touch of wit which appears everywhere in his work. More importantly, however, the title calls attention to and reinforces what many of Frye's readers have felt about the creative nature of his achievement. We will examine this aspect of his work in chapter 7.

In order to illustrate how his conception of specific continuous forms can help to illuminate a complex hybrid work, Frye applies his formulas to Joyce's *Ulysses*. The traditions of the novel, he says, are manifested in "the clarity with which the sights and sounds and smells of Dublin come to life, the rotundity of the character-drawing, and the naturalness of the dialogue"; the conventions of the romance, in "the elaborate way that the story and characters are parodied by being set against archetypal heroic patterns, notably the one provided by the *Odyssey*"; those of the confession, in "the revelation of character and incident through the searching use of the stream-of-consciousness technique"; and, finally, the traditions of the anatomy, in "the constant tendency to be encyclopaedic and exhaustive both in technique and in subject matter, and to see both in highly intellectualized terms" (AC, 313). These distinctions seem to indicate that a hybrid work does not so much combine *forms* as it integrates *techniques*. The conventions of realism ("clarity," "rotundity," "naturalness"), the parody of heroic patterns, the manner of revealing character and incident ("stream-of-consciousness"), and the tendency to intellectualize content are all matters of rhetorical technique, whatever their affinity might be with the four "pure" species. This observation serves to underline once again the intimate relation between genre and the manner of representation in Frye's thinking; the reason for his calling his theory of genres "rhetorical criticism" should, by this point in the argument, cause us little difficulty. What makes *Ulysses* an integrated work and not an aggregate of conventions is the fact that all four of the prose traditions are "of practically equal importance, and are essential to one another" (AC, 314). This too is essentially a matter of rhetorical technique, as we can see in Frye's discussion of Joyce's unifying his work by the method of "parallel contrasts" (AC, 314).

One final prose form deserves comment: the fifth or quintessential form, which does not depend for its existence upon "the commonsense dichotomies of the daylight consciousness" (AC, 314). Frye's example is *Finnegans Wake,* a form in which, because its "setting is a dream, no contrast is possible between confession and novel, between a stream of consciousness inside the mind and the appearances of other people outside it. Nor is the experiential world of the novel to be separated from the intelligible world of the anatomy" (AC, 314). The form of *Finnegans Wake,* Frye adds, is commonly associated with those scriptural or sacred works which treat human life in terms of fall and redemption, and nature in terms of creation and apocalypse. Other examples include the Bible, the Egyptian Book of the Dead, and the Icelandic Prose Edda. Since these encyclopaedic works are not restricted to prose, Frye treats them in his next section.

Specific Encyclopaedic Forms In his glossary, Frye defines "encyclopaedic form" as "a genre presenting an anagogic form of symbolism, such as sacred scripture, or its analogues in other modes. The term includes the Bible, Dante's *Commedia,* the great epics, and the works of Joyce and Proust" (AC, 365). This definition draws upon much of what has come before and thus illustrates the perils of approaching Frye *in medias res,* for it shows that to discover what Frye means by encyclopaedic form requires some understanding of both his theory of modes and his theory of symbols; it requires, moreover, though this is not explicit in the definition, some knowledge of his theory of myths. Even then, unless we are prepared to see that the meaning of genre, as it is used here, is quite different from the meaning it has when applied to drama, *epos,* fiction, and lyric, we are likely to encounter difficulties.

In the First Essay Frye argues that encyclopaedic forms manifest themselves throughout the sequence of modes. The encyclopaedic form for the mythical mode is usually sacred scripture of some kind, which in the other modes takes the shape of an analogy of mythical or scriptural revelation (AC, 54–57). These analogues have been represented in Figure 2. In chapter 1 we observed that Frye's concept of thematic modes would figure importantly in his analysis of the specific encyclopaedic forms. It figures importantly because Frye makes explicit here the kind of encyclopaedic form characteristic of each historical mode. To see how this is the case, we must consider the complex framework of cycles and epic forms which precedes the actual taxonomy of examples.

Frye's argument begins with the assumption that the Bible, seen as a definitive and integrated myth in itself, is the single most important influence on Western literary symbolism. Mythically, the Bible is "a single archetypal structure extending from creation to apocalypse" (AC, 315), or a "total cyclical *mythos*" (AC, 316). Within this large cyclical structure, Frye says, we can observe the heroic quest of a Messiah, a quest which follows the stages and employs the symbols of romantic *mythos*: "A mysterious birth is followed by an epiphany or recognition as God's son; symbols of humiliation, betrayal, and martyrdom, the so-called suffering servant complex, follow, and in their turn are succeeded by symbols of the Messiah as bridegroom, as conqueror of a monster, and as the leader of his people into their rightful home" (AC, 316). The quest, in other words, leads from "incarnation to apotheosis" (AC, 316). Such would be the form of the Biblical *mythos* from the perspective of romance. As we move from the mythical or divine view through romance to the lower human perspectives, we encounter still other cyclical paradigms in the Biblical narrative, expressed either in individual, sexual or social, or ironic terms. The six cycles, along with the objects to and from which they move, can be represented as follows:

I Mythical (divine or apocalyptic)	from creation to apocalypse
II Romantic (heroic or Messianic)	from incarnation to apotheosis
III Individual ⎤	from birth to salvation
IV Sexual ⎬ (human)	from Adam and Eve to apocalyptic wedding
V Social ⎦	from law to kingdom (or from rebuilt Zion of the Old Testament to the millennium of the New)
VI Ironic ("all too human")	from birth to death

Because the movement of the first five of these cycles is "first down and then up to a permanently redeemed world," Frye calls them "completed or dialectic cycles" (AC, 317). At the ironic level, however, we have the "*mere* cycle of human life without redemptive assistance. . . . Here the final cadence is one of bondage, exile, continuing war, or destruction by fire (Sodom, Babylon) or water (the flood)" (AC, 317). These cycles become the basis for Frye's discovery, either by analogy or by opposition, of four encyclopaedic (epic) frameworks: the epic of return; the epic of wrath; the analogical epic; and the contrast epic (AC, 317). The epic of return is produced by the completed or dialectic cycles (the first through the fifth), since all of them involve a movement back to the redeemed world. The epic of wrath, on the other hand, has its source in the sixth or "all too human" cycle, where the "final cadence" is that of death only. The analogical epic, one which embodies any process from life through death to rebirth, derives from the romantic influence or the second cycle, since this process is analogous to the Biblical version of the Messianic cycle.[16] Finally, the fourth type is dialectical, being based on a contrast between the ironic human situation, at one pole, and the divine society at the other; thus it derives from an opposition between the sixth cycle and any of the other five.

This complex series of cyclic and epic structures provides the framework for Frye's analysis of the specific encyclopaedic forms. His problem is to determine which kinds of epic forms manifest themselves in each of the modes—myth, romance, high and low mimesis, and irony. The framework itself appears to be essentially a product of his study of the first three modes; at least he is more successful in discovering examples for them than he is for the last two.[17] Rather than reviewing the taxonomy in detail, I shall simply indicate how the larger framework is applied by noting some of the epic forms which Frye locates in the first three modes.

Three of the four epic forms can be found in the mythical mode. First, the apocalyptic epic of return, Frye says, "occurs in Northern mythology, in the Eddas and the *Muspilli,* and the last book of the *Mahabharata* is an entry into heaven" (AC, 317). Second, the myth of apotheosis is to be found in the legend of Hercules; the myth of salvation, in the Book of the Dead; and the myth of ceremonial law, in almost all sacred books (AC, 317). As can be seen from the discussion above and from the preceding list, these are all analogical epics: the first one is of the Messianic variety, and the last two are, respectively, individual and social manifestations of the encyclopaedic form. Third, the epic of Gilgamesh, the collections of myth by Ovid and Hesiod, and the works of Boethius are all examples of the contrast epic, with its opposition between the human and the divine (AC, 317).

In the romantic mode, encyclopaedic works take the form of both the analogical and the contrast epic. Three examples of the former, which are imitations or analogues of the Messianic myth, are Dante's quest in *The Divine Comedy,* St. George's in *The Faerie Queene,* and the medieval knight's quest for the Holy Grail (AC, 317). Langland's "great vision" in *Piers Plowman,* on the other hand, is the "first major English treatment of the contrast-epic. At one pole is the risen Christ and the salvation of Piers: at the other is the somber vision of human life which presents at the end of the poem something very like a triumph of Antichrist" (AC, 318).

"In the high mimetic," Frye says, "we reach the structure that we think of as typically epic, the form represented by Homer, Virgil, and Milton" (AC, 318). The *Iliad* is Frye's example of the nondialectic cycle, that is, the epic of wrath; the *Odyssey* is his illustration of the epic of return, displaced, of course, in the direction of the heroic. A third form, represented by the *Aeneid,* "develops the theme of return into one of rebirth, the end in New Troy being the starting-point renewed and transformed by the hero's quest" (AC, 319). Finally the prototypical epic poet in the high-mimetic mode is Milton, who, because he is writing a Christian or Biblical epic, carries the three classical forms "into a wider archetypal context" (AC, 319) and whose work therefore shows a "completeness of theme (not in any kind of value)" beyond that of Homer and Virgil (AC, 320).

In the low-mimetic and ironic modes the encyclopaedic structure tends to dissolve into other forms. Sometimes it takes the form of *epos,* as in Blake's *Mental Traveller* (AC, 320–22), and at other times the form of prose fiction, as in *Finnegans Wake* (AC, 323), which has the distinction in Frye's schema of being a continuous prose form as well as an epic one.

An understanding of Frye's specific forms should give us a better perspective on the relationship between this aspect of his theory of genres and the first major pair of categories we encountered in our study: fictional and thematic. Fictional works, we recall from the First Essay, are those in which the primary interest derives from *ethos* and *mythos*. Frye calls these *internal* fictions, and he says they usually take the generic form of novels and plays. We have seen how he isolates the specific forms of each of these genres, the modal paradigm of the First Essay having an especially important function in his analysis of the dramatic forms and the concept of *ethos* having a similar function in his treatment of the continuous forms (the novel and its congeners). The primary interest of thematic works, on the other hand, is *dianoia*. These works, as we also recall from the First Essay, are divided into episodic and encyclopaedic kinds. The typical forms of this latter category are made explicit in Frye's treatment of the epic. What remains, then, are those works which fall into the first thematic category, the episodic: works which take the form of lyric, *epos,* and oratorical prose.[18]

Specific Thematic Forms: Lyric and Epos We have seen repeatedly that Frye characteristically employs cyclical, rectilinear, quadrantal, and hierarchical models to organize his thought. Sometimes his categories are set in order by the use of only one of these, as in his discussion of prose fiction where the specific continuous forms combine with each other to produce a tabular organization. Most often, however, he works with several models simultaneously, superimposing them on each other, as it were. Thus we find in his study of drama, for example, a cyclical pattern of specific forms, a quadrantal pattern of cardinal points, and several hierarchical patterns—these last deriving from a conception of higher and lower levels of both reality and literature.

Frye's conceptual arrangement of the specific thematic forms employs a combination of models like these, and thus the skeletal shape of his argument is quite similar to that of the dramatic forms. Specifically, it relies on the same four conceptual principles we met in the discussion of drama: a cyclical organization of forms, based on a movement from "spectacle" to "mimesis" and then back to "spectacle" again; a division of spectacular forms, based on the *melos* and *opsis* analogues; a dialectical separation of forms, based on the innocence-experience dichotomy; and a fourfold division of forms, based on the notion of "cardinal points."[19]

These are the principles that underlie Frye's study of those specific forms which manifest themselves thematically. Although his section heading reads "specific thematic forms," he says that his survey of the cycle of themes "will not give, and is not intended to give, a classification of specific forms of lyric: what it attempts to give is an account of the chief conventional themes of lyric and *epos*" (AC, 293). These conventions, as they appear in the lyric, can be located around the perimeter of a circle, as in Figure 22. Since Frye's aim, however, "is not to 'fit' poems into categories, but to show empirically how conventional archetypes get embodied in conventional genres" (AC, 293), the terms used in the diagram should be understood to correspond only roughly to lyric species. "Forms," in short, can be translated in this context as lyric conventions.

The content of Frye's argument is an elaborate series of these conventions, placed within the general framework just outlined. He begins with the cardinal point corresponding to the epiphany in drama. This is the convention, he says, "of the oracular associative process," discussed earlier in this chapter as the typical rhythm of the lyric. One of its "most

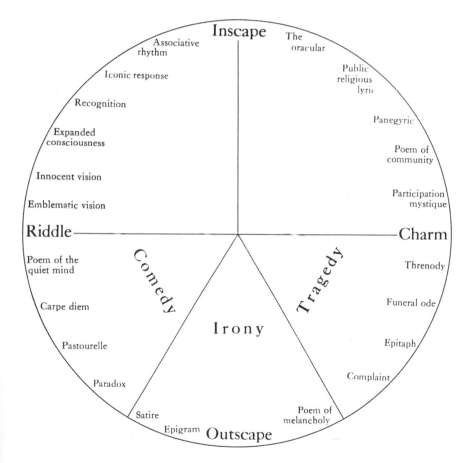

Figure 22. Thematic conventions of the lyric.

direct products . . . is a type of religious poetry marked by a concentration of sound and ambiguity of sense" (AC, 293). Since Frye cites Hopkins's poetry as a typical modern example of this convention, I have labeled the first cardinal point "inscape." Frye's own label for the second cardinal point is "charm," the same term he used earlier to characterize the radical of *melos* in the lyric. Between these two points are various lyric forms and conventions. In the tradition of the religious lyric, located near the "inscape" pole, Frye places such works as "the *Pearl* and many poems of Herbert," poems which combine intricate stanzaic and verbal patterns (AC, 294). This oracular tradition, preserved in much of the King James version of the Bible, also includes "the curious sing-song chant of the Koran . . . and the poetic ambiguities of the Classical oracles" (AC, 294). The religious poem, when it becomes more dignified and less ambiguous, Frye argues, produces such forms as the "Apollonian paean, the Hebrew psalm, the Christian hymn, or the Hindu Vedas" (AC, 294). He calls these forms "poems of community," and this category in turn is expanded to include various types of the panegyric: odes to heroes and kings as the representatives of deity, to victorious athletes, to the state, to the courtly love mistress; the epithalamium; poems of triumph, festivity, and procession (AC, 295).

The fact that all of these forms and conventions are seen as instances of the oracular lyric is a result once again of Frye's analogical method. How does his application of the method produce the various examples cited? In Figure 22 we observe that Frye's first category—what I have called the poem of "inscape"—lies midway between riddle and charm, representing respectively the *opsis* and *melos* elements of associative or lyrical rhythm. The coming together of these two elements, according to Frye, produces the oracular associative process, distinguished by incantatory sound patterns (charm) and ambiguous meaning (riddle) in combination. This observation leads to the establishment of Frye's primary field of reference, from which descend, by a series of parallels and correspondences, his conventions and forms. First he observes that the combination of charm and riddle is to be found in some kinds of religious poetry, Hopkins's, for example. Once this type of lyric is established as the exemplary, oracular poem, Frye can enumerate other sacred types of literary forms and styles, including the psalm and hymn.

But observe what he says about these forms: "In the more public type of religious lyric . . . the rhythms become more stately, simple, and dignified, the 'I' of the poem is one of a visible community of worshippers, and the syntax and diction become less ambiguous" (AC, 294). The hymn and psalm, in other words, are some distance removed from the Hopkins-type lyric; the former is analogous to the latter only because they are both religious lyrics. The degree of arbitrariness in this kind of analogy will be considered later. Similarly, Frye's next category, the panegyrical ode, is introduced into the discussion because it is analogous—"closely related," he says—to the hymn (AC, 295). Next we discover that there are many forms analogous to the panegyric: the Pindaric ode, the poem praising the courtly love mistress, the St. Cecelia ode, the poetic tributes to music, the epithalamium, the triumph poem, and poems of festivity or procession.

The poem of community, Frye says, "brings us to the next cardinal point of the lyric," namely, charm (AC, 295). Charm is defined as the "response to some kind of physical or quasi-physical compulsion—perhaps propulsion is the word." "One's education in this type of charm," Frye adds, "begins with nursery rhymes, where the infant is swung or bounced to the rhythm, or where the theme includes some form of affectionate assault on the child. It continues through college yells, sing-songs, and similar forms of *participation mystique*" (AC, 295; see also 278–79). The convention of *participation mystique* is communal in nature and thus lies toward the extreme right of our diagram, alongside the panegyric and other poems of community. When the form of the panegyric, however, becomes the funeral ode, we pass from the lyric conventions corresponding to those of the dramatic *auto* into the lower half of the cycle. In Figure 22 the three divisions of this lower half represent the lyric counterparts of the tragic, ironic, and comic forms of drama. These lyric forms can be briefly recounted.

Funeral odes, pastoral elegies, threnodies, epitaphs, and the like, are "tragic" forms—tragic insofar as their conventional theme is related to death. Moving toward irony, we encounter "the complaint, the poem of exile, neglect or protest at cruelty" (AC, 297). More ironic still is the poem of melancholy or ennui, which brings us, in Frye's diagrammatic framework, to the nadir of the cycle, or to the cardinal point of "outscape," as he calls it, parodying Hopkins's term. This is "the lyrical counterpart," Frye adds, "of what in drama we call the mime, the center of the irony which is common to tragedy and comedy. It is a convention of pure projected detachment, in which an image, a situation, or a mood is observed with all the imaginative energy thrown outward to it and away from the poet" (AC, 297). From this point, Frye proceeds to elaborate the lyric forms of the cycle as it moves through satire and comedy toward the fourth cardinal point, the riddle. These conventions include the epigram; the satiric features of the lyric, as in Housman and Hardy, who combine epigram and proverb; the paradoxical conventions of metaphysical poetry and the pastourelle; and, finally, the "less ambiguous" forms of lyric comedy that we find in the *carpe diem* poem or the "poem of the quiet mind" (AC, 299).

At this point in Frye's schema we pass over the boundary of experience into the area of innocence. This brings us into the fourth quadrant, those lyric conventions which fall between "riddle" and "inscape" and which have their dramatic counterpart in the masque. Since this is the quadrant of *opsis,* Frye characteristically speaks of the lyric conventions located here as those of "vision," "expanded consciousness," or "recognition" (AC, 300–302). We observe here once again the crucial role performed by the method of analogy: *opsis* is an analogue for that aspect of poetic diction which depends on imagery and which is related to sense rather than sound; "vision" is an analogue for *opsis;* "recognition" is an analogue for vision; the oracular gifts of the visionary poet, finally, are an analogue for recognition—which brings us back to the beginning of the cycle.

This abbreviated checklist of Frye's lyric conventions is intended to suggest the manner in which they are related to, indeed dependent upon, the larger framework of principles outlined at the beginning. As is so often the case with Frye, it is difficult to determine whether his general framework for discussing a topic, in this case the lyric, derives from an inductive survey of forms and conventions or whether he proceeds in a more *a priori* manner, establishing his generic principles first and then illustrating them with particular examples. Both procedures are certainly involved. Frye says in the Polemical Introduction that he bases his study on an inductive survey of literature and yet that he is going to proceed deductively. Since what is at issue here obviously applies to more than his discussion of the lyric, we shall return to it in the final chapter.

Frye's discussion of the thematic forms is not restricted to the lyric. He also calls attention to the *epos* and prose conventions which fall within the range of his thematic categories, thus producing two more cyclical organizations of forms. A brief outline of the *epos* conventions—to select only one of these—will be sufficient to indicate his conceptual arrangement of the remaining forms, which are represented in Figure 23. The *epos* form corresponding to the religious lyric is the mythical narrative which gives some account of a god. "This myth," Frye claims, "has two main parts: legend, recounting the god's biography or his former dealings with his people; and the description of the ritual he requires" (AC, 294). Examples include, on the legendary side, the Homeric hymns and the "priestly" narrative of creation in Genesis; and on the ritualistic side, the Vedic hymns (AC, 294–95). The *epos* form of the panegyric is difficult to isolate. Frye gives no examples, saying only that, as the panegyric is "naturally a public convention, [it] is often an extended form which combines both lyric and *epos* characteristics" (AC, 295).

The *epos* form corresponding generally to the poem of community and its convention of *participation mystique* is the ballad, which brings us to the second cardinal point (AC, 296). The first quadrant of the lower half of the cycle is represented, in turn, by such *epos* forms as the tragic panegyric (Marvell's ode on Cromwell), the historical epitaph, and Shakespeare's narrative poems (*Venus and Adonis* and *The Rape of Lucrece*), all of which more or less correspond to their lyric counterparts, the elegy, epitaph, and complaint (AC, 296–97). The third cardinal point is represented by the epigram and proverb, *epos* varieties of which are to be found in the conventions of satire used by Dryden and Pope (AC, 298). Next, in the comic section of the cycle are located the

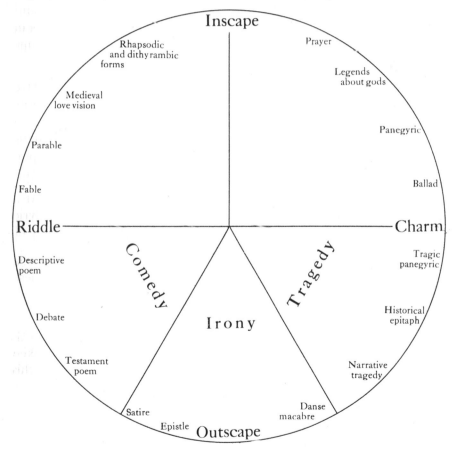

Figure 23. Thematic conventions of *epos* forms.

"testament" poem (Swift's poem on his death, Donne's Anniversaries) and the "debate" (*The Owl and the Nightingale,* Chaucer's *Parliament of Fowls,* and Spenser's *Mutabilitie Cantoes*), corresponding to the lyric conventions of the satire and pastourelle respectively. A final example of comic *epos* is the "expression of serenity" we frequently find in descriptive poems, "where the poet climbs a hill and surveys a landscape below, an imitation in experience of the point of epiphany" (AC, 299). Its lyric parallel is the "poem of the quiet mind."

Finally, the fourth cardinal point is the parable or fable, which corresponds to the riddle of the lyric cycle and which begins the fourth quadrant. In this area Frye is able to recognize several *epos* conventions, including the medieval love vision (AC, 301), Swinburne's poetry, and Blake's prophecies; the first of these is parallel to the recognition poem of the lyric cycle, and the last two are parallel to the poem of iconic response (AC, 302).

Although Frye devotes very little attention to the *epos* forms, I have reviewed his catalogue of conventions in order simply to suggest the way in which he aligns the *epos* cycle to that of the lyric, both of which are a part of the larger conceptual framework used to organize the thematic forms. Frye's argument in the section moves swiftly and depends upon many distinctions developed earlier. Perhaps the most obvious feature of the argument is once again its use of the analogical method. To give a specific illustration of the method at work, let us return to the lyric conventions of Frye's first quadrant, where he mentions a number of forms similar to the panegyric, such as the Pindaric ode, the St. Cecelia ode, and the epithalamium. Although Frye suggests that all of these forms are species of the panegyric, he does not seem concerned to show how they are related to his initial observation about the oracular combination of sound and sense. Indeed this would be difficult, if not impossible, to do anyway, since the rapid sequence of analogical leaps has taken him far from his original distinction. The argument proceeds in this manner: the oracular associative process is *like* what we find in some religious lyrics, both being oracular; these in turn are *like* some hymns and psalms, which are *like* some religious panegyrics, all being in some sense religious; the religious panegyric in turn is *like* other odes of praise, both being laudatory; these odes are *like* patriotic verse, both being poems of community; and so on. This is a classic instance of the analogical procedure at work, and it represents the characteristic method of Frye's argument throughout this section. Only by drawing analogies like these can he move, say, in the first quadrant of his cycle, from the highly individual and ambiguous poetry of Hopkins to the highly social and unambiguous "poem of community."

Even though Frye is able to distinguish a number of lyric and *epos* forms and to organize them in an ingenious way, his entire discussion still represents but a bare outline of those thematic conventions which, as he says, "get embodied in conventional genres" (AC, 293). He does refer briefly to some forms of oratorical prose, and they can be seen as forming still another thematic cycle. But some conventions are omitted altogether from Frye's survey. "An extremely complicated problem," he says, "the problem of the intervening generic stages between lyric and *epos,* has to be omitted from this discussion" (AC, 363). We observe also that he devotes little attention to the purely narrative poem. Although this kind of poem, which in Frye's schema would be a fictional rather than a thematic work, is omitted from his discussion, the framework for its inclusion is not: if the narrative poem is episodic, as opposed to encyclopaedic, its forms would correspond to those of the dramatic cycle; if continuous, to those of the specific forms of prose fiction (AC, 293).

There is, however, one final literary type included in his analysis of the specific forms. It is what Frye calls the "brief" or "miniature" epic. In his book on Milton he refers to it as "a somewhat undeveloped conception in criticism, though examples of it in English literature stretch from *Beowulf* to *The Waste Land.*"[20] In the *Anatomy* it is treated briefly at the end of the section on encyclopaedic forms. As a specific form, however, it requires separate treatment, since it does not fall neatly into Frye's episodic-encyclopaedic dichotomy. It is like both the epic and the lyric, insofar as it is in the thematic mode. But it is unlike the epic because it is less encyclopaedic, and it is unlike the lyric because its treatment of a conventional theme is more concentrated. "In encyclopaedic forms," Frye says, "we see how the conventional themes, around which lyrics cluster, reappear as *episodes* of a longer story. . . . The reverse development occurs when a lyric on a conventional theme achieves a concentration that expands it into a miniature epic: if not the historical 'little epic' or epyllion, something very like it generically" (AC, 324). Although the concentration of theme is one of the primary characteristics of the miniature epic, the range of the theme, as we see in Frye's examples, is what really counts: "*Lycidas* is a miniature scriptural epic extending over the whole range covered by *Paradise Lost,* the death of man and his redemption by Christ. Spenser's *Epithalamion* also probably contains in miniature as much symbolic range as the unwritten conclusion to his epic would have had. In modern times the miniature epic becomes a very common form: the later poems of Eliot, of Edith Sitwell, and many cantos of Pound belong to it" (AC, 324). Moreover, the brief epic can sometimes be found within the larger, encyclopaedic kind. Michael's prophecy in *Paradise Lost,* Frye says, "presents the whole Bible as a miniature contrast-epic, with one pole at the apocalypse and the other at the flood" (AC, 324). Similarly, the Book of Job is "a kind of microcosm of [the Bible's] total theme" (AC, 324).

This brings us back to the observation with which Frye began his survey of encyclopaedic forms: the parabolic dramatic structure of the Bible is the most expansive of all myths. A story like the Book of Job can be studied, Frye argues, as a complete cyclic drama in itself, or it can be studied as an integral part of the five-act drama which is the Bible: creation, fall, exile, redemption, restoration. From the larger thematic perspective, the Book of Job may appear as a discontinuous, fragmentary work. But since the literary critic should view the Bible "not as the scrapbook of corruptions, glosses, redactions, insertions, conflations, misplacings, and misunderstandings revealed by the analytic critic, but as the typological unity which all these things were originally intended to help construct" (AC, 315), the contradiction between the continuous and discontinuous perspectives on the Book of Job is more apparent than real.

What Frye wants to guard against here is the critic's complete reliance on the methods of historical Biblical scholarship ("higher" criticism). In Frye's synoptic perspective, this kind of study is purely "descriptive" criticism, as he has defined this term in the Second Essay. His own version of "higher" criticism is myth criticism, that version which always assumes the "typological unity" of a literary work. And in the face of myth criticism, the descriptive aspect of literary meaning "dissolves" (AC, 325). Perhaps "transforms" is a more appropriate word, since Frye states that only when the critic assumes the "priority of myth to fact" does "the analytic view of the Bible begin to come into focus as the thematic aspect of it. In proportion as the continuous fictional myth begins to look illusory, as the text breaks down into smaller and smaller fragments, it takes on the appearance of a sequence of epiphanies, a discontinuous but rightly ordered series of significant moments of apprehension or vision."[21]

The consequences of this view are enormous. Frye is saying that the Bible (and by extension, all literary works, since the Bible is the "major informing influence on literary symbolism") can be read in two ways: either as total *mythos* or as a series of epiphanies. Since the priority of myth permits "higher" criticism to absorb analytic criticism within itself, the two seemingly different and opposed perspectives are "reconciled." Frye's own statement of the principle is this:

> The Bible may . . . be examined from an aesthetic or Aristotelian point of view as a single form, as a story in which pity and terror, which in this context are the knowledge of good and evil, are raised and cast out. Or it may be examined from a Longinian

point of view as a series of ecstatic moments or points of expanding apprehension. . . . Here we have a critical principle which we
can take back to literature and apply to anything we like, a
principle in which the "holism," as it has been called, of Coleridge and the discontinuous theories of Poe, Hulme, and Pound
are reconciled. (AC, 326)

When we have arrived at this point, Frye says, "we have gone as far as
we can within literature" (AC, 326). This conclusion to Frye's discussion
of the specific literary forms recalls the final part of his theory of
modes where he first argued the necessity of synthesizing the Aristotelian and Longinian views.

While Frye is speaking here about the application of a critical
principle to the Bible, it is one which can be applied, and indeed is, by
Frye, to "anything we like." As just said, the consequences of this view
are of great importance for Frye's theory; but they are not unexpected
consequences, since the critical principle to which he refers has been
with us all along. It is the principle which seeks to do justice to both the
Aristotelian and the Longinian views of art; to both the aesthetic and
the psychological experiences; to the idea of literature both as product
and as process; to detachment and catharsis, on the one hand, and to
absorption and ecstasis, on the other.

5

Autonomy and the Context of Criticism

If Frye's reconciliatory aim takes us back to that part of the First Essay where he seeks to unite the Aristotelian and Longinian approaches, it takes us back to the Introduction to the *Anatomy* as well, for here he argues that the development of a unified structure of knowledge about literature should serve, if not to reconcile the differences among the public critic, the scholar, and the man of taste, at least to provide them a common body of principles on which to proceed with their separate tasks.[1] Although we have had several occasions to glance at statements Frye makes in his Introduction, we have not yet considered two important theoretical claims he makes there: one regarding the autonomy and the scientific nature of criticism; the other regarding the status of value judgments in critical theory. The Introduction has aroused more controversy than any other single part of Frye's writing. Some of his detractors, in fact, have become so caught up in debating the issues raised here that they have never gotten beyond the first two dozen pages, which is one of the reasons I have chosen to analyze these issues only after having looked at the *Anatomy* itself in some detail. Another reason is that the Introduction is admittedly a polemical one. As a reaction against some emphases in the 1950s which Frye felt to be badly motivated, it tends toward an overstatement of views expressed more cautiously elsewhere. The Polemical Introduction is important, however, and our first obligation in dealing with it is to understand what Frye is saying.

Critical Autonomy

I have remarked previously that Frye's theory of literature is developed from an attempt to answer two questions: What is the total subject of study of which criticism forms a part? and how does one arrive at poetic meaning? In answering the first question, Frye rejects the notion that criticism is a subdivision of literature, a rejection based on the commonsense observation that apart from some aspect of criticism literature is not a subject of study at all. Instead it is an object of study which can be neither understood nor taught except as criticism develops its own autonomous principles. The fact that literature consists of words, Frye says,

> makes us confuse it with the talking verbal disciplines. The libraries reflect our confusion by cataloguing criticism as one of the subdivisions of literature. Criticism, rather, is to art what history is to action and philosophy to wisdom: a verbal imitation of a human productive power which in itself does not speak. And just as there is nothing which the philosopher cannot consider philosophically, and nothing which the historian cannot consider historically, so the critic should be able to construct and dwell in a conceptual universe of his own. (AC, 12)

Such a conceptual universe is what Frye sets out to build. His goal is stated forthrightly: to give his reasons for believing that "a synoptic view of the scope, theory, principles, and techniques of literary criticism" is both possible and necessary and "to provide a tentative version" of one such synoptic view.[2] His first assumption, therefore, is the existence of a unified structure of knowledge about literature which criticism should progressively and systematically develop.

The *Anatomy* itself is witness to Frye's claim that such a structure of knowledge is possible. That it is necessary, on the other hand, derives from two convictions. First of all, critics are in need of a handbook, a contemporary *Poetics*, which can perform the same function as basic theoretical manuals do in other disciplines. The book reviewer, the literary historian, the philosophical and the formal critic all need a shareable body of theoretical knowledge which, by involving them in a large context, can serve as a common point of reference and thereby work to reconcile the differences among their opposing "schools." A synoptic view is required in the second place because criticism itself needs an autonomy, an independence from externally derived frameworks. Autonomy is a concept frequently encountered in Frye's work and needs to be examined in greater detail.

His argument for *critical* independence is rooted in his view that criticism has tended to attach itself to, and thereby derive its conceptual framework from, other disciplines or ideologies. "Critical principles," he says, "cannot be taken over ready-made from theology, philosophy, politics, science, or any combination of these" (AC, 7). If they are, the result is the fallacy of "determinism," that is, the fallacy which sets up a causal relationship between one's primary interest and a particular subject of study, as when a geographer or an economist, for example, seeks to explain all historical events solely in terms of geographical or economic causes. To assimilate criticism to another discipline is to give "one the illusion of explaining one's subject while studying it, thus wasting no time" (AC, 6). There are many such determinisms in criticism, according to Frye, each of which—whether Marxist, Freudian, existentialist, Thomist, liberal-humanist, Jungian, neoclassical, or whatnot—uses some framework external to literature as its conceptual base. This is parasitism (AC, 6). It assumes that the conceptual framework for criticism cannot be derived from literature itself and thus forces the critic to become a second-class academic citizen, dependent upon the postulates of some other discipline. "To subordinate criticism to an externally derived critical attitude," Frye argues,

> is to exaggerate the values in literature that can be related to the external source, whatever it is. It is all too easy to impose on literature an extra-literary schematism, a sort of religio-political color-filter, which makes some poets leap into prominence and others show up as dark and faulty. All that the disinterested critic can do with such a color-filter is to murmur politely that it shows things in a new light and is indeed a most stimulating contribution to criticism. Of course such filtering critics usually imply, and often believe, that they are letting their literary experience speak for itself and are holding their other attitudes in reserve, the coincidence between their critical valuations and their religious or political views being silently gratifying to them but not explicitly forced on the reader. Such independence of criticism from prejudice, however, does not invariably occur even with those who best understand criticism.[3]

The obvious question now is in what respect Frye's own conceptual framework differs from those of the deterministic methods he seeks to avoid. Is his method free of what he calls "extra-literary schematisms" and "color-filters"? The superficial answer is that Frye's claim for the autonomy of his theory is suspect, since he goes to other disciplines for a large part of his conceptual apparatus: witness the terminology he has appropriated from psychoanalysis (projection, displacement, dream), Biblical symbology (levels of meaning, anagogic phase), and cultural anthropology (ritual, myth, archetype). These obvious intellectual debts are the reason Frye is sometimes identified as a critic who has derived his primary assumptions from psychology, anthropology, and Biblical symbology. The contradiction, however, between his theoretical statements about critical autonomy and his practice of freely borrowing from other disciplines is more apparent than real.

In the first place, Frye's borrowings are less substantive than terminological. Being a "terminological buccaneer," as he calls himself (AC, 362), means that he can pirate a word like "displacement" without feeling an obligation to retain the meaning which the term has in Freudian psychology. Similarly, the meaning which Frye attaches to the word "archetype" is altogether different from Jung's use of the term.[4] Even those terms he appropriates from other literary critics are often redefined to suit his own purposes, Aristotle's *mythos* and Coleridge's "initiative," for example.

Tzvetan Todorov has called into question Frye's claim for autonomy, pointing out that he devotes very little attention to a theoretical discussion of such pairs of categories as superior/inferior, verisimilitude/fantasy, real/ideal, introvert/extrovert, intellectual/personal, social reconciliation/social exclusion.

> What is striking in this list from the very first is its arbitrariness: why are these categories and not others useful in describing a literary text? One looks for a closely reasoned argument which would prove this importance; but there is no trace of such an argument. Further, we cannot fail to notice a characteristic common to these categories: their non-literary nature. They are all borrowed from philosophy, from psychology, or from a social ethic, and moreover not from just any psychology or philosophy. Either these terms are to be taken in a special, strictly literary sense; or—and since we are told nothing about such a sense, this is the only possibility available to us—they lead us outside of literature. Whereupon literature becomes no more than a means of expressing philosophical categories. Its autonomy is thus profoundly contested—and we again contradict one of the theoretical principles stated, precisely, by Frye himself.[5]

"As destructive criticism," remarks David H. Richter, "this is devastating."[6] But it is hardly devastating if we keep separate, as we should, the issues of critical assumptions and principles, on the one hand, and critical language, on the other. Todorov confuses these.[7] The issue is not whether extraliterary influences can be found in Frye, for they are obvious and abundant; many discursive thinkers "interpenetrate" Frye's critical vision, as he freely admits.[8] The issue rather is what function these influences perform in his total discourse. This in turn depends upon the criteria he uses to separate criticism from other disciplines. These criteria show, in the second place, that the inconsistency between his theory and practice is only apparent.

In *The Critical Path*, where Frye discusses again the relationship of criticism to other disciplines, he says: "I have always insisted that criticism cannot take presuppositions from elsewhere, which always means wrenching them out of their real context, and must work out its own" (CP, 16). The question thus becomes defining the "real context" of criticism; and Frye's answer boils down to whether literary meaning is conceived of in intentional or nonintentional terms. He says that when he first began to write on critical theory, "all meaning in literature seemed to be referred first of all to the context of intentional meaning, always a secondary and sometimes the wrong context. That is, the primary meaning of a literary work was assumed to be the kind of meaning that a prose paraphrase could represent. This primary meaning was called the 'literal' meaning, a phrase with a luxuriant growth of semantic tangles around it" (CP, 15). Placing poetry in this literal or intentional context is to see poetic meaning as "related to some verbal area of study outside literature" (CP, 16). This is a familiar New Critical dictum and one we have seen Frye appeal to before.[9] But it lies at the heart of his distinction between an autonomous criticism and one dependent upon the presuppositions of another discipline. Literature, in short, is different from other kinds of verbal expression in that it is nondiscursive, nonintentional, nondescriptive. And a criticism which does not begin with this assumption, according to Frye's argument, will inevitably move outward into some other discipline for its conceptual presuppositions.

The polemic against deterministic approaches is much less absolute in *The Critical Path* than in the *Anatomy*. We find, for example, that Frye does not condemn all biographical approaches as deterministic, only those which assume that biography is the "essential key" to poetic meaning (CP, 17). Moreover, only "some" centrifugal methods are "badly motivated" (CP, 14), and documentary approaches must be used by the centripetal critic with "tact," not banned altogether (CP, 18). Frye therefore admits into critical discourse the contributions of other disciplines as long as the nonintentional rather than the intentional view of poetry is primary. Studying literature in the context of other literature means we will be less likely to capitulate to some "extra-literary schematism" even though other disciplines may interpenetrate the literary context.

Criticism as Science

To achieve his goal, Frye proposes "an examination of literature in terms of a conceptual framework derivable from an inductive survey of the literary field" (AC, 7). He suggests that such an examination can and should be scientific. The view of criticism as science has proved to be a troublesome point for some of Frye's readers, not all of whom have been aware of the two distinct senses in which he uses the word "scientific."[10]

The first sense derives from his claim, simply, that critical inquiry should be systematic, inductive, and causal as opposed to random and intuitive; that it should be self-contained rather than dependent upon the principles of other disciplines; and that it should attempt a coherent and progressive consolidation in organizing its materials (AC, 7–8). Because there is a kind of critical inquiry based on rational and systematic analysis—a kind of criticism distinguishable from what R.S. Crane calls, on the one hand, "cultivated *causerie*," and, on the other, the application to literature of general systems of ideas[11]—then Frye's use of the term *scientific* can be said to describe such an approach.

But the second sense of the word arises from Frye's claim that criticism, considered historically, still exists in a state of naive induction, whereas other disciplines, such as physics, history, biology, and astronomy, have moved beyond primitivism to the status of pure science. The transition from naive induction is accomplished when a discipline, rather than taking the data of immediate experience as its explanatory and structural principles, conceives of the data themselves as the phenomena to be explained. Physics, for example, "began by taking the immediate sensations of experience, classified as hot, cold, moist, and dry, as fundamental principles. Eventually physics turned inside out, and discovered that its real function was rather to explain what heat and moisture were" (AC, 15). The study of history has passed through a similar revolution. In the chronicles of the naive historian there is no distinction between the recorded events and the structure of the chronicle, whereas the scientific historian, rather than merely cataloguing events chronologically, sees them as data to be explained and is thus forced to view them from the perspective of a larger interpretative framework. Frye argues by analogy that criticism, currently in a state of naive induction because its practitioners insist on treating every literary work as a datum, needs to pass beyond the primitive state to a scientific one. And this can be accomplished only when criticism seeks to explain literary works in terms of a conceptual framework which is independent from the datum itself. Just as physics has discovered the theoretical framework of relativity, so criticism needs "to leap to a new ground from which it can discover what the organizing or containing forms of its conceptual framework are. Criticism seems to be badly in need of a coordinating principle, a central hypothesis which, like the theory of evolution in biology, will see the phenomena it deals with as parts of a whole" (AC, 16).

Frye's boldly stated purpose is to develop such a synoptic hypothesis, and his first step in doing so is to assume that there is a total coherence among literary works.

> We have to adopt the hypothesis, then, that just as there is an order of nature behind the natural sciences, so literature is not a piled aggregate of "works," but an order of words. A belief in an order of nature, however, is an inference from the intelligibility of the natural sciences; and if the natural sciences ever completely demonstrated the order of nature they would presumably exhaust their subject. Similarly, criticism, if a science, must be totally intelligible, but literature, as the order of words which makes the science possible, is, so far as we know, an inexhaustible source of new critical discoveries, and would be even if new works of literature ceased to be written. (AC, 17)

It is clear that when Frye speaks of criticism as scientific in this sense he means something much different from the systematic and rational formulation of a theory; one could develop a systematic and internally rational theory which would be an "anatomy of nonsense," to use Yvor Winters's phrase. But to say that hypothetical structures of criticism and natural science are or should be the same means that the kinds of tests that are applied to purely scientific hypotheses may be applied to critical hypotheses and statements as well. Whether Frye's theory can meet the demands of such tests is problematic and will be examined later. For the moment I want only to observe, first, that Frye's concern to establish the autonomy of criticism stems from his belief that criticism is not a second-class subdivision of anything, but a discipline deserving its own theoretical structure, and, second, that Frye's view of "criticism as science" has two different meanings.

Value Judgments

Lying behind Frye's effort to free criticism from a dependence upon other disciplines and his concern to make critical inquiry scientific is an assumption which we encounter at a number of places in his writings: the radical disjunction between knowledge and experience, criticism and taste, fact and value, objective intellect and subjective feeling. This assumption is perhaps most clearly evident in his much-discussed yet often misunderstood ideas about value judgments. In seeking to understand his position, we should recognize that Frye has never claimed the discussion of value to lie altogether outside the function of criticism. What he does contend is that certain kinds of evaluative statements do not properly belong to the kind of criticism which he is mainly concerned to establish. Or to put the matter differently, Frye is not intent on purging all value judgments from criticism: his own work is replete with expressions of value, implicit and explicit. He is intent rather on arguing that value judgments should be neither the starting point nor the goal of criticism. Since the basis of this claim is the fundamental dichotomy between fact and value, or between knowledge and experience, it is not difficult to see why criticism, defined as a structure of thought derived inductively from the total order of words which constitutes literature, cannot embrace evaluation as its proper end. In one sense Frye's argument is circular and, if we grant his assumption, irrefutable: if criticism is a structure of knowledge, and if knowledge and value are separate, then value cannot be a part of criticism. But this is too simple an account of Frye's view.

In the *Anatomy* he distinguishes between what he calls comparative and positive value judgments (AC, 20). Most of his polemic is directed against two kinds of comparative judgments: biographical evaluations, which view a literary work as a product, and tropical evaluations, which view the work as possession (AC, 20–21). Both kinds of comparative evaluations are rhetorical: critics who use them praise or censure literary works in terms either of the author, in which case questions about the greatness of the author's personality are paramount, or of the audience, in which case the issue is the effect of style and meaning on the reader. But in either case, Frye insists, the basis of appeal is some "concealed social, moral, or intellectual analogy" (AC, 23). Such analogies, he claims, lie behind all attempts at evaluative comparison; and since any effort to promote or demote authors, like Arnold's touchstones of high seriousness, will betray the subjective preferences hidden in the analogy, such efforts belong to the history of taste rather than to criticism. "Comparative estimates of value are really inferences, most valid when silent ones, from critical practice, not expressed principles guiding its practice" (AC, 25).

Positive evaluations, on the other hand, treat the goodness or genuineness of a poem, and because they derive in part from one's direct experience of literature rather than from an extraliterary prejudice, Frye regards them as somewhat less suspect than comparative judgments. Positive values, he says, are born of "informed good taste" (AC, 27), that is, taste founded on both experience and knowledge. Nevertheless, Frye insists that positive value judgments can never serve as the aim of criticism, and he issues several caveats against overestimating their importance.

In the first place, he says, "it is superstition to believe that the swift intuitive certainty of good taste is infallible. Good taste follows and is developed by the study of literature; its precision results from knowledge, but does not produce knowledge. Hence the accuracy of any critic's good taste is no guarantee that its inductive basis in literary experience is adequate" (AC, 27). Here we have an explicit formulation of the priority of criticism to taste: positive value judgments depend on good taste which depends in turn on disinterested knowledge.

Second, Frye claims that however important to criticism the experience of literature may be, such experience is, "like literature itself, unable to speak" and thus can never be recaptured by critical terminology (AC, 27). The important assumption here is the disjunction between knowledge and experience. In another essay Frye says that criticism proper

> is categorical and descriptive: it tries to *identify* a writer's work. Now even judicial criticism [criticism based on taste] never leads logically to a value-judgement: value-judgements may be assumed at one end or emitted at the other, but the relation between them is rhetorical only. The source of the confusions involved here is the failure to distinguish criticism from the direct experience of literature. Direct experience, developed by practice and habit, is the basis of good taste, and the normal result of good taste is a value-judgement. Good taste in itself is inarticulate: it feels and knows, but cannot speak. Value-judgements may be asserted, intuited, assumed, argued about, explained, attacked or defended: what they can never be is demonstrated.[12]

They cannot be demonstrated, of course, because of the prior assumption that categorical and descriptive fact, which constitutes knowledge, is entirely separate from opinionated and prejudicial judgment, which constitutes taste. Frye's emphasis, however, is that a scientific criticism must always assume the priority of the former. This conviction is reiterated in the following passage, intended by Frye to be a succinct summary of his views on value judgments:

> (1) Every value-judgment contains within it an antecedent categorical judgment, as we obviously cannot tell how good a thing is until we know what it is. (2) Inadequate value-judgments nearly always owe their inadequacy to an insufficient knowledge of what the categories of literature are. (3) Categorical judgments are based on a knowledge that can be learned and which should constantly increase; value-judgments are based on a skill derived only from such knowledge as we already have. (4) Therefore, knowledge, or scholarship, has priority to value-judgments, constantly corrects their perspective, and always has the power of veto over them, whereas subordinating knowledge to value-judgments leads to impossible pendantries. (FI, 43–44)

Frye's view of value judgments is another example of his attack on critical provincialism. It permits him to grant equal status, in his synoptic perspective, to all literary works. Popular, primitive, and prophetic art can take its place alongside the elite, sophisticated, and urbane. "Provincialism," writes E.W. Mandel, "clearly has something to do with boundaries, and it is revealing to notice what a difference can be suggested in the quality of a work simply by altering the boundaries within which it is placed." In a criticism concerned with "first principles," he adds, we are interested in

> the foundations and structure of one of the central humanistic disciplines, and it follows that we are not interested in personality or gossip, but in theory or idea. From this point of view we can define provincialism, as in effect Professor Frye defines it in the *Anatomy of Criticism,* as the failure to suspect the existence of a systematic criticism distinct from the history of taste. Provincialism here appears to be a derivative of a particular theory of criticism, the theory that criticism is parasitic rather than autonomous, and that therefore it can never deserve serious attention on its own merits.[13]

This is certainly one of the reasons for Frye's wanting to expel matters of taste and comparative judgments from the house of critical knowledge: provincialism in both art and criticism has no place in the free and classless society which is his cultural ideal.[14]

Literature and Life: The Question of Literary Autonomy

Frye's doctrine of value judgments derives from a fundamental assumption which separates knowledge from experience. The same assumption underlies his strong and recurring emphasis on the independence of criticism from other disciplines and of literature from life. We should not be deceived by the polemics of his Introduction, however, into thinking of his solution to these matters as simplistic. The question of literary autonomy has been an especially thorny problem for Frye. He refers to it as the "central dilemma of literature," a dilemma suggested by the traditional opposition between delight and instruction (SS, 169).

If literature is made out of other literature, as Frye says, then its relationship to life would not appear to figure importantly. And if it is unrelated to life, there is little danger of its integrity being injured by appeals to ethical or instructive ends: it can remain an autonomous object of disinterested study, detached from all value except aesthetic contemplation for its own sake. Such a view, however, does not accurately represent Frye's position. It is true that he has often been accused of ignoring historical, moral, and social realities, of slighting any literary response which is not disengaged from direct experience, and of retreating into the timeless and amoral vacuum of literary archetype and vision. The feeling is widespread that his views on the nature and function of both literature and criticism commit him to an art-for-art's-sake elitism and to a view of poetry as nothing more than convention.[15] But this assessment is a caricature of Frye's views. One such caricature has been drawn by Frederick Crews. In an outspoken essay entitled "Anaesthetic Criticism," Crews takes the position that Frye represents everything that is wrong with contemporary poetics, and he sets out to develop a critical framework in conscious opposition to Frye's method.[16] Crews's strictures against Frye are best understood in terms of the constructive theory he himself advances. And this is based on the assumption that contemporary criticism has paid too little attention to the direct experience of literature. In his effort to redirect criticism toward a concern for the literary response, he turns to psychoanalysis for his theoretical foundations.

Crews's argument proceeds deductively. He begins with a definition of man and draws from it certain inferences about the power of psychoanalytic explanation and the nature of art. He rejects the "work-itself" doctrine of recent poetics, and thus he seldom speaks of poetry as if it has some kind of reality apart from the writer or reader. If, in order to characterize Crews's position, we adopt the familiar rhetorical poet-poem-audience division, it is clear that his fundamental interests relate to the creative process and to the response of the audience—in his words, to "the making and apprehension of art works" (14). Most often he focuses upon the latter. The first requisite of good criticism, he says, is "the capacity to be moved" (19). And this emphasis is most readily apparent in the reasons which underlie his indictment of contemporary criticism. He claims that recent poetic theory has become "anaesthetic" because it has not properly conceived of the function of art:

> A criticism that explicitly or implicitly reduces art to some combination of moral content and abstract form and genre conventions is literally an anaesthetic criticism. It insulates the critic and his readers from the threat of affective disturbance. . . . All literary criticism aims to make the reading experience more possible for us, but anaesthetic criticism assumes that this requires keeping caged the anxieties that the artist set free and then recaptured. (13)

Since this dialectic of liberation and recapture constitutes the essence of literature, Crews believes that criticism needs not a procedure for cataloguing various forms of the contest—a procedure he attributes to Frye—but a method for interpreting responses. How artistic effects come about is the question that most intrigues him, and he argues that a psychoanalytically oriented criticism can answer this question more completely than rival approaches. More than once he suggests that the disinterested posture of many critics springs from some deep-seated aversion to actually confronting literature. "The very routine of one's method," he says, "becomes a barrier to the deep involvement which should energize all criticism" (18). His ultimate concern, then, is not with what literature *is* abstractly but with what is *does* concretely, with what issues from the reader's confrontation with the literary text.[17]

The first part of Crews's essay is devoted largely to establishing the methodological validity of using an extraliterary framework, one that is "neither derived from literature nor primarily meant to apply to literature" (1). His polemic is directed against the prevalent tendency to renounce "methods that would plainly reveal literary determinants" (1). This becomes his *bête noire,* and he sees Frye as the chief promulgator of the doctrine that critics should not stray outside literature in developing their fundamental principles. Such a notion, he says, is "intellectually indefensible" (2).

As Crews's polemic progresses, it becomes clear that he objects not so much to Frye's argument for the autonomy of criticism as he does to the entire enterprise outlined in *Anatomy of Criticism.* He finds the *Anatomy* to be symptomatic of current critical anaesthesia. He regrets that critics neglect the "urges" of literary causality and that they have too much "reverence for the all-sufficient text." He sees their systems as apologies "for the most routine academic drudgery." He says that they make a simple equation between merit and borrowed thematic content, that they are too rational and disinterested, that they are not concerned with how literature moves us, and that their criticism leads only to an unhumanistic and pretentious gentility. Crews advances, in fact, two distinct complaints. On the one hand, he presents an apology for using extraliterary hypotheses: thus Frye becomes his whipping boy for failing to see that criticism cannot be autonomous. On the other hand, he is objecting to the "dull, safe, provincial work" (10) which he feels criticism of Frye's variety supports: thus his implicit suggestion that Frye has not properly conceived of the function of art, that he has been asking the wrong questions.

There are several attractive suggestions in the constructive theory Crews advances, but his critique of Frye rests upon half-truth and misrepresentation. In the first place, it is important to recognize that much of Crews's complaint makes sense only in terms of premises which are not Frye's. Unless it can be established that Frye and Crews are talking about the same thing, there can be no basis for either agreement or disagreement. As R.S. Crane has cogently argued, "there can be no genuine refutation of a critical position except within the particular framework of concepts and rules of inference in which it has been asserted." Most critical disagreements, he adds, "can be reduced to quarrels between opponents who are really talking about different things or who are talking about them in different ways."[18] A case in point is Frye's insistence in the Polemical Introduction on the autonomy of criticism. Crews views this as "intrinsically anti-humanistic" and calculated "to close off the possibility that one line of investigation might be fruitfully pursued to its end" (13). But Frye's claim is intelligible only in terms of his purpose, which, in the *Anatomy,* is not to discover the proper ends or uses of literature but to determine the principles by which the whole of literature can be organized and by which individual works can be understood as they relate to other works. Frye does not say that literature is unrelated to life or to the direct experience of the reader. He says simply that these relations cannot be the basis for systematic critical knowledge.

Crews's complaint does not take account of the separation in the *Anatomy* between knowledge and experience, between fact and value. To frown upon Frye's caveat about taking "definite positions," as Crews does, without seeing this statement in the context of Frye's insistence that the direct experience of literature lies outside the kind of knowledge he is attempting to establish, is to misrepresent his argument. Frye's statement about "definite positions" comes in the course of an extended discussion about the subjective basis of comparative value judgments. Thus Crews distorts Frye's statements about externally derived critical attitudes by not placing them in the context of Frye's argument. He deals only with Frye's inference, refusing to confront the hypothesis from which the inference is drawn. The result is that the two critics are really talking about different things.[19]

Frye's case for the autonomy of criticism is perhaps somewhat overstated in the Polemical Introduction. But his central intent is clear: to caution against using literature for the purpose of documenting some sociological, religious, or psychological thesis. He would claim that to corroborate Freud by finding literary illustrations for Freudian hypotheses is not very illuminating for criticism, though it may be for psychoanalysis. Crews maintains, however, that Frye means much more than this: "Frye is asserting that the critic, if he is to retain his objectivity, must derive his principles 'solely' from his inductive survey of literary works" (2). What Frye in fact says is that such a survey is merely the first step a literary critic should take (AC, 6–7). He also says that "the next step is to realize that criticism has a variety of neighbors, and that the critics must enter into relations with them in any way that guarantees his [*sic*] own independence" (AC, 19).

We have already seen that Frye himself goes to a number of other disciplines, not the least of which is psychoanalysis, for his own conceptual apparatus. His discussions of manifest and latent content, his concepts of displacement and existential projection, and his emphasis on the relationship of literature to dreams indicate a clear indebtedness to Freud. A number of passages in the *Anatomy* are clearly influenced by psychoanalysis: Frye's discussion, for example, of the relationship of poetry to desire and repugnance, to wish fulfillment and anxiety. These remarks are not meant to represent Frye as a disguised psychoanalytic critic; they are intended simply to illustrate that Frye's principles are not—Crews's claim to the contrary—derived solely from literature itself. The issue for Frye is not that criticism is prevented from appropriating terminology or concepts from intellectual developments outside its own field. It is rather the use to which these borrowings are put within the framework of a given critical discourse. The framework of Crews's position is pragmatic; he is interested in the effects of literature interpreted psychologically. In such a framework it would make little sense to speak of the autonomy of either literature or criticism. The framework of Frye's position is contextual; he is interested in looking at literature—at least as an initial step—as a nonintentional form of writing. In such a framework, it does make sense to speak of literature as self-contained.

Part of Crews's failure to understand Frye results from his refusal to place Frye's statements in the framework of general assumptions from which they derive. Part of his failure comes from an unwillingness to reveal the context of Frye's statements on a particular issue, like that of value judgments. Moreover, there are several inconsistencies between Crews's own position and his overall assessment of Frye. After condemning Frye's concerns as useless and irrelevant, for example, he urges that his position not be misunderstood:

> Let me emphasize that psychoanalytic discourse properly seeks to show how individuals and groups *respond to* a totality of inner and outer conditions, and that for this task an awareness of nonpsychological forces is indispensable. As applied to literature this position not only welcomes but insists upon knowledge of every operative factor, including genre, convention, rhetorical devices, philosophical intent, audience, class, and personal background. What psychological analysis disputes is not the usefulness of such information, but the equation of it with literary experience. (22)

Now this concession cuts across Crews's earlier claims about the dehumanizing implications in Frye's study of genre, archetypal themes, and historical context. None of these things, moreover, is ever equated in

Frye's criticism with the literary experience. To indict Frye for a position he does not hold is unfair; and at the same time to welcome and insist upon the kind of knowledge he has contributed to criticism is to be guilty of an inconsistency.[20]

Crews's essay raises the question as to whether Frye does in fact show an unqualified reverence for the "all-sufficient text." Does his system always point inward to the work itself? Is he unconcerned with the relationship of literature to life? Does his attention to questions of form and convention necessarily mean that he must abandon all interest in the social context of literature and criticism? A formidable amount of Frye's writing, especially in recent years, has been directed toward precisely the issues Crews accuses him of slighting or neglecting altogether. Even in the *Anatomy,* where Frye's primary concern is the formal nature of literature, we see his willingness to confront such questions as the role of literature in society, the ethical ends of art, and the social function of criticism. These issues are but a part of a much larger concern, what we might call a general theory of culture. Because of the popular conception of Frye as an exclusively formal theorist, this aspect of his work has been either slighted or, as in the case of critics like Crews, overlooked. "As some of those who write about me are still asserting that I ignore the social reference of literary criticism," Frye says in the Preface to *The Stubborn Structure* (1970), "the sub-title [*Essays on Criticism and Society*] calls the attention of those who read me to the fact that I have written about practically nothing else" (SS, x). The same point applies to *The Critical Path: An Essay on the Social Context of Literary Criticism,* a book published the following year. The social reference of criticism, in short, forms an important part of Frye's work; we will not have accounted for his critical theory without examining it.

It is clear from the Tentative Conclusion to the *Anatomy* that Frye neither endorses the view that criticism is finally autonomous nor accepts the idea that literature is aesthetically self-contained. He speaks of the necessity for critics becoming "more aware of the external relations of criticism as a whole with other disciplines" (AC, 342), of the "revolutionary act of consciousness" involved in the response to literature (AC, 344), and of the obligation of criticism to recover the social function of art (AC, 345). It is "hardly honest," he says, for criticism "to shrink altogether from [these] larger issues" (AC, 343). In confronting the "larger issues," Frye examines a number of alternatives the critic might take, rejecting some and trying to reconcile others to his Romantic view of the imagination. His approach is not altogether systematic, but it does appear that he wants to suggest a way that each of the four kinds of criticism in the *Anatomy* (historical, ethical, archetypal, and rhetorical) is related to a wider area of humanistic concern.

First, Frye expands the reference of "historical criticism" to mean not just the codification of the heritage of the past but the recreation of the past in a new context. "The preoccupation of the humanities with the past," he says,

> is sometimes made a reproach against them by those who forget that we face the past: it may be shadowy, but it is all that there is. Plato draws a gloomy picture of man staring at the flickering shapes made on the wall of the objective world by a fire behind us like the sun. But the analogy breaks down when the shadows are those of the past, for the only light we can see them by is the Promethean fire within us. The substance of these shadows can only be in ourselves, and the goal of historical criticism, as our metaphors about it often indicate, is a kind of self-resurrection, the vision of a valley of dry bones that takes on the flesh and blood of our vision. The culture of the past is not only the memory of mankind, but our own buried life, and study of it leads to a recognition scene, a discovery in which we see, not our past lives, but the total cultural form of our present life. It is not only the poet but his reader who is subject to the obligation to "make it new." (AC, 345–46)

Therefore a historical criticism which sees art only in terms of the past must be balanced by a sense of the contemporary relevance of the past. Such an approach, Frye claims, can lead to an expansion of our perspective in the present. This view has been anticipated in the Polemical Introduction where he says (1) that in historical criticism, we study literature "as we do the stars, seeing their interrelationships but not approaching them"; and (2) that historical criticism therefore "needs to be complemented by a corresponding activity growing out of tropical criticism" (AC, 24). He does not mean that the critic should use art to support social or political causes; at least criticism cannot be based on these ends, for they lead to a moral or revolutionary perspective which slights the present in favor of the future. "As soon as we make culture a definite image of a future and perhaps attainable society, we start selecting and purging a tradition, and all the artists who don't fit (an increasing number as the process goes on) have to be thrown out" (AC, 346). Thus, just as an uncorrected historical criticism can lead to a deadening reverence for the archaic, so an uncorrected ethical criticism can lead to a futurism based on indoctrination. Both approaches are provincial, and neither, according to Frye, is anchored in the present in any positive way.

This leads him to reconsider the implications of ethical criticism as he has defined it in the Second Essay. There, in his discussion of fourth-phase symbolism, he maintains that art in its archetypal aspect is an ethical instrument. That is, it becomes more than an object of aesthetic contemplation because, archetypically, it is a product of civilization, "a vision of the goals of human work" (AC, 113). "In terms of his moral significance," Frye says in the Second Essay, "the poet reflects, and follows at a distance, what his community really achieves through its work. Hence the moral view of the artist is invariably that he ought to assist the work of his society by framing workable hypotheses, imitating human action and thought in such a way as to suggest realizable modes of both."[21] As attractive as this view is for Frye, he finally rejects it because it represents art as "useful and functional," serving the external goals of truth and goodness (AC, 112–15). Thus he is led (in the Second Essay) from the archetypal phase, where poetry is related to civilization, to the anagogic phase, where it is "disinterested and liberal, and stands on its own feet" (AC, 115).

In the Tentative Conclusion, Frye raises the issue again, and his solution turns out to be the same, though it is formulated in somewhat different terms. Beginning with Arnold's axiom that "culture seeks to do away with classes," he says:

> The ethical purpose of a liberal education is to liberate, which can only mean to make one capable of conceiving society as free, classless, and urbane. No such society exists, which is one reason why a liberal education must be deeply concerned with works of imagination. The imaginative element in works of art, again, lifts them clear of the bondage of history. Anything that emerges from the total experience of criticism to form a part of liberal education becomes, by virtue of that fact, part of the emancipated and humane community of culture, whatever its original reference. Thus liberal education liberates the works of culture themselves as well as the mind they educate. . . . No discussion of beauty can confine itself to the formal relations of the isolated work of art; it must consider, too, the participation of the work of art in the vision of the goal of social effort, the idea of a complete and classless civilization. This idea of complete civilization is also the implicit moral standard to which ethical criticism always refers. (AC, 347–48)

There are two poles of reference in this passage, the imagination and society, and Frye is unwilling to let either of them be his ultimate norm. If society becomes the goal of criticism, then art becomes subservient to morality or one of the practical sciences, and the detachment of the imaginative vision Frye seeks is lost. Thus, he adds, "the goal of ethical criticism is transvaluation, the ability to look at contemporary social values with the detachment of one who is able to compare them in some degree with the infinite vision of possibilities presented by culture" (AC, 348). On the other hand, if the aesthetic norm is given priority, the social function of criticism withers. Thus he appeals to archetypal criticism to right the balance. "We tried to show in the second essay," he says, "that the moment we go from the individual work of art to the sense of the total form of the art, the art becomes no longer an object of aesthetic contemplation but an ethical instrument, participating in the work of civilization. In this shift to the ethical, criticism as well as poetry is involved" (AC, 349).

But Frye also argued in the Second Essay that both ethical and aesthetic norms must ultimately give way, at the anagogic level, to a self-contained literary universe where the critic is a model of Arnold's disinterestedness, freed from all external goals. Reflecting on this leap, however, he remarks (in the Conclusion) that he was perhaps merely restoring "the aesthetic view on a gigantic scale, substituting Poetry for a mass of poems, aesthetic mysticism for aesthetic empiricism" (AC, 350). Thus, to right the balance once more, he appeals to the critical approach of his Fourth Essay, the argument of which, he says, "led to the principle that all structures in words are partly rhetorical, and hence literary, and that the notion of a scientific or philosophical verbal structure free of rhetorical elements is an illusion. If so, then our literary universe has expanded into a verbal universe, and no aesthetic principle of self-containment will work" (AC, 350).

These are sweeping generalizations, yet they illustrate Frye's concern to establish, on the one hand, an autonomous conceptual universe while insuring, on the other hand, that this universe is not isolated from culture, society, and humane letters. "I am not wholly unaware," he says, "that at every step of this argument there are extremely complicated philosophical problems which I am incompetent to solve as such" (AC, 350). Not the least of these is how criticism can be both disinterested and engaged at the same time. Or, we might ask Frye, what is criticism really, the study of self-contained literary form or the relation of literature to social value? His system, of course, will not easily permit these kinds of questions to be asked, for he conceives of criticism as a dialectical axis, having "as one pole the total acceptance of the data of literature, and as the other the total acceptance of the potential value of those data" (AC, 25). This dyadic framework permits him to pursue practically any critical problem he wants, depending on whether his gaze is centripetal or centrifugal—to use the terms of the Second Essay. His primary interest in the *Anatomy* is centripetal, the inward gaze toward the structure of literature itself. Much of his other work, however, is directed outward toward the social context of literature. In the final analysis Frye does not see "detachment" and "concern," to use his familiar terms, as contradictory at all; he sees them simply as contrary, that is, as different in emphasis and direction. This is why he can say that

> seeing literature as a unity in itself does not withdraw it from a social context: on the contrary, it becomes far easier to see what its place in civilization is. Criticism will always have two aspects, one turned toward the structure of literature and one turned toward the other cultural phenomena that form the social environment of literature. Together, they balance each other: when one is worked on to the exclusion of the other, the critical perspective goes out of focus. If criticism is in proper balance, the tendency of critics to move from critical to larger social issues becomes more intelligible. Such a movement need not, and should not, be due to a dissatisfaction with the narrowness of criticism as a discipline, but should be simply the result of a sense of social context. (CP, 24–25)

This passage comes from a work published a decade and a half after the *Anatomy,* but it represents what Frye is reaching for in the Conclusion to the earlier work. The *application* of the principle expressed here, in such later works as *The Critical Path* and *The Modern Century*[22] as well as in a number of individual essays,[23] should dispel the view that Frye's work represents a myopic commitment to the disinterested study of literary structure.

Another way of describing Frye's view is to see it as a combination of poetics, which separates literature from other areas of verbal expression, and rhetoric, which does not. Frye himself uses this traditional distinction in *The Well-Tempered Critic* (1963), a book which seems consciously intent on giving a kind of moral and philosophic rationale for the *Anatomy of Criticism.* In the last chapter of the later book, he returns once again to consider the two principal ways literature can be viewed, the Aristotelian and Longinian (or Platonic). The difference between the two, according to Frye, is whether art is seen fundamentally as product or as process. He describes the difference by appealing to another series of opposing concepts: Classical versus Romantic, aesthetic versus psychological, hieratic versus demotic, artifact versus expression, imitation versus creation, and the like. From the perspective of "poetics," Frye says, *poeta* and *poema* are assumed to be embedded in a context of *nature,* whatever concepts or metaphors a critic uses to discuss them. In the Aristotelian tradition nature has reference to the physical order, or to structure and system. In the Longinian tradition it refers to the total creative process (WTC, 111–22).

But when *poeta* and *poema* are seen in the context of experience, rather than nature, we leave the province of poetics and enter the realm of rhetoric—the area where authors' intentions, direct appeals, moral value, evidence, and truth become important considerations. And in this area, Frye argues, criticism, like literature, can also be discussed in terms of either product or process, either detachment or participation. The critic, therefore, "is concerned with two kinds of experience. First, he has to understand and interpret the experience which forms the content of the work he is reading. Second, the impact of the work on him itself is an experience, 'an experience different in kind from any experience not of art,' as T.S. Eliot puts it" (WTC, 128). Frye wants to balance the two conceptions of criticism which derive from the two contexts of experience. The disinterested critical response, he says, is fundamental, but never an end in itself (WTC, 140), for the ultimate aim of "literary education is an ethical and participating aim" (WTC, 142).

The reconciliation of the two poles of Frye's critical axis is accomplished, as already suggested, in terms of his Blakean view of the imagination. The schema I have just been outlining is, after all, a dualistic one. And since Frye is looking for a more unified conception of criticism than any approach that splits off the intellect from the emotions, nature from experience, beauty from truth, and aesthetic from social value, such a dualism for him is inadequate. His solution is to say that these opposites are "inseparable, two halves of one great whole which is the *possession* of literature" (WTC, 144–45). Perhaps this should really read "possession *by* literature," for when we ask what it means to "possess" literature, our answer can only be that it means finally to affirm Frye's view of the imagination and his conception of the central place of art in culture. He defines cuture as "a total imaginative vision of life with literature at its center. . . . It is, in its totality, a vision or model of what humanity is capable of achieving, the matrix of all Utopias and social ideals" (WTC, 154). And he defines literature as "a total imaginative form which is . . . *bigger* than either nature or human life, because it contains them, the actual being only a part of the possible" (WTC, 155). To speak of culture and literature in these terms takes us directly to the heart of Frye's critical system. Or, to put it in the language of the Second Essay, it takes us to the highest of the five critical phases. "When we pass into anagogy," he says, "nature becomes, not the container, but the thing contained" (AC, 119). To possess literature, in other words, means really to be possessed by it, and this happens at the highest level of imaginative experience. Frye puts it this way at the end of *The Well-Tempered Critic*:

Literature, we say, neither reflects nor escapes from ordinary life: what it does reflect is the world as human imagination conceives it, in mythical, romantic, heroic and ironic as well as realistic and fantastic terms. This world is the universe in human form, stretching from the complete fulfillment of human desire to what human desire utterly repudiates, the *quo tendas* [i.e., anagogic, "where you should be going"] vision of reality that elsewhere I have called, for reasons rooted in my study of Blake, apocalyptic. . . . Some religions assume that such a world exists, though only for gods; other religions, including those closer to us, identify it with a world man enters at death, the extremes of desire becoming its heavens and hells; revolutionary philosophies associate it with what man is to gain in the future; mystics call it the world of total or cosmic consciousness. A poet may accept any of these identifications without damage to his poetry; but for the literary critic, this larger world is the world man exists and participates in through his imagination. It is the world in which our imaginations move and have their being while we are also living in the "real" world, where our imaginations find the ideals that they try to pass on to belief and action, where they find the vision which is the source of both the dignity and the joy of life. (WTC, 155–56)

The Imagination

The keystone of Frye's theoretical arch is, as the passage above suggests, his doctrine of the imagination. This itself distinguishes his poetics from the positions of those who find the source of their general philosophic principles in (1) the nature of "things" (e.g., Plato and Aristotle, who use "imitation" as the basic term for their discussion of art) and in (2) operations or processes (e.g., Horace and Tolstoy, who use poetic effects as their basic term). Frye's emphasis on the imagination aligns him rather with the tradition of those, such as Kant, who have located the source of their general principles in the human understanding or the faculties of the mind and who use the word "imagination" itself as their basic term for discussing art.[24] This is not to say that Kant's aesthetic views are the source of Frye's conception of the imagination;[25] its chief source is the Romantic tradition, mainly Blake. Like Blake, Frye understands the imagination as both a creative and perceptive faculty. His fullest discussion of the topic appears in a fellowship lecture, "The Imaginative and the Imaginary," presented to The American Psychiatric Association (1962).[26] Here he equates the imagination with the "creative force in the mind." What it has produced is "everything that we call culture and civilization. It is the power of transforming a sub-human physical world into a world with a human shape and meaning" (FI, 152). "Imagination creates reality" (FS, 27), Frye says: it creates culture out of nature; it also produces literary language (EI, 23). The most important thing it creates is not the surface texture of literature but its deeper structures and designs.

Frye is careful to emphasize this point. It is the structuring power of the imagination, in fact, which distinguishes his understanding of the imaginative faculty from Coleridge's. In the well-known passage in chapter 13 of the *Biographia,* Coleridge speaks of the imagination as a vital, recreative force which struggles to idealize and unify. Frye often uses the same kind of language to describe the imagination;[27] yet Coleridge, in Frye's view, did not actually believe in the power of the imagination to create the total structures of literature, even though he talks almost obsessively about the imagination as the creative force which is able to make one thing out of many. Coleridge "intended the climax of the *Biographia Literaria,"* Frye says,

> to be a demonstration of the "esemplastic" or structural nature of the imagination, only to discover when the great chapter arrived that he was unable to write it. There were doubtless many reasons for this, but one was that he does not really think of imagination as a constructive power at all. He means by imagination . . . the reproductive power, the ability to bring to life the texture of characterization and imagery. It is to this power that he applies his favorite metaphor of an organism, where the unity is some mysterious and elusive "vitality." His practical criticism of work he admires is concerned with texture: he never discusses the total design. . . . Coleridge is in the tradition of critical naturalism, which bases its values on the immediacy of contact between art and nature that we continuously feel in the texture of mimetic fiction.[28]

Because the imagination "is the constructive power of the mind, the power of building unities out of units" (SeS, 36), the designs it creates are most obvious in undisplaced literary works—those which are most formulaic. "What the imagination, left to itself, produces is the rigidly conventionalized" (SeS, 36). And since literary works displaced in the direction of the plausible move toward realism, where formulaic structures are less rigid, the context of the imagination can be seen as occupying a space opposite that of the context of realistic, representational, or displaced literary works. In *The Secular Scripture,* in fact, Frye appropriates Wallace Stevens's use of the word "imagination," meaning "the shaping spirit, the power of ordering which seems so mysterious to the poet himself, because it often acts as though it were an identity separate from him" (SeS, 35). Thus while the imagination, by means of displacement, does produce credibility and lifelikeness, it also produces "total design," and this is its most important power for Frye.

One of Frye's readers argues that his views on the imaginative and the imaginary "establish the fact that for Frye imagination is a constructive faculty as opposed to a perceptive faculty," and that it "is *not* primarily an *originating* faculty."[29] But this is to misunderstand Frye's view, especially those ideas on imaginative perception which he has taken over from Blake's theory of knowledge. We have already seen (in chapter 2) how Blake's view of reality, in which the imagination by the process of "identity" transforms the nonhuman world (Nature) into something with human shape and meaning (Culture), is opposed to the commonsense view of Locke in which the perceiving subject is separated from the perceived object. Frye agrees with Blake. Sometimes he speaks of two basic modes of apprehending reality, as in the *Anatomy* where the scientific mode, which perceives an objective nature, is opposed to the poetic mode, which perceives a transformed one. Sometimes he speaks of three basic modes of perceiving the world: the egocentric perception of the unreal world of reflection and abstract ideas, which he calls the world of memory; the ordinary perception of the world we live in, called the world of sight; and the imaginative perception of the world we desire and want to create, called the world of vision (FS, 26). Whether there are three orders of perception or only two is not so important for understanding Frye as is his conviction that there are different kinds or levels of perception and that these depend, as they did for Blake, on differing ways men can apprehend the relationships between subject and object.

If the visionary imagination is a *perceptive* faculty, is it one common to all men? In the *Anatomy* Frye draws back from speculating about the universality of the human mind. He says, for example, that the literary critic should not worry about the origins of archetypes: he "is concerned only with the ritual or dream patterns which are actually in what he is studying, however they got there" (AC, 109). Or again, he remarks that the Jungian theory of a collective unconscious is "an unnecessary hypothesis in literary criticism, so far as I can judge" (AC, 111–12). Yet the universality of archetypes does suggest, as Lawrence Lipking observes, "that they belong to a single human imagination shared by all men."[30]

If in the *Anatomy* Frye shies away from speculating about the universality of the imaginative faculty, in *Fearful Symmetry* he does not:

[Blake's] "All Religions Are One" means that the material world provides a universal language of images and that each man's imagination speaks that language with his own accent. (FS, 28)

What makes the poet worth studying at all is his ability to communicate beyond his own context in time and space. . . . It is here that Blake comes in with his doctrine that "all had originally one language, and one religion." If we follow his own method, and interpret this in imaginative instead of historical terms, we have the doctrine that all symbolism in all art and all religion is mutually intelligible among all men, and that there is such a thing as an iconography of the imagination. (FS, 420)

Neither the study of ritual nor of mythopoeic dreams takes us above a subconscious mental level, nor does such a study, except in rare cases, attempt to suggest anything more than a subconscious unity among men. But if we can find such impressive archetypal forms emerging from sleeping or savage minds, it is surely possible that they would emerge more clearly from the concentrated visions of genius. . . . A comparative study of dreams and rituals can lead us only to a vague and intuitive sense of the unity of the human mind; a comparative study of works of art should demonstrate it beyond conjecture. (FS, 424)

Art therefore demonstrates the universality of the human imagination, a belief reinforced by Frye's conviction that all men, whether creators (artists) or creatures, are motivated by "desire." He does not use the word in a biological or psychological sense. He means simply that all men have some conception of a "world" they want to live in— some mental model of an imaginatively possible experience. "Desire," he says, "is part of imagination" (FS, 27). It is "the impulse toward what Aristotle calls *telos,* realizing the form that one potentially has. . . . It works dialectically, separating what is wanted from what is not wanted" (FI, 152). Thus while all men are limited in nature, their desire is infinite: "In the imagination anything goes that can be imagined. . . . In the human world the imagination has no limits" (EI, 29, 30).

If all men possess the imaginative faculty because of the teleological impulse, they do not possess it to the same degree. As the titles of several of Frye's works suggest, the imagination must be educated; it must develop. And it is the artist who develops the perceptive power of the imagination into a constructive one. The artist "catches and trains the objects of his vision: he can put human imagination into them, make them intelligible and responsive" (FS, 41–42). Therefore only those who have the "energy" (another Blakean concept which Frye often identifies with the imagination) to train themselves to see clearly, to pass "through sight to vision" (FS, 25), possess imagination as a structural power. "The artist is *par excellence* the man who struggles to develop his perception into creation, his sight into vision" (FS, 26).

If the imagination is a universal perceptive faculty for Frye, it varies among men according to the degree they can create the forms of culture from their perceptions.[31] Not all men, obviously, are artists, but all men, for Frye, can at least educate their imaginations into a constructive or creative awareness. If all men do not actually produce the universal forms of the imagination, the unity of the human mind makes it possible for them at least to perceive these visionary forms. Frye has had his own vision, as it were, of the total order of words produced by the imagination. What this vision looks like—"the iconography of the imagination," as he puts it—is the entire elaborate map of cyclical and dialectical structures we have analyzed in chapters 1–4.

To sum up, we began this chapter by looking at several recurrent ideas in Frye's work: ideas about the autonomy and the scientific nature of criticism, about value judgments, and about literature as self-contained. And we found that however strongly these principles are emphasized in the *Anatomy,* Frye's conception of criticism is always broad enough to include the dialectically opposite emphasis: the moral and social reference of criticism, taste and "positive" value judgments, and the centrifugal aspect of literary meaning. We saw, moreover, how each of Frye's four types of criticism is continually qualified or corrected by the succeeding type, the result being a breadth of reference which permits him to discuss literature in both its poetic and its more-than-poetic contexts. And, finally, we observed how the several pairs of categories he opposed to each other are ultimately subsumed under the most expansive of all his critical categories, the visionary imagination. All of these matters are an integral part of Frye's critical theory, the understanding of which has been our main concern up to this point. But a critical theory, even one as intricately and artistically fashioned as Frye's, does not exist for its own sake. As R.S. Crane says, "the principles and methods of any distinguishable mode of [critical] discourse are tools of inquiry and interpretation."[32] Since the ultimate *raison d'être* for critical theory is therefore pragmatic and utilitarian, the most important requirement it must fulfill is external to its own system. Thus we must determine how the theory works practically—which brings us to Frye's applied criticism.

6

Applied Criticism

Separating Frye's theoretical from his applied criticism suggests a
sharper disjunction between them than actually exists in much of his
work. *Fearful Symmetry,* ostensibly a work of practical criticism on
Blake's prophecies, is heavily laden with theoretical speculation. At
some places in this book it becomes difficult, especially in retrospect, to
determine whether the theory exists for the commentary or vice versa.
And since poetry and criticism at the anagogic level are often indistinguishable for Frye, it is not surprising that his commentary on Blake
merges into his theory of criticism. Nevertheless, the difference between the theory of criticism and the application of the theory is a
distinction Frye himself makes in referring to his own work.

After completing *Fearful Symmetry* he began a study of *The Faerie
Queene.* But the work was never completed, developing instead, as he
tells us in the preface to the *Anatomy,* into a theory of allegory. This in
turn directed his attention toward much larger theoretical issues, the
culmination of which, after more than a decade, was the *Anatomy* itself.
"The theoretical and practical aspects of the task I had begun," he says,
"completely separated," and he speaks of the need for a volume of
"practical criticism, a sort of morphology of symbolism," to complement the "pure critical theory" of the *Anatomy* (AC, vii). Frye's critical
theory is seldom "pure," insofar as his continual reference to specific
works suggests, at least, the general shape a more detailed commentary
would take. Conversely, his commentary on individual writers and
works is, at the same time, theoretical, as it must be for any critic, since
all critical methods include theoretical assumptions, if but implicit ones.
Nonetheless, we can classify most of Frye's criticism into two broad
categories, depending upon whether his aim is primarily to develop a
method for doing practical criticism or whether he is actually engaged
in specific interpretation, explication, or commentary on individual
writers.[1]

Frye has produced a substantial body of this latter kind of criticism. In *Fables of Identity* he treats a number of specific works and

writers, even though this book is hardly the sequel, he says, that he had in mind when he wrote the *Anatomy* (FI, 1). It contains discussions of *The Faerie Queene,* Shakespeare's sonnets, *Lycidas,* Blake, Byron, Emily Dickinson, Yeats, Wallace Stevens, and *Finnegans Wake.* Frye has written two books on Shakespeare, one on Milton, still another on Eliot, and a major book on the Bible is in progress. A large body of practical criticism is included in his three other volumes of selected essays: *The Stubborn Structure, Spiritus Mundi,* and *The Bush Garden,* a collection of his essays and reviews on Canadian writers.[2] His book on English Romanticism contains long essays on Beddoes's *Death's Jest-Book,* Shelley's *Prometheus Unbound,* and Keats's *Endymion.* The list of such studies is lengthy.[3]

The practical criticism is by no means single in aim or approach. Frye can analyze poetic texture after the manner of the New Critics. He can use his discussion of individual works as a means for defining literary periods, the procedure followed in his book on English Romanticism and his essay on the "Age of Sensibility" (FI, 130–37). He can engage in interpretative commentary on individual passages. As we might expect from our study of the *Anatomy,* however, none of these practices is typical of Frye's approach. More often than not he is concerned not with detailed commentary on individual poems but with the whole of a writer's work.[4]

> The great merit of explicatory criticism was that it accepted poetic language and form as the basis for poetic meaning. On [this] basis it built up a resistance to all "background" criticism that explained the literary in terms of the non-literary. At the same time, it deprived itself of the great strength of documentary criticism: the sense of context. It simply explicated one work after another, paying little attention to genre or to any larger structural principles connecting the different works explicated. (CP, 20)

Frye's own sense of context, however, is not that of documentary or historical criticism. The following passage, in which Frye recounts his reaction to deterministic, historical, and exclusively rhetorical approaches, spells out clearly the kinds of contexts he has in mind:

> It seemed to me obvious that, after accepting the poetic form of a poem as its primary basis of meaning, the next step was to look for its context within literature itself. And of course the most obvious literary context for a poem is the entire output of its author. . . . Every poet has his own distinctive structure of imagery, which usually emerges even in his earliest work, and which

does not and cannot essentially change. This larger context of the poem within its author's entire "mental landscape" is assumed in all the best explication—Spitzer's, for example. I became aware of its importance myself, when working on Blake, as soon as I realized that Blake's special symbolic names and the like did form a genuine structure of poetic imagery. . . . The structure of imagery, however, as I continued to study it, began to show an increasing number of similarities to the structures of other poets. . . . I was led to three conclusions in particular. First, there is no private symbolism. . . . Second, as just said, every poet has his own structure of imagery, every detail of which has its analogue in that of all other poets. Third, when we follow out this pattern of analogous structures, we find that it leads, not to similarity, but to identity. . . . I was still not satisfied: I wanted a historical approach to literature, but an approach that would be or include a genuine history of literature, and not simply the assimilating of literature to some other kind of history. It was at this point that the immense importance of certain structural elements in the literary tradition, such as conventions, genres, and the recurring use of certain images or image-clusters, which I came to call archetypes, forced itself on me. (CP, 21–23)

The convictions outlined in this passage determine the way Frye characteristically approaches literature. As a practical critic he typically seeks to place individual works within the context of a writer's entire canon and to relate them in turn by way of generic and archetypal principles to the literary tradition, what he calls the total order of words. Frye's practical criticism therefore is contextual, using the word in both the senses just mentioned. His conception of the total order of words is not unlike Eliot's belief (in "Tradition and the Individual Talent") that the literature from the time of Homer has a simultaneous existence and composes a simultaneous order. More than once Frye echoes this belief, arguing that the literary tradition operates creatively on the poet as a craftsman (AC, 17; CP, 23). But he goes beyond Eliot in attempting to identify the conventions that permit the poet to create new works of literature out of earlier ones.[5]

When we consider the writers to whom Frye has devoted the most attention, another characteristic of his practical criticism becomes apparent: his Romantic sensibilities and his predisposition to the forms of romance. He refers to Coleridge's division of literary critics into either Iliad or Odyssey types, meaning that one's "interest in literature tends to center either in the area of tragedy, realism, and irony, or in the area of comedy and romance." "I have always," he says, "been temperamentally an Odyssean critic" (NP, 1, 2). In another context he remarks, "Romance is the structural core of all fiction" (SeS, 15). This helps to explain the prominence which Blake, Spenser, Milton, and later Shakespeare, Shelley, Keats, William Morris, and Wallace Stevens assume in Frye's view.

Moreover, these are writers whom he locates in the "central tradition of mythopoeic poetry" (FI, 1). This is the tradition, Frye says, whose primary tendencies are Romantic, revolutionary, and Protestant. There is a note of ironic parody here, directed against the Classical, royalist, and Anglo-Catholic pronouncements of Eliot. But Frye means to be taken quite seriously. Despite his disclaimers about preferring one of these traditions to the other (FI, 149), there is no question about the locus of his deepest sympathies. He is convinced that the prejudices of modernism are still with us, and thus much of his practical criticism is part of a larger effort to right the balance. He sees the Catholic, Tory, and Classical emphases of modernism as a "consciously intellectual reaction" to the Romantic tradition (FI, 149). The "most articulate supporters" of the reaction, he says,

> were cultural evangelists who came from places like Missouri and Idaho, and who had a clear sense of the shape of the true English tradition, from its beginnings in Provence and mediaeval Italy to its later developments in France. Mr. Eliot's version of this tradition was finally announced as Classical, royalist, and Anglo-Catholic, implying that whatever was Protestant, radical, and Romantic would have to go into the intellectual doghouse. Many others who did not have the specific motivations of Mr. Eliot or of Mr. Pound joined in the chorus of denigration of Miltonic, Romantic, liberal, and allied values. . . . Although the fashion itself is on its way out, the prejudices set up by it still remain. (FI, 149)

This passage comes from an essay on Blake and is a part of Frye's argument that Blake must be seen in the context of his own tradition. And the "fashionable judgments" about this tradition, he says, have consisted mainly of "pseudo-critical hokum" (FI, 149). Frye has written a great many pages about the Romantic tradition in an effort to rescue it from these "fashionable judgments." He sees Romanticism as "one of the most decisive changes in the history of culture, so decisive as to make everything written since post-Romantic, including, of course, everything that is regarded by its producers as anti-Romantic" (FI, 3). Although his polemic against the prejudices of modernism is couched in the language of value, belief, and intellectual commitment, his several essays toward a definition of Romanticism approach the issue from a different perspective.[6] "What I see first of all in Romanticism," he says, "is the effect of a profound change, not primarily in belief, but in the spatial projection of reality. This in turn leads to a different localizing of the various levels of that reality. Such a change in the localizing of images is bound to be accompanied by, or even cause, changes in belief or attitude. . . . But the change itself is not in belief or attitude, and may be found in, or at least affecting, poets of a great variety of beliefs" (SS, 203). In other words, Romanticism as a literary phenomenon represents a profound change in poetic imagery and an equally profound modification of the traditional idea of four levels of reality, that background or "topocosm" against which images are portrayed. The point I want to emphasize is that the significance Frye attaches to Romanticism as a revolutionary cultural movement has important consequences for his practical criticism. This emphasis, along with his taste for comedy and romance (most fully developed in *The Secular Scripture*), and his liberal and Protestant sympathies, goes a long way toward explaining the selection of those writers he has discussed in some detail. One of these is Milton.

Milton

Frye's book on Milton, *The Return of Eden,* is a typical example of his work and one that specifically applies many of the principles set forth in *Anatomy of Criticism.* In addition, Milton is central in the development of Frye's own thought. The realization that Blake and Milton were connected by their use of the Bible is what pulled Frye toward the study of mythological frameworks in the first place (SM, 17). *The Return of Eden* is not a work of historical scholarship: Frye disclaims having "knowledge of Milton sufficiently detailed to add to the body of Milton scholarship or sufficiently profound to alter its general shape" (RE, 3). And although subtitled "Five Essays on Milton's Epics," it is more than a work on *Paradise Lost* and *Paradise Regained*; Frye continually moves beyond these poems, engaging finally a large part of Milton's thought and art.[7]

Each of the five essays is organized around a central theme: the encyclopaedic nature of epic forms and the hierarchical structure of Renaissance imagery; Milton's cosmology and its relation to his doctrine of good and evil; the Miltonic view of reason, will, and appetite as these manifest themselves on each of the levels of reality outlined in the first and second chapters; the themes of liberty and Milton's revolutionary art; and the typology or structure of *Paradise Regained* and its relation to *Paradise Lost.* Such a summary of topics says very little about Frye's method of study or the unity of his argument. His method depends on a number of the assumptions and principles outlined in the *Anatomy*. How does his argument illustrate the relation between theory and practice?

The central theme of Milton's epics, according to Frye, is the return of Eden. Eden represents the condition of freedom to which man aspires. It is to be found only *within* man, because for Milton the proper locus of God's presence is not in nature or history. Frye assumes, then, that Eden is the central archetype of Milton's epics. Their central myth is the loss and recovery of this "paradise within."

To illustrate this central theme, Frye calls upon a number of broad parallels, recurring analogues, and symmetrical patterns. In the *Anatomy* he maintains time and again that literature can be viewed in two ways, temporally and spatially. These two concepts are defined variously, according to the context of his discussion. Most often they are related to *mythos* and *dianoia,* to the narrative movement in time and the static structure of imagery. Both categories are fundamental to his study of Milton. The spatial aspect of Milton's work is especially emphasized in Frye's first three chapters, where he uses the Renaissance framework of four levels of existence to organize the characteristic themes, concepts, and imagery of *Paradise Lost.* This part of his discussion is a specific application of what I have previously called "the *dianoia* of archetypal imagery."

Frye begins his study, however, with the question of genre. For Milton the epic ideal was "a poem that derived its structure from the epic tradition of Homer and Virgil and still had the quality of universal knowledge which belonged to the encyclopaedic poem and included the extra dimension of reality that was afforded by Christianity" (RE, 7). *Paradise Lost,* Frye argues, incorporates each of these Renaissance assumptions. In the first place, since Milton's is a Christian epic, its shape derives "ultimately from the shape of the Bible" (RE, 9), which, as Frye has claimed in the *Anatomy,* is the prototypical or definitive encyclopaedic form. *Paradise Lost,* he says, follows the Biblical pattern from the Creation to the Last Judgment, surveying the complete history of man in between. A condensed version of this encyclopaedic pattern is to be found in the speech of Michael (RE, 9–10).

Second, Milton is influenced by those prose forms which the Renaissance critics accepted as major genres. The most familiar of these were the Platonic dialogue, the description of the ideal commonwealth, and the educational treatise or cyropaedia. We have a versified form of these genres, according to Frye, in the speech of Raphael: "the colloquy of Raphael and Adam is a Socratic dialogue without irony, a symposium with unfermented wine, a description of an ideal commonwealth ending with the expulsion of undesirables, and (for Adam is the king of men) a cyropaedia, or manual of royal discipline. It is essentially the education of Adam, and it covers a vast amount of knowledge, both natural and revealed" (RE, 12). Third, Milton draws upon the tradition of Homer and Virgil. There are three important ways in which *Paradise Lost* is influenced by the *Odyssey* and the *Aeneid*: all three epics are organized in twelve books (or a multiple of twelve); their narratives are neatly divisible into two parts; and, as Frye has argued in the *Anatomy*, their total actions follow a cyclical design (RE, 12–14).

This formal symmetry is what fascinates Frye, and to carry the design "much further," he proposes that we "visualize the dial of a clock, with the presence of God where the figure 12 is" (RE, 18). He then distributes the "main events" of *Paradise Lost* around the face of the clock as follows:

1. First epiphany of Christ: generation of Son from Father.
2. Second epiphany of Christ: triumph after three-day conflict.
3. Establishment of the natural order in the creation.
4. Establishment of the human order: creation of Adam and Eve.
5. Epiphany of Satan, generating Sin and Death.
6. Fall of the human order.
7. Fall of the natural order: triumph of Sin and Death.
8. Re-establishment of the natural order at the end of the flood.
9. Re-establishment of the human order with the giving of the law.
10. Third epiphany of Christ: the Word as gospel.
11. Fourth epiphany of Christ: the apocalypse or Last Judgment.
    (RE, 20–21)

The first four of the phases "represent the four main events in the speech of Raphael" (RE, 18); and the last four, the events in the speech of Michael (RE, 19).

Frye's argument for this grand design depends more on assertion than on demonstration: he gives no reason from the poem itself which would lead us to believe Milton intended to use this kind of pattern. The symmetrical scheme depends rather upon his prior assumptions about the epic as a genre and about Milton's relation to the epic tradition. The form of Frye's argument is this: the total action of an epic is by definition cyclical (a major premise taken over from the *Anatomy*); Milton was influenced by the formal symmetry and duodecimal organization of the classical epic; therefore we can expect the structural pattern of *Paradise Lost* to follow a symmetrical, twelve-part cycle. Some of the problems attendant on this kind of argument will be considered later.

As a pattern of themes, the diagram of Milton's formal symmetry represents what Frye in the *Anatomy* calls poetic *dianoia*; as a cyclical movement, it represents poetic *mythos*. In the *Anatomy* Frye classifies *Paradise Lost* as a thematic epic in the high-mimetic mode (AC, 58), which means that in reading it our interest is directed primarily toward its idea or poetic thought, rather than toward its internal fiction. Because one of Milton's chief themes is heroic action, we might expect Frye's analysis of heroism to rely upon the principles of the First Essay, where fictions are classified according to the hero's power of action. But Frye does not follow this course, the reason being that *Paradise Lost* is primarily a thematic (rather than a fictional) work. He turns rather to his familiar hierarchical paradigm: the idea of four orders of existence (divine, angelic, human, and demonic). These orders underlie his discussion of Milton's view of heroic action.[8]

His argument, briefly, is this. First, Milton conceives of God as the source of all real action. "It is only the divine," Frye says, "that can really act, by Milton's own definition of an act" (RE, 23); and this, according to what Milton says in *The Christian Doctrine,* is the power of expression of a free and conscious being (RE, 21). More specifically, the action of *Paradise Lost* at the divine level is revealed as "an act of creation, which becomes an act of re-creation or redemption after the fall of man" (RE, 23). Second, at the angelic order, the norm for heroic action is to be found in the moral models provided by Gabriel (responsibility), Raphael (instruction), Michael (command), Uriel (vigilance), and especially by Abdiel (obedience). The power of action possessed by the angels, however, derives from God and is contained by Christ (RE, 24–25); thus the difference between the divine and angelic orders is really one of degree. Third, in the human order of existence—the order of Adam—action is defined negatively as the "surrendering of the power to act" (RE, 21). Adam's fall, symbolized by his eating the forbidden fruit, is an act by which he loses his freedom. Thus, Frye says, for Milton, "a typically fallen human act is something where the word 'act' has to be in quotation marks. It is a pseudo-act, the pseudo-act of disobedience, and it is really a refusal to act at all" (RE, 22). Finally, at the demonic level, action involves rivalry with God. Hence demonic action, as manifested by Satan and Nimrod, is a parody of divine action because it aims at destructiveness rather than creation.

Frye sees these four orders of existence as the background against which the total action of *Paradise Lost* is played out. It involves a conflict between divine and demonic heroism, between fallen man's inability to act and the angelic models for the truly heroic act. The resolution to this conflict will come about when true heroism is seen as the free, creative, and redemptive act. Milton's poem therefore contravenes the traditional concept of heroism. "The fact that conventional heroism, as we have it in Classical epic and medieval and Renaissance romance, is associated with the demonic in Milton means, of course, that *Paradise Lost* is a profoundly anti-romantic and anti-heroic poem" (RE, 28). Milton will not identify freedom with "consciousness centered in the ego" or with "the works of God in our present world," both of which characterize the traditional epic hero. Human freedom, for Milton, is above nature. Frye puts it this way in the concluding words to his first chapter:

> [For Milton] the free intelligence must detach itself from this world and unite itself to the totality of freedom and intelligence which is God in man, shift its centre of gravity from the self to the presence of God in the self. Then it will find the identity with nature it appeared to reject: it will participate in the Creator's view of a world he made and found good. This is the relation of Adam and Eve to Eden before their fall. From Milton's point of view, the polytheistic imagination can never free itself from the labyrinths of fantasy and irony, with their fitful glimpses of inseparable good and evil. What Milton means by revelation is a consolidated, coherent, encyclopaedic view of human life which defines, among other things, the function of poetry. Every act of the free intelligence, including the poetic intelligence, is an attempt to return to Eden, a world in the human form of a garden, where we may wander as we please but cannot lose our way. (RE, 31)

This passage, with its Blakean overtones, is Frye's initial formulation of Milton's central theme. In order to understand Milton's treatment of this theme, Frye believes it necessary for us to know something about the genre in which it is found; thus his discussion of the epic and the encyclopaedic conventions. But it is also necessary for us to know how Milton adapts and goes beyond the classical conventions; thus Frye's discussion of Milton's particular conception of heroic action. In both cases, Frye draws upon principles set forth in *Anatomy of Criticism*.

In the remainder of the book the cosmological or hierarchical model is especially important. It guides Frye's discussion in the second and third chapters. In the *Anatomy* he observes that "in studying poems of immense scope, such as the *Commedia* or *Paradise Lost,* we find that we have to learn a good deal of cosmology" (AC, 160). He suggests that the form of cosmology is quite close to that of poetry and that "symmetrical cosmology may be a branch of myth. If so, then it would be, like myth, a structural principle of poetry" (AC, 161). In the *Return of Eden,* he finds that he cannot discuss crucial events in *Paradise Lost,* like the fall, without reference to its cosmology. Milton's is a four-storied cosmos, the orders of which Frye represents as follows:

I. The order of grace or heaven (the place of God's presence).
II. The "proper" human order (symbolized by Eden and the Golden Age).
III. The physical order.
IV. The order of sin, death, corruption.

There is an obvious similarity between this hierarchy and the four orders Frye employs in his first chapter to discuss heroic action (divine, angelic, human, and demonic). The difference is that the possibilities for human existence are not restricted to the third (human) level of his initial paradigm: man can exist on any of the last three levels. In Milton's view, man is born into the physical order. He can either rise above this station into his proper humanity, living the way God intended him to live, or he can sink below into the world of sin and corruption. In other words, man does not really belong in the world of physical nature; true nature or proper humanity for him is found at the angelic level. Milton makes certain modifications, however, in this traditional view of the cosmos:

> In the first place, heaven itself is a creation of God like the angels, and consequently heaven is a part of the order of nature. The angels in Milton are quite familiar with the conception of nature: Abdiel says to Satan, for example: "God and Nature bid the same." Then again, in *Paradise Lost,* the whole of the order of nature falls with the fall of Adam, and with the fall of nature, as described in Book Ten, the stars turn into beings of noxious efficacy, meeting "in Synod unbenign." *As far as man is concerned* (I italicize this because it is a hinge of Milton's argument), the entire order of nature is now a fallen order. The washing away of the Garden of Eden in the flood symbolizes the fact that the two levels of nature cannot both exist in space, but must succeed one another in time, and that the upper level of human nature can be lived in only as an inner state of mind, not as an outward environment. (RE, 41)

This is typical of the way Frye uses the cosmological framework to explain Milton. In other words, Milton selects what he wants from the Ptolemaic tradition and from the Great Chain of Being and adapts it to fit his own theological concerns. And we cannot understand Milton, Frye would argue, unless we are aware of this larger cosmological framework, for the activity of God, regularly symbolized in Milton by music and harmony, takes place within this framework.

"The Creator," says Frye, "moves downward to his creatures, in a power symbolized by music and poetry and called in the Bible the Word, releasing energy by creating form. The creature moves upward toward its Creator by obeying the inner law of its own being, its *telos* or chief end which is always and at all levels the glorifying of God" (RE, 50).

There is a corresponding demonic dialectic which takes a number of forms, and which Frye refers to as the demonic parody of the divine. We see the upward demonic movement, for example, in "the destructive explosion from below associated in Milton's mind from earliest days with the Gunpowder Plot" (RE, 50–51). The same movement is repeated in the Limbo of Vanities, "the explosion of deluded souls trying to take heaven by storm" (RE, 51). The downward movement is expressed by the descent into hell by the devils. This is just one of the many details of the "vast symmetrical pattern" of the demonic parody of good. A number of details, Frye says, are obvious: the council of hell versus the council of heaven; Christ's journey into chaos to create the world versus Satan's journey to destroy it; the City of Pandemonium versus the City of God (RE, 51). But some details, according to Frye, are not so obvious to the modern reader, though they would be to Milton's ideal reader—to one, that is, who read the Bible typologically. Frye's examples are drawn from Milton's imagery, like his juxtaposition of the tower of Babel, a demonic image, with the ark atop Mount Ararat, the symbol of the end of the flood.

These details of Frye's interpretation are a direct consequence of his method, depending as it does upon the assumption that the larger framework of correspondences and antitheses are present throughout Milton's epic. In other words, the cosmology which Frye assumes to be operative throughout *Paradise Lost* determines the direction of his commentary. Consider, for example, his interpretation of Galileo's function in Book I:

> The references of Galileo are by no means hostile, and it is clear from the use made of him in the argument of *Areopagitica* that in Milton's ideal state he would be a highly respected citizen. But if they are not hostile they are curiously deprecatory. Milton seems to regard Galileo, most inaccurately, as concerned primarily with the question of whether the heavenly bodies, more particularly the moon, are habitable—as a pioneer of science fiction rather than of science. As Satan hoists his great shield, the shield, in a glancing parody of the shield of Achilles which depicted mainly a world at peace, is associated with Galileo peering through his telescope at the moon:

>   to descry new lands,
>   Rivers or mountains in her spotty globe.
> Galileo thus appears to symbolize, for Milton, the gaze outward
> on physical nature, as opposed to the concentration inward on
> human nature, the speculative reason that searches for new
> places, rather than the moral reason that tries to create a new
> state of mind. (RE, 58)

Now this interpretation depends on Frye's dialectical division of
Milton's world into the demonic and the "properly human poles." Galileo's philosophic vision, which "sees man as a spectator of a theatrical
nature" (RE, 59), is rooted in a demonic conception of the cosmos. It is
the view of fallen man, pulling humanity away from the vision of liberty because it is attached to the external world and not to the "world
within." For Galileo, Frye says, "the form of God's creation has been
entirely replaced by space, and while he may hope, like Satan, that
space may produce or disclose new worlds, there is nothing divine in
space that man can *now* see, nothing to afford him a model of the new
world he must construct within himself" (RE, 58).

Whether or not Frye is correct about Galileo's function is problematic. At least one Miltonist thinks not.[9] The point I want to make,
however, is that Frye's interpretation derives from his broad, cosmological perspective. If Milton's poetic world is hierarchical, then every
image he uses must have its appropriate place on one of the levels of
existence. If heroic action, defined in terms of man's proper place in
the four orders, is the "paradise within," then Milton's imagery must
either support the ultimate vision or be a demonic parody of it. Frye
follows this kind of reasoning throughout.

We can see Frye "standing back," as it were, in an effort to grasp
the large dialectical patterns. Once these have been found, his usual
procedure is to let them determine the direction of his commentary.
To illustrate the point again: In *The Return of Eden* Frye discusses four
kinds of heroic action, whereas in an earlier essay he considers only
three.[10] The reason for the discrepancy is that the earlier essay assumes
a three-storied cosmology: Milton's universe, Frye argues, consists of
heaven, earth, and hell; therefore we find three corresponding kinds
of action. But in *The Return of Eden* an additional order makes its way
into the Miltonic hierarchy, which means that Frye must locate an
additional form of heroic action. In short, the way Frye views Milton's
cosmological framework determines the specific details of his analysis.

In his third chapter Frye turns from the macrocosmic to the micro-
cosmic perspective: "In the soul of man, as God originally created it,
there is a hierarchy. This hierarchy has three main levels: the reason,

which is in control of the soul; the will, the agent carrying out the decrees of the reason; and the appetite" (RE, 60). In an unfallen state—that is, when reason controls the soul—the will is free "because it participates in the freedom of the reason." "The appetite is subordinate to both, and is controlled by the will from the reason" (RE, 60). Milton accepts this traditional division of the soul, according to Frye. It is implicit in his presentation of Adam and Eve before the fall. And after the fall, the hierarchy which God implants in the soul is reversed. Appetite now assumes the topmost place, Frye says, "and by doing so it ceases to be appetite and is transformed into passion, the drive toward death" (RE, 68–69). Frye does not develop the application of this hierarchy and its reversal. His emphasis rather is upon Milton's intellectual framework itself, especially as it relates to the fall. And this framework, we come to discover finally, consists not of three levels after all, but of five.

> Reason is subordinate to a higher principle than itself: revelation, coming directly from the Word of God, which emancipates and fulfils the reason and gives it a basis to work on which the reason could not achieve by itself. The point at which revelation impinges on reason is the point at which discursive understanding begins to be intuitive: the point of the emblematic vision or parable, which is the normal unit in the teaching of Jesus. The story of the fall of Satan is a parable to Adam, giving him the kind of knowledge he needs in the only form appropriate to a free man. (RE, 74)

Here we have a clear indication of the categories of the *Anatomy* being put to use, especially those of the Second Essay. The emblematic vision which Milton holds out to Adam is not unlike the anagogic vision in whose presence, according to Frye, the poet and critic become almost indistinguishable. In defining anagogic criticism, we recall, Frye turns to the heightened poetic moments of writers like Blake and Eliot (in the *Quartets*), whose epiphanic visions of the incarnate Word embody a *critical* doctrine of the imagination. He does not go quite so far with *Paradise Lost,* but he does see Milton's concept of revelation as approaching the Romantic view of the imagination: "for the poet, who has brought his poetic gifts into line with revelation, the same point [i.e., the point of emblematic vision] would be the point of inspiration. Milton does not have exactly the later Romantic conception of imagination, but Keats was right in seeing in Adam's dream the corresponding conception, a mental image that becomes a reality" (RE, 74). In other words, Milton the poet becomes Milton the anagogic critic, illuminating the nature of what, for Frye, is the highest level of criticism.

At the opposite pole from revelation, so Frye's argument continues, is still another level in the hierarchical structure of existence lying
behind *Paradise Lost*. "Below the appetite . . . there is a parody of revelation, the fancy or fantasy, the aspect of the mind that is expressed in
dreams, including daydreams, and which has the quality of illuminating the appetite from below, as revelation illuminates the reason from
above" (RE, 75). The dream of Eve represents this fantasy, "a microscopic example of the upward demonic explosive movement, from
chaos into order" (RE, 75). What happens, then, after the fall is that
fantasy and revelation are reversed. Fantasy becomes the demonic emblematic vision: it "is now on top illuminating the passion" (RE, 75).

Milton's conception of the various divisions of the unfallen soul—
to summarize Frye's view of it—would be organized as follows:

> I. Revelation.
> II. Reason.
> III. Will.
> IV. Appetite.
> V. Fantasy.

After the fall this hierarchy, of course, is reversed. Frye's chief procedure in the third chapter is to use this model for illuminating Milton's
conception of sin. Behind the discussion, which is primarily doctrinal
or theological, we can observe the ever-present method of analogy. To
take one example, the "appetite," before the fall, is represented by
hunger and sexual desire. When the soul is inverted, these energies are
transformed into greed and lust respectively. By analogy, greed and
lust on the demonic level become fraud and force, inward and outward
vices, inquisition and indulgence, excess and mechanical repetition (RE,
68–78). In other words Frye keeps altering, or at least expanding, the
meaning of his terms, depending on whether he is examining the behavior of Adam and Eve or of human society, and on whether the examination relates to a prelapsarian or postlapsarian state.

Frye devotes all this attention to Milton's conceptual universe because he believes the structure of *Paradise Lost* depends on it. "If we
knew nothing of Milton except *Paradise Lost*," he says at one point, "we
should still be aware that the structure was supported by a powerful
and coherent skeleton of ideas" (RE, 82), which is to say that the poem
is primarily a "thematic" work. But at the same time *Paradise Lost* contains "fictional" elements. Frye does not actually use the fictional-thematic terminology, speaking rather of the two interests as "dramatic"
and "conceptual." But the difference is the same. In fact, one of the
issues he confronts is the relationship of these two interests in *Paradise
Lost*. Sometimes he takes the view that the tension between the dramatic

and conceptual emphases is deliberate on Milton's part and necessary to the structure of the entire poem. He says, for example, that after the fall

> Adam is motivated by his desire to live with Eve and his feeling that he cannot live without her. Conceptually and theologically, he is entirely wrong. . . . He should have "divorced" Eve at the moment of her fall. But . . . the conceptual and theological situation is not the dramatic one. Adam's decision to die with Eve rather than live without her impresses us, in our fallen state, as a heroic decision. We feel a certain nobility in what Adam does: Eve also feels this and expresses it. (RE, 79)

Yet, Frye concludes, the sense of this contrast between the fictional and the thematic aspects of the poem is necessary: it satisfies our feelings of what is appropriate for Adam to do, and it fits the structure of the Christian myth and its classical precedents (RE, 79).

At other times, however, Frye takes the view that the dramatic and conceptual aspects of the poem are simply inconsistent, as in the speech of God in Book Three:

> [When] God the Father, in flagrant defiance of Milton's own theology, which tells us we can know nothing about the Father except through the human incarnation of the Son, does speak, [it is] with disastrous consequences. The rest of the poem hardly recovers from his speech, and there are few difficulties in the appreciation of *Paradise Lost* that are not directly connected with it. Further, he keeps on speaking at intervals, and whenever he opens his ambrosial mouth the sensitive reader shudders. Nowhere else in Milton is the contrast between the conceptual and dramatic aspects of the situation . . . so grotesque: between recognizing that God is the source of all goodness and introducing God as a character saying: "I am the source of all goodness." The Father observes the improved behaviour of Adam after the fall and parenthetically remarks: "my motions in him." Theologically, nothing could be more correct: dramatically, nothing is better calculated to give the impression of a smirking hypocrite. (RE, 99)

More often than not, however, Frye's attention is focused less on the details of the dramatic situation than on Milton's larger thematic vision. This vision is central to Frye's main argument about *Paradise Lost*. It concerns the imaginative return of Eden, that internal paradise emblematic of the free intelligence. The theme receives its fullest treatment in Frye's fourth chapter. But in the other four chapters, especially toward the conclusion of each of them, Frye manages to relate this theme to whatever his special topic happens to be. He relates it to Milton's concept of heroic action in the first chapter and to the speculative reason of Galileo's philosophic gaze in the second. In the heavily doctrinal third chapter the major theme returns once again, this time in relation to Milton's view of the Mosaic code. Milton conceives of Mosaic law as "a higher gift than moral law, because it prevents morality from becoming an end in itself. Its meaning is typological, the acts it enjoins being symbols of the spiritual truths of the gospel. Hence it corresponds in society to what we have called the emblematic vision in the individual, the point at which reason begins to comprehend revelation" (RE, 84).

In the fourth chapter Frye analyzes this emblematic vision as it relates to the revolutionary nature of Milton's art. The argument, briefly, is this: True liberty for Milton will come not through political or social action but through revelation. Milton is a revolutionary artist insofar as he discards external and historical conceptions of liberty in favor of an internal and visionary freedom. "Everything Milton associates with liberty is discontinuous with ordinary life. . . . The source of liberty is revelation: why liberty is good for man and why God wants him to have it cannot be understood apart from Christianity" (RE, 96). Where, in Milton's perspective, is man to obtain such a vision? "Not from the nature outside us," answers Frye, "because . . . the fall of man was the fall of Narcissus, and what we see in nature is like ourselves. It can only come from something inside us which is also totally different from us. That something is ultimately revelation, and the kernel of revelation is Paradise, the feeling that man's home is not in this world, but in another world (though occupying the same time and space) that makes more human sense" (RE, 97). Or again: "In *Paradise Lost* . . . it is Paradise itself that is internalized, transformed from an outward place to an inner state of mind. . . . The heaven of *Paradise Lost,* with God the supreme sovereign and the angels in a state of unquestioning obedience to his will, can only be set up on earth inside the individual's mind" (RE, 110–11).

It is obvious that Frye's Romantic aesthetic helps to shape his central thesis about Milton. He is most captivated by that aspect of Milton's work which, to use the language of the *Anatomy,* approaches the imaginative limits of desire. By emphasizing Milton's mythopoeic vision, Frye locates him among those liberal and Romantic writers, like Blake, whose view of the imagination is consistent with his own. "Milton's 'liberty,' " he says in *Fearful Symmetry,* "is practically the same as Blake's imagination" (FS, 159). Many statements in *The Return of Eden,* if taken out of context, sound as if they might have come from *Fearful Symmetry.*

Milton, like Blake, is for Frye a fifth-phase symbolic poet. "We have got far enough with *Paradise Lost*," he says toward the end of his fourth chapter, "to see that we have to turn the universe inside out, with God sitting within the human soul at the centre and Satan on a remote periphery plotting against our freedom. From this persective, perhaps, we can see what Blake meant when he said that Milton was a true poet and of the devil's (i.e., revolutionary) party without knowing it" (RE, 112–13). In another essay Frye observes that the revolutionary aspect of Milton's art "shows how near he is to the mythology of Romanticism and its later by-products, the revolutionary erotic, Promethean, and Dionysian myths of Freud, Marx, and Nietzsche."[11]

We began by observing that Frye's discussion is influenced by his dyadic framework of *mythos* and *dianoia*. The thrust of his argument derives from the ideas associated with the latter of these categories: the structure of Milton's imagery; his conceptual universe; and his thematic emphasis, which is "the garden within." But Frye also conceives of Milton's work in terms of *mythos*. On the one hand, he envisions the narrative of *Paradise Lost* as an episodic sequence. Milton invites us to read the events of his poem not as a great cycle of cause and effect but "as a discontinuous series of crises" (RE, 102). "At each crisis of life the important factor is not the consequences of previous actions, but the confrontation, across a vast apocalyptic gulf, with the source of deliverance. So whatever one thinks of the Father's argument, some argument separating present knowledge and past causation is essential to Milton's conception of the poem" (RE, 103). On the other hand, when Frye looks at Milton's work as a whole, he sees it comprising a total cyclical action. Thus he views the epics not simply as a vast symmetrical ordering of themes and images but also as an equally vast narrative movement. In the *Anatomy* he calls this the "central unifying myth" (AC, 192), or the total action of literature comprised by the four *mythoi*. His own version of this monomyth is an expansive, cyclical narrative of exile, quest, and return. Frye does not provide a detailed application of his theory of *mythos* to Milton's work. But it is clear that he views the two epics as separate parts of a total action which begins and ends "not at precisely the same point, but at the same point renewed and transformed by the heroic action itself" (RE, 14). Transformation comes about by man's quest, which for Milton is an interior journey. It is a quest for the recovery of that vision of freedom man possessed in Eden before the fall. And the narrative movement of Milton's epics, Frye believes, is directed precisely toward this renewal of man's true identity: "To use terms which are not Milton's but express something of his attitude, the central myth of mankind is the myth of lost identity: the goal of all reason, courage, and vision is the regaining of identity. The recovery of identity is not the feeling that I am myself and not another, but the realization that there is only one man, one mind, one world, and that all walls of partition have been broken down forever" (RE, 143). These are the concluding words to *The Return of Eden,* and they indicate, more clearly perhaps than anywhere else in the book, Frye's view of Milton as a Blakean visionary, the understanding of whom depends ultimately on anagogic criticism.

The study of conventions and genres, Frye says in the *Anatomy,* is the basis of archetypal criticism (AC, 99), the principles of which are outlined in the Third and Fourth Essays of that book. I have been attempting to show how he applies these principles in his study of Milton. It is not always easy to distinguish the biographical and historical from the archetypal approaches in *The Return of Eden.* And yet the study as a whole remains a work of archetypal criticism insofar as Frye is interested primarily in Milton's use and adaptation of conventional literary forms and imagery, of conventional cosmologies and myths.

The same interest directs Frye's other studies of Milton. In "The Revelation to Eve" (SS, 135–59) he examines Milton's imagery in terms of "two great mythological structures on which the literature of our own Near Eastern and Western traditions has been founded" (SS, 158). One structure is dominated by the masculine father principle with its emphasis on the rational order of nature; the other is dominated by the female-goddess archetype, with its stress on the mystery of Eros. The father-god archetype is inherently conservative, while the mother-goddess archetype is Romantic, revolutionary, and Dionysian. Milton, according to Frye, understood the claims of both of these mythical structures on the imagination, and Frye uses the dreams of Adam and Eve in *Paradise Lost* to illustrate the way Milton holds them in tension.

Frye's other essay on Milton, "Literature as Context: Milton's *Lycidas*" (FI, 119–29), is an excellent example of his theoretical principles applied to a single poem. He seeks to relate *Lycidas,* first of all, to the conventions of the pastoral elegy, which involves him in a discussion of such things as the dying-god imagery of the Adonis lament and its association with the cyclic imagery of nature, the "sanguine flower" archetype, and the archetypes of the poet (Orpheus) and the priest (Peter). He also sets the poem against the background of the four-storied framework of Renaissance imagery, showing how *Lycidas* is connected with each of the levels of existence. Frye himself summarizes the principles that guide his discussion:

> In the writing of *Lycidas* there are four creative principles of particular importance. To say that there are four does not mean, of course, that they are separable. One is convention, the reshap-

ing of the poetic material which is appropriate to this subject. Another is genre, the choosing of the appropriate form. A third is archetype, the use of appropriate, and therefore recurrently employed, images and symbols. The fourth, for which there is no name, is the fact that the forms of literature are autonomous: that is, they do not exist outside literature. (FI, 123)

To these structural and generic principles we should add a fifth, for Frye goes on to argue that the structure of *Lycidas* as a whole is informed by myth, specifically the Adonis myth. He says, in fact, that the structure of Milton's poem *is* the Adonis myth: "It is in *Lycidas* in much the same way that the sonata form is in the first movement of a Mozart symphony. It is the connecting link between what makes *Lycidas* the poem it is and what unites it to other forms of poetic experience" (FI, 127). In other words, myth as a structural principle is what holds together the unique and the conventional tendencies in the poem.

Studies of Literary Periods

Frye's several essays in literary history are also based on the application of principles and assumptions laid down in the *Anatomy*. We will consider two of these studies, each of which employs a separate method and depends upon a distinctive set of assumptions.

The Age of Sensibility The first is an essay entitled "Towards Defining an Age of Sensibility" (FI, 130–37). Although a brief study, it is a classic example of Frye's use of the Aristotelian versus the Longinian approach. His aim is to define the period of English literature covering roughly the last half of the eighteenth century. His method depends on the assumption that "in the history of literature we become aware, not only of periods, but of a recurrent opposition of two views of literature. These two views are the Aristotelian and the Longinian, the aesthetic and the psychological, the view of literature as product and the view of literature as process" (FI, 130–31). These pairs of opposites are the basis for Frye's study in contrast. On the Aristotelian side of the dichotomy he locates those writers and literary tendencies which preceded the Age of Sensibility; and on the Longinian side, those of the post-Augustan age itself. These broad distinctions are refined in the course of Frye's discussion.

What does it mean to say one age views literature as product, another as process? For Frye it means that in the area of prose fiction, to take his first example, the typical question we ask about (say) a Fielding novel is, "How is this story going to turn out?" The emphasis, in other words, is on the novel as a finished product: "The suspense is thrown forward until it reaches the end, and is based on our confidence that the author knows what is coming next" (FI, 131). But in writers like Richardson, Boswell, and especially Sterne our interest, Frye says, is focused not upon what is coming next in the story but upon what the author will think of next. In the case of Sterne, for example, "we are not being led into a story, but into the process of writing a story" (FI, 131). Similarly, in Richardson and Boswell our interest is in the continuous process of experience in the present.

The dichotomy between product and process is also apparent, he argues, in the poetry of the two periods. In Pope's verse, for example, the sense of a finished product greets us in the regularly recurring meter of the heroic couplet and in the continually fulfilled expectations of sound and sense. But in the succeeding period "we get something of the same kind of shock that we get when we turn from Tennyson or Matthew Arnold to Hopkins. Our ears are assaulted by unpredictable assonances, alliterations, interrhymings, and echolalia" (FI, 132). These intensified sound patterns, which we find in such poets as Smart, Chatterton, Burns, Ossian, and Blake, are a result, Frye maintains, of an interest in poetry as process; they are close to the primary stage of poetic composition where free association predominates.

Frye proposes a whole list of opposites which might be used to differentiate these two interests: conscious versus unconscious control, regular versus irregular meter, concentration of sense versus diffusion of sense, epigrammatic versus incantatory quality, wit versus dream, continuous versus discontinuous lyrics, clarity of syntax versus fragmentary utterances, and so on (FI, 133–34).

A third opposition Frye uses is one we have already met in the First Essay of the *Anatomy*.[12] This is the distinction between the aesthetic and the psychological reaction of the reader to the emotions of pity and fear.

> Where there is a strong sense of literature as aesthetic product, there is also a sense of its detachment from the spectator. Aristotle's theory of catharsis describes how this works for tragedy: pity and fear are detached from the beholder by being directed towards objects. Where there is a sense of literature as process, pity and fear become states of mind without objects, moods which are common to the work of art and the reader, and which bind them together psychologically instead of separating them aesthetically.[13]

Although Frye does not say so, he implies that in the Age of Pope aesthetic detachment is the typical response. In any case, all of his attention is directed toward defining what it means to say that in the Age of Sensibility fear and pity are emotions without objects. "Fear without an object, as a condition of mind prior to being afraid *of* anything, is called *Angst* or anxiety, a somewhat narrow term for what may be almost anything between pleasure and pain" (FI, 135). Frye finds the source of this kind of reaction in the eighteenth-century conception of the sublime, with its qualities of "austerity, gloom, grandeur, melancholy, or even menace." Such qualities produce romantic or penseroso emotions, which are the basis of appeal in Ossian and "graveyard" poetry, in Gothic novels and tragic ballads, and in "such *fleurs du mal* as Cowper's *Castaway* and Blake's Golden Chapel poem" (FI, 135).

Pity without an object, on the other hand, "expresses itself as an imaginative animism, or treating everything in nature as though it had human feelings or qualities" (FI, 135). Frye is able to isolate four types of this state of mind or mood: (1) the apocalyptic celebration of nature, as in Smart's *Song of David* and the ninth Night of Blake's *The Four Zoas*; (2) imaginative sympathy with the folklore of elemental spirits, as in Collins, Fergusson, Burns, and the Wartons; (3) intense awareness of the animal world, as in Burns's *To a Mouse,* Cowper's snail poem, Smart's lines on his cat, the starling and ass episodes in Sterne, and Blake's opening to *Auguries of Innocence*; and (4) sympathy with man himself, as in the protests against slavery and misery in Cowper, Crabbe, and Blake (FI, 135).

When Frye turns to elaborate on the primitive process of writing itself, his method, once again, is that of dichotomous division. It involves three additional sets of subcategories, descending from the "process" side of his main opposition. Figure 24 is a diagram of the three-tiered taxonomy. The primitive process of writing, Frye is saying, can be projected toward one of two poles: nature or history. If projected toward nature, the poetry of sensibility will tend toward one or the other of two additional poles, either the creative or the decaying natural process. In other words the poet will be attracted either by the "primeval and 'unspoiled' " or by "the ruinous and the mephitic" (FI, 135). On the other hand, the "projection into history assumes that the psychological progress of the poet from lyrical through epic to dramatic presentations . . . must be the historical progress of literature as well. Even as late as the preface to Victor Hugo's *Cromwell* this assumption persists. The Ossian and Rowley poems are . . . pseudepigrapha, like the book of Enoch, and like it they take what is psychologically primitive, the oracular process of composition, and project it as something historically primitive" (FI, 135–36).

Frye's final point about the "primitive" quality of the Age of Sensibility relates to the poet himself. It is an age, he points out, of the *poète*

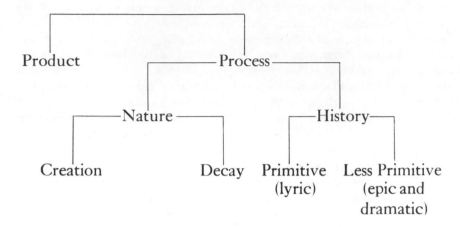

Figure 24. Literature as process.

maudit. He then connects this personal or biographical quality with "its central technical feature," the metaphor, drawing upon the principles of analogy and identity we encountered in the Second Essay of the *Anatomy*:

> For Classical and Augustan critics the metaphor is a condensed simile: its real or common-sense basis is likeness, not identity, and when it obliterates the sense of likeness it becomes barbaric. . . . For the Romantic critic, the identification in the metaphor is ideal: two images are identified within the mind of the creating poet. But where metaphor is conceived as part of an oracular and half-ecstatic process, there is a direct identification in which the poet himself is involved. To use [a] phrase of Rimbaud's, the poet feels not "je pense," but "on me pense." (FI, 136–37)

Thus the fundamental metaphoric feature of the Age of Sensibility is neither an analogy nor an equation between two things or images but a psychological identification between the poet himself and something else. These self-identifications of the *poète maudit,* which work against his social personality, take strange and poignant forms: they may seem "manic, like Blake's [identification] with Druidic bards or Smart's with Hebrew prophets, or depressive, like Cowper's with a scapegoat figure, a stricken deer or castaway, or merely bizarre, like Macpherson's with Ossian or Chatterton's with Rowley" (FI, 137). The most complete and intense expressions of this "primitive" self-identification are to be found, Frye says, in Collins's *Ode on the Poetical Character,* Smart's *Jubi-late Agno,* and Blake's *Four Zoas,* poems in which "God, the poet's soul and nature are brought into a white-hot fusion of identity, an imaginative fiery furnace in which the reader may, if he chooses, make a fourth" (FI, 137).

It is certainly not unusual for critics, in their attempts to define literary periods, to refer to the conception which the poet has of himself. In this respect, Frye's point about the *poète maudit* is typical of what a historical critic might do. What is highly unexpected, however, is the way Frye goes about doing it: his relating the poet's personality (a biographical matter) to the technical principle of metaphor (a rhetorical matter) in order to define the "primitive" quality of an age's poetry. If we ask how all of this relates to Frye's initial category of literature as process, his answer would be that the typical image we have of the post-Augustan poet is that of an oracle, one who freely associates words in a trancelike state, one who utters rather than addresses; so that our interest is focused—to use his earlier distinction—not upon how the poem is going to turn out but upon what is coming next.

The chief methodological feature of this essay is the deductive manner by which Frye proceeds, for what he does is to establish broad pairs of categories and then use them as a framework for generalizing about the Age of Sensibility. There is nothing particularly striking about his a priori categories: few would disagree that it is possible to view literature both as product and as process, that there are two poles to the natural process, or that some literary works are both historically and psychologically more primitive than others. Rather, the extraordinary feature is the kind of insight that results from the application of the theoretical assumptions. What really defines the Age of Sensibility is not the fact that its literature can be viewed as "process"; this is a commonplace, not a definition. But when Frye applies this principle specifically, working back and forth between his general hypothesis and his inductive survey of literature itself, a meaningful set of defining characteristics does emerge. I said previously that the essay is a study in contrast, by which I meant that Frye defines the Age of Sensibility by differentiating it from the previous and, to a lesser extent, the succeeding ages. And yet, since Frye is seeking to discover the broad "tendencies" and "interests" of the period, his definition does remain highly generalized.[14] When we look at the essay as a whole, what stands out is the conceptual breadth which characterizes Frye's criticism.

Frye's readers have sometimes questioned the freedom and assurance of his broad categorizing, especially when he seems to be trespassing into their own special fields of competence.[15] There seems to be no one, however, who has questioned Frye's authority in the field of English Romanticism. His book on the subject will be our second example of his studies in literary history.

Romanticism   A Study of English Romanticism treats the Romantic movement as primarily a change in the mythological structure of poetry, brought about by various cultural and historical forces. This, in fact, is Frye's thesis, argued in an introductory chapter entitled "The Romantic Myth."[16] The three remaining chapters, intended to illustrate the thesis, are critical discussions of Beddoes's *Death's Jest-Book,* Shelley's *Prometheus Unbound,* and Keats's *Endymion.*

Frye claims that Romanticism gives birth to a new mythological structure in Western culture. The argument rests upon his conceptions of myth and mythology, which he summarizes as follows:

> The informing structures of literature are myths, that is, fictions and metaphors that identify aspects of human personality with the natural environment, such as stories about sun-gods or tree-gods. The metaphorical nature of the god who is both a person and a class of natural objects makes myth, rather than folktale or legend, the direct ancestor of literature. It also gives to myth, in primitive cultures, a particular importance in establishing a society's views of its own origin, including the reasons for its divisions into different classes or groups, its legal sanctions, and its prescribed rituals. The canonical significance which distinguishes the myth from less important fictions also causes myths to form large unified structures, or mythologies, which tend to become encyclopedic in extent, covering all aspects of a society's vision of its situation and destiny. As civilization develops, mythology divides into two main aspects. Its patterns of stories and images, attracting and absorbing those of legend and folktale, become the fictions and metaphors of literature. At the same time, there are also germs of conceptual ideas in myths which extend into theology, philosophy, political theory, and, in earlier ages, science, and become informing principles there as well. (SER, 4–5)

The assumption here is that myths manifest themselves in two ways, artistically and conceptually. On the one hand, literature and other forms of art descend from mythology, inheriting its fictional and metaphorical patterns. One can study these patterns formally, which is what the *Anatomy* is all about. On the other hand, because myth is related to certain social features in a society, there is a body of ideas which descends from myth. Both the literary and the conceptual forms are a part of what Frye calls a culture's "total mythological structure"; it "may not be explicitly known to anyone, but is nevertheless present as a shaping principle" (SER, 5). The closest realization we have of this total mythological structure is found in encyclopaedic cultural forms, in literary works like the *Commedia* and *Paradise Lost* and in conceptual works like St. Thomas's *Summa*. The total structure in Western culture was for centuries characterized by an encyclopaedic myth derived mainly from the Bible.

It is this mythological structure that Frye sets out initially to define, for his argument depends on showing how the Romantic myth is opposed to the myth which dominated the centuries preceding Romanticism. There are a number of differences between the two mythological structures. First, they are based on different myths of the creation. For pre-Romanticism (i.e., from the beginning of the Christian era down to the last part of the eighteenth century) the creation myth was an "artificial" one in that it assumed "the world was made, as an artefact or creature, by a divine artisan or demiurge" (SER, 6). The idea that the gods are not a part of nature and that man should view nature as evidence for intelligent design gave prominence to subject-object relations and heightened the rational attitude toward the world. The Christian version of the myth postulates that God, man, and nature were once identified, but that man fell and thus broke his harmonious relation with nature. Therefore man's chief end is to regain his lost identity, and the means for achieving this is through rational and social discipline, that is, through law, morality, and religion. Behind the entire Christian myth lies a dichotomy in which nature is set over against human consciousness: man is assumed to be a social rather than a natural being; he must constantly maintain the barrier between himself and the forces of nature, Eros and Dionysus (SER, 5–10).

But in Romanticism, acording to Frye, the subject-object relationship recedes into the background. When we begin reading Wordsworth and Coleridge we discover that "the reason founded on a separation of consciousness from nature is becoming an inferior faculty of the consciousness, more analytic and less constructive, the outside of the mind dealing with the outside of nature; determined by its field of operation, not free; descriptive, not creative" (SER, 12). Frye sees this change as the first important difference between the Romantic and pre-Romantic mythological structures. Blake, who saw the implications of this change more completely than any other English Romantic poet, realized that the god of the older paradigm was "a projected God, an idol constructed out of the sky and reflecting its mindless mechanism" (SER, 13). Thus Blake concluded that if God exists, he exists as an aspect of man's own identity. Frye sees this recovery of projection as the "one central element of [the] new mythological construction" (SER, 14). "In the older myth," he says,

> God was ultimately the only active agent. God had not only created the world and man: he had also created the forms of human civilization. The traditional images of civilization are the city and the garden: the models of both were established by God before Adam was created. Law, moral principles, and, of course, the myth itself were not invented by man, but were a part of God's revelation to him. Gradually at first, in such relatively isolated thinkers as Vico, then more confidently, the conviction grows that a great deal of all this creative activity ascribed to God is projected from man, that man has created the forms of his civilization, including his laws and his myths, and that consequently they exhibit human imperfections and are subject to human criticism. (SER, 14)

A second aspect of the imaginative revolution of Romanticism is a splitting away of the scientific vision of nature from the poetic and existential vision. These last two are what Frye calls the "myth of concern," what society sees as its situation and destiny. And when the myth of concern is separated from science, it becomes an "open" mythology, as distinct from the previous Christian, or "closed," mythology of compulsory belief. Romanticism, then, ushers in not merely a new myth but a new attitude toward other myths. Moreover, conceiving of mythology as a structure of the imagination changes the spirit of belief: new types of belief are possible (SER, 15–16). Two of these are especially important for Frye's argument: "One is the revived sense of the numinous power of nature, as symbolized in Eros, Dionysus, and Mother Nature herself" (SER, 16). The second "comes from the ability that Romantic mythology conferred of being able to express a *revolutionary* attitude toward society, religion, and personal life" (SER, 17).

The first of these means that in Romanticism the older cyclical myth of the Bible from fall to reconciliation assumes a different shape. The old unfallen state becomes the original identity between individual man and nature. The myth of alienation is changed from a fall into sin to a fall into a self-conscious awareness of the subject-object relation to nature: man's primary conscious feeling is one of separation not from God but from nature. Thus the myth of redemption in Romanticism "becomes a recovery of the original identity" (SER, 18). Redemption proceeds from human-centered *eros* rather than from divine *agape* (SER, 20).

The transposition of the older mythology brings with it a revolutionary change in the poet's social freedom. If the poet himself creates the forms of his civilization, then he becomes a central figure who aims not to please but to expand society's consciousness. The poet, Frye says, gains an authority of his own, completely separate from the moral context of the traditional mythology (SER, 21–22).

Third, Romanticism profoundly alters the traditional schema of four levels of reality. This chain of being includes a divine world, an unfallen world of the proper or original human nature, a lower world of experience (the physical order), and a demonic world of death. As we know from the *Anatomy,* Frye conceives of this schema both cyclically and dialectically. The divine and demonic worlds (heaven and hell) are eternally separated, whereas the two middle worlds describe a condition from which man fell and to which, at the end of the historical cycle, he should return. According to Frye it is still possible to think of the mythological structure of Romanticism as a scheme of four levels, but the structure as a whole is much more ambiguous and much less concretely related to the physical world. He says, for example, that in Romanticism

> what corresponds to heaven and hell is still there, the worlds of identity and alienation, but the imagery associated with them, being based on the opposition of "within" and "without" rather than of "up" and "down," is almost reversed. The identity "within," being not purely subjective but a communion, whether with nature or God, is often expressed in imagery of depth or descent. . . . On the other hand, the sense of alienation is reinforced, if anything, by the imagery of what, since Pascal, has increasingly been felt to be the terrifying waste spaces of the heavens. (SER, 46–47)

Similarly, the worlds of human and physical nature are also present in Romanticism, but their relation is reversed too. In the traditional mythology, social and civilized life was necessary for man's regaining his identity, whereas in "a great deal of Romantic imagery human society is thought of as leading to alienation rather than identity" (SER, 47). The Romantics most often appeal to the order of nature outside of society as the source for what is creative and healing.

I have been summarizing Frye's understanding of the chief differences between the two major mythological structures of Western culture. His method of defining Romanticism is to show how three aspects of the older mythology are profoundly transformed. What emerges in the Romantic mythology is a new myth of creation, a new myth of the fall and redemption, and a new understanding of the four-tiered structure of reality. In what respects is Frye's method different from that which a historian of ideas might follow? My summary of his discussion might suggest that nothing would be much changed if we were to substitute a word like "doctrine," "idea," or "conception" for his word "myth." But Frye's study actually differs from a history of ideas in that mythology for him is never simply the conceptual product of culture. Myths are originally stories, and when they are codified to form a mythology, he says, two cultural products result. One is conceptual, a body of cohering ideas; the other is fictional and metaphorical, a body of artistic patterns and conventions. Frye sees mythology then—to use the language of the *Anatomy*—as a combination of *dianoia* and *mythos*. When he defines the myth of creation, for example, it is not only in terms of a set of concepts, like the relationship between God, man, and nature, but also in terms of imagery and story. More important than this, however, is the fact that even when Frye uses "myth" as a synonym for "idea," he does not primarily mean "idea" as an object of belief but "idea" as part of a structure of imagery. Conceptually, the Romantic myth is mainly fictional, an imaginative construct, a spatial projection of reality. "For the literary critic," Frye says, "the word Romanticism refers primarily to some kind of change in the structure of literature itself, rather than to a change in beliefs, ideas, or political movements reflected in literature" (SER, 4).

The remainder of Frye's book is devoted to an analysis of the three English Romantic works already mentioned. Frye's commentary, however, is not primarily directed toward an interpretation of the works themselves, even though much of what he says would be useful in developing an interpretation. Rather, the three writers are used to illustrate Frye's conception of Romanticism: his commentary exists for the sake of the theory rather than vice versa. "Any reader who finds [my] approach to these poets somewhat peripheral," Frye says, "is asked to remember that this is not a book on Beddoes or Keats or Shelley, but a book on Romanticism as illustrated by some of their works."[17]

I have called Frye's book on Romanticism a study of literary history in order to help distinguish among his several kinds of applied criticism. Yet Frye sees "Romanticism" as both more than and less than a term referring to a literary period. It is a cultural as well as a literary term, even though it is not used to characterize all the products of culture between, say, 1780 and 1830. It hardly occurs to us, as Frye points out, to speak of a Romantic movement in the history of science (SER, 3–4). To see "Romanticism" as a cultural term means then that it has its center of gravity in the creative arts, which distinguishes it from a more general historical term like "medieval." But Frye does maintain that Romanticism has a historical center of gravity as well, a period of about fifty years beginning in England around 1780.[18] It is therefore appropriate to call Frye's work a study in literary history insofar as (1) he is concerned mainly with the literary implications of the term Romanticism, and (2) he believes the term characterizes a new sensibility which comes into Western culture during the last part of the eighteenth century.

Frye's method for defining this new sensibility rests upon principles which are by now familiar. First, there is the principle of opposition, represented by the broad historical dialectic of the traditional mythological structure versus the Romantic one. Second, there is Frye's assumption that literature can be viewed spatially, as a static structure of imagery, and temporally, as a narrative movement in time. In the *Anatomy* Frye's discussion of the meaning of imagery (Third Essay) is set against the background of the orders-of-reality or levels-of-existence model. He follows the same procedure, as we have seen, in his study of English Romanticism, showing how the older model is reversed by the newer one. Also in the *Anatomy* Frye analyzes the narrative aspect of literature (its *mythoi*) in terms of a total mythic pattern stretching from creation to apocalypse. In the present work we see this general principle applied in his analysis of the differences between the two "total mythological structures." Third, there are Frye's assumptions about the inherent relationship between literature and myth, assumptions such as the following: the permanent significance of myth is reflected in literature; poetry descends ultimately from myth; both the form and content of myth are subjects of critical study; the social function of mythology is to provide men with an imaginative vision of the human situation, and so on.

These are the three main ways in which *A Study of English Romanticism* is an application of theoretical assumptions which Frye brings to his subject matter. His method consists in applying these assumptions to two large bodies of mythological (fictional and conceptual) data. The exposition which results, while ranging from prehistory to the twentieth century, is a rather complete account (in forty-six pages) of the differences between the Romantic myth and its predecessors. Certainly one of the values of Frye's study is its demonstration that Romanticism is not a chaotic age of relativism and subjectivity or a period of contradictory tendencies which follows the breakup of the Great Chain of Being but a consistent imaginative structure in its own right. The essay is a substantive piece of work, deserving a place alongside the efforts of Wellek, Lovejoy, Abrams, and Peckham to define Romanticism. One of the essay's values is that the work of a largely overlooked writer like Beddoes can be brought properly into focus. Beddoes's preoccupation with death as an imaginative realm outside the world of experience permits us to see him, according to Frye, as a central, even potentially a major, figure of English Romanticism: "Beddoes revolves around the heart of Romantic imagery, at the point of identity with nature of which death is the only visible form" (SER, 48). Thus he is not simply a "morbid" writer whose place is somewhere on the fringes of the Romantic myth. Frye's study, in short, provides the kind of background necessary for understanding a writer like Beddoes.[19]

The Social Context of Criticism

In chapter 5 we observed that Frye has devoted himself in recent years to subjects less strictly literary than the kinds of studies we have just been reviewing. We looked at *The Well-Tempered Critic* as one of his efforts to mark the intimate relationship between literary style and social meaning. Much of Frye's later work is in the same vein, reaching out across literature into areas of social concern. It would be a mistake, however, to lump all of his later writings together; such works as *The Modern Century* and the essays collected in Part I of *The Stubborn Structure* are completely different in emphasis. But there is a similarity among them in that the focus of Frye's attention is on what could be called a criticism of culture—an analysis of the social, philosophic, and moral aspects of the products of culture. The most extensive of these studies is *The Critical Path,* a book which, if it deals with subjects less strictly literary than his previous writings, is no less a work of criticism. It stands as an example of what, for Frye, would be the centrifugal direction that criticism must ultimately take. It is the logical outcome of the *Anatomy's* Tentative Conclusion. Frye himself refers to the book as a rewriting of his "central myth" (CP, 9).

The *Critical Path* is a highly theoretical work, and even though it draws upon many of the assumptions and categories Frye uses to discuss literature, it is not "applied" criticism in the sense that I have been using the word. Labeling the work is not important in the final analysis, but since it is a typical example of Frye's expanding conception of criticism, it is important that we consider briefly his aim, his method of argument, and his conclusions about the social context of criticism.[20]

An indication of Frye's approach is suggested by his claim that the process of interpreting the social myths of culture is "very similar to criticism in literature" and that "the different forms of critical interpretation cannot be sharply separated, whether they are applied to the plays of Shakespeare, the manuscripts of the Bible, the American Constitution, or the oral traditions of an aboriginal tribe. In the area of general concern they converge, however widely the technical contexts in law, theology, literature or anthropology may differ" (CP, 123). This aptly describes the main assumption on which the book is based: while the literary critic is not qualified to handle all the "technical contexts" of culture, he is especially prepared, particularly if he is an archetypal critic, to interpret the cultural phenomena that form the social environment of literature. "The modern critic," he says, "is . . . a student of mythology, and his total subject embraces not merely literature, but the areas of concern which the mythical language of construction and belief enters and informs. These areas constitute the mythological subjects, and they include large parts of religion, philosophy, political theory, and the social sciences" (CP, 98).

The book treats a far-ranging body of such subjects, including the difference between oral and writing cultures, Renaissance humanism, the critical theories of Sidney and Shelley, Marxism and democracy, the idea of progress, advertising and propaganda, social contract theories and conceptions of Utopia, contemporary youth culture, McLuhanism, and theories of education. What holds these apparently unrelated subjects together is the dialectical framework of Frye's discussion. Whatever issue he confronts, it always is set against the background of what he sees as the two opposing myths of Western culture, the myth of concern and the myth of freedom.

The myth of concern comprises everything that a society is most concerned to know. It is the disposition which leads man to uphold communal rather than individual values. It exists, Frye says, "to hold society together. . . . For it, truth and reality are not directly connected with reasoning or evidence, but are socially established. What is true, for concern, is what society does and believes in response to authority, and a belief, so far as a belief is verbalized, is a statement of willingness to participate in a myth of concern. The typical language of concern therefore tends to become the language of belief" (CP, 36). A myth of concern has its roots in religion and only later branches out into politics, law, and literature. It is inherently traditional and conservative, placing a strong emphasis on values of coherence and continuity. It originates in oral or preliterate culture and is associated with continuous verse conventions and discontinuous prose forms. And it is "deeply attached to ritual, to coronations, weddings, funerals, parades, demonstrations, where something is publicly done that expresses an inner social identity" (CP, 45).

The myth of freedom, on the other hand, is committed to a truth of correspondence. It appeals to such self-validating criteria as "logicality of argument or (usually a later stage) impersonal evidence and verification." It is inherently "liberal," helping to develop and honoring such values as objectivity, detachment, suspension of judgment, tolerance, and respect for the individual. It "stresses the importance of the non-mythical elements in culture, of the truths and realities that are studied rather than created, provided by nature rather than by a social vision" (CP, 44). It originates in the mental habits which a writing culture, with its continuous prose and discontinuous verse forms, brings into society.

The way Frye uses this broad dialectic of freedom and concern can be illustrated by his treatment of two classic defenses of poetry, Sidney's and Shelley's. Placing Sidney's view of poetry against the background of Renaissance humanism, Frye concludes that Sidney accommodates the role of the poet to the values of a reading and writing culture, to the norms of meaning established by writers of discursive prose. "The conception of poetry in Sidney," he says, "is an application of the general humanistic view of disciplined speech as the manifestation or audible presence of social authority" (CP, 66). For Sidney, "what is most distinctive about poetry is the poet's power of illustration, a power which is partly an ability to popularize and make more accessible the truths of revelation and reason" (CP, 67). In other words poetry is not qualitatively distinct from the other verbal disciplines. What actually occurs in Sidney's view of poetry, according to Frye, is that the original characteristics of the myths of freedom and concern are interchanged: "The myth of concern takes on a reasoning aspect, claiming the support of logic and historical evidence; the myth of freedom becomes literary and imaginative, as the poet, excluded from primary authority in the myth of concern, finds his social function in a complementary activity, which liberalizes concern but also . . . reinforces it" (CP, 75).

In Shelley's defense, on the other hand, we return to a conception of poetry as mythical and psychologically primitive.

> Shelley begins by neatly inverting the hierarchy of values assumed in Sidney. . . . Shelley puts all the discursive disciplines into an inferior group of "analytic" operations of reason. They are aggressive; they think of ideas as weapons; they seek the irrefutable argument, which keeps eluding them because all arguments are theses, and theses are half-truths implying their own opposites. . . . The works of imagination, by contrast, cannot be refuted: poetry is the dialectic of love, which treats everything it encounters as another form of itself, and never attacks, only includes. . . . This argument assumes, not only that the language of poetry is mythical, but that poetry, in its totality, is in fact society's real myth of concern, and that the poet is still the teacher of that myth. . . . In Sidney's day, it was accepted that the models of creation were established by God: for Shelley, man

makes his own civilization, and at the centre of man's creation are the poets, whose work provides the models of human society. The myths of poetry embody and express man's creation of his own culture, rather than his reception of it from a divine source. (CP, 94, 95–96)

There is no denying the fact the Frye's sympathies lie on the side of Shelley, for both of them believe that the language of literature represents the imaginative possibilities of concern. And both of them are opposed to the constrictive view of Sidney which makes the critic an evaluator and which makes poetry subservient to whatever established framework of concern an elite society happens to be championing at the moment. To say that literature contains the imaginative possibilities of concern means, for Frye, that it displays "the total range of verbal fictions and models and images and metaphors out of which all myths of concern are constructed" (CP, 98). Frye's conclusion is that while Shelley's (and his own) view of poetry takes us back to the areas of concern expressed in primitive and oracular mythology, the critic's approach to the values expressed by a myth of concern must derive from the myth of freedom. "The critic *qua* critic," Frye says, "is not himself concerned but detached" (CP, 99).

The merging of freedom and concern, however, is what produces the social context of literature. If there is a central thesis to *The Critical Path* it is the dialectical tension Frye seeks to establish between the myths of freedom and concern. This tension comprises his own central myth, as it were, and the cultural phenomena he examines throughout the book are interpreted from the perspective of this tension. A corollary to the tension is the necessity for a pluralism of myths of concern, which can only occur in societies with open mythologies.

The basis of all tolerance in society, the condition in which a plurality of concerns can co-exist, is the recognition of the tension between concern and freedom. . . . Concern and freedom both occupy the whole of the same universe: they interpenetrate, and it is no good trying to set up boundary stones. Some, of course, meet the collision of concern and freedom from the opposite side, with a naive rationalism which expects that before long all myths of concern will be outgrown and only the appeal to reason and evidence and experiment will be taken seriously. . . . I consider such a view entirely impossible. The growth of non-mythical knowledge tends to eliminate the incredible from belief, and helps to shape the myth of concern according to the outlines of what experience finds possible and vision desirable. But the growth of knowledge cannot in itself provide us with the social vision which will suggest what we should do with our knowledge. (CP, 108–10)

This is where Frye's view of the social function of criticism enters the argument; the literary critic, or at least Frye's ideal critic, is prepared to see that myths of concern in society are like those in literature in that they represent the range of imaginative possibilities of belief. Frye will not be cornered into accepting the Kierkegaardian "either-or" position. He wants the best of both possible worlds: the detached, liberal, impersonal values of the "aesthetic" attitude which Kierkegaard rejects and the values of commitment which come from the primacy of concern. He, of course, does not think Kierkegaard's own solution is satisfactory: "If we stop with the voluntary self-blinkering of commitment, we are no better off than the 'aesthetic': on the other side of 'or' is another step to be taken, a step from the committed to the creative, from iconoclastic concern to what the literary critic above all ought to be able to see, that in literature man *is* a spectator of his own life, or at least of the larger vision in which his life is contained" (CP, 129).

This is Frye's answer as to how man can be detached yet joined to the community of concern at the same time. It is an answer in which the visionary imagination once again becomes the ultimate criterion, for only in the world of imagination can the tension between freedom and concern be properly maintained. It is out of this tension, Frye concludes,

> that glimpses of a third order of experience emerge, of a world that may not exist but completes existence, the world of the definitive experience that poetry urges us to have but which we never quite get. If such a world existed, no individual could live in it. . . . If we could live in it, of course, criticism would cease and the distinction between literature and life would disappear, because life itself would then be the continuous incarnation of the creative word. (CP, 170–71)

The doctrine of the imagination being proposed here takes us back to the Blakean ideas set forth in the Second Essay of the *Anatomy*. *The Critical Path* is a logical outcome of the *Anatomy*. If we "stand back" from the later work, we cannot help but observe that the twin values of detachment and concern are, in fact, the same values adumbrated in the *Anatomy*; for throughout that work Frye seeks to hold in tension an ethical or social criticism, which is forever extended toward the myth of concern, with a detached and disinterested criticism of literary structure and convention. He holds them in tension, finally, by his all-encompassing doctrine of the imagination.

7

Powers and Limitations

To this point my treatment of Frye has been largely analytical. To be sure, value judgments of various kinds have entered the discussion, and the entire effort is based on the value-laden premise that Frye's work is important enough to merit the close study I have attempted to give it. But on the whole my aim has been expository and my approach disinterested. I have tried to examine Frye's criticism on his own terms, seeking to understand what he has said and why he has said it. My commitment has been to the simple truth that understanding precedes judgment.

But there is no escaping, finally, the issue of assessment. The very nature of Frye's work will not permit us simply "to murmur politely that it shows things in a new light and is indeed a most stimulating contribution to criticism."[1] There is hardly a page in Frye which does not invite controversy or reaction. A student of his work cannot rest content with having described the details of his method, the nature of his argument, the example of his practice, the large claims and audacious scope of his entire undertaking. Part of our task is to take stock of the entire effort, to assess its powers and limitations, and to suggest at least some of its problematic areas.

To begin with a general question, one that relates to the theoretical system as a whole: Does literary criticism need the kind of conceptual universe Frye seeks to provide? In one respect, this question lies outside the issue of critical method. It is a precritical issue, best decided in terms of the individual critic's interests, sensibility, and predisposition. What I have in mind is R.S. Crane's principle that critical methods themselves are "immune to theoretical questioning," since a critic's choice of a subject matter and his method of reasoning are, more than anything else, practical decisions, stemming from his own interests and the kinds of problems he wants to solve.[2] Related to this is the distinction Crane draws, following Carnap, between internal and external questions. Internal questions pertain to the logical and conceptual aspects of a critical framework, whereas external questions are "not propositions within a framework but about the justification of the framework itself."[3] From this perspective my initial question about Frye's system as a whole is external and therefore, in Crane's words, "immune to theoretical questioning."[4]

Certainly Frye's concern to formulate a synoptic view of criticism will be of minimal value to critics intent primarily on explaining the unique texture of single literary works. While the conception of criticism outlined in the Second Essay is clearly broad enough to include such study, archetypal and myth criticism, by definition, precludes it. The same point could be made about a good many critical treatises, Coleridge's *Biographia,* for example. His concern to marry German idealism with nineteenth-century British poetics and thereby produce a theory of the imagination is not indispensable for explaining the peculiar or unique qualities of a given work. The point is that if one is predisposed to relating literature to other literature, then he cannot be faulted for not explicating poems, which is precisely where a large number of Frye's critics have faulted him. The implicit conflict here is between two kinds of interests, and it cannot be resolved by appealing to any universal *critical* principle. As Meyer Abrams puts it, "all those who, in the course of time, emerge with the reputation of major theorists of art have in fact contributed important new knowledge . . . and they have succeeded in doing so not despite their basic discrepancies, but as a direct result of these discrepancies."[5] The differences among critical purposes and methods is not something we need to lament. All we need to acknowledge at this stage is that Frye's analogical and archetypal criticism is a completely legitimate activity and that it deserves the best theoretical principles that can be devised. The better these principles can be systematically described and classified, the better his kind of criticism will be as a body of theoretical and practical knowledge.

Scientific versus Literary Theory

If we can agree, then, that one kind of critical interest depends on a synoptic view like Frye's, the next question is how well his own system meets the demands of such a view. This is an internal question, for it takes us inside Frye's framework and forces us to confront the logical and conceptual aspects of his theory. We can begin with Frye's claim that the nature of criticism is "scientific," using the word in the second sense referred to in chapter 5. Frye often points to the similarity between the hypotheses he wants to develop and those of the natural sciences. It is not at all clear, however, that such a similarity can or does exist or, even if it does, that Frye's understanding of the relationship among hypotheses, theory, and observation is very meaningful or useful. Is he right, for example, about the role which theories play in the development of a science?

His claim that revolutions in conceptual thought fundamentally alter the method of investigation within a discipline is unobjectionable: it goes without saying that such ideas as Newton's "forces" and "attractions" or Darwin's theory of evolution effected major changes within their respective scientific traditions. But it is not universally agreed that such revolutions are always as progressive, empirically cumulative, and revitalizing as Frye implies. He says, for example, that "the development of [a scientifically organized criticism] would fulfil the systematic and *progressive* element in research by assimilating its work into a unified structure of knowledge, as other sciences do." He speaks of a "central *expanding pattern* of systematic comprehension" in criticism and talks of how revolutions in theory *revitalize* conceptual thought (AC, 11, 12, 15, italics added).

Thomas Kuhn's study of scientific revolutions reminds us, however, that there is more than one kind of scientific discovery. On the one hand, there are discoveries which take place within a particular scientific tradition, discoveries which are not revolutionary in themselves but which develop from a framework of concepts and principles established by some great originator, like Aristotle, Newton, or Einstein. Kuhn refers to these theories as "paradigms," or "universally recognized scientific achievements that for a time provide model problems and solutions to a community of practitioners."[6] His study of the history of science leads him to believe that most scientific study is paradigm-governed; that is, within a given discipline most problem-solving is largely controlled by a dominant conceptual structure which is accepted as true. Kuhn calls this activity "normal science." Its concern is not to test the paradigm but to fit its experimental findings into the dominant conceptual model. And when discrepancies are discovered—anomalies which do not quite fit the accepted structure—normal science simply adjusts the data so as to leave the paradigm intact.

Now it is clear that Frye thinks of science as a cumulative enterprise, progressively building upon the theories and laws established by previous scientists. He conceives of all scientific activity to be like Kuhn's "normal science." But according to Kuhn, "Cumulative acquisition of unanticipated novelties proves to be an almost non-existent exception to the rule of scientific development. The man who takes historic fact seriously must suspect that science does not tend toward the ideal that our [empirical] image of its cumulativeness has suggested."[7] This means that most scientific activity (or all of normal science), the aim of which is to solve the remaining problems in the field by using the paradigm theory which is current, tends toward a kind of dogmatism. The reason for this, according to Kuhn, is simply that most scientists are concerned not with testing the paradigm but with interpreting new data and new problems according to its principles. The paradigm, in other words, becomes entrenched. On the other hand, nonparadigmatic changes in the scientific tradition are the revolutions themselves, those periods when the dominant theory breaks apart.

There *is* an analogy between what Frye calls the period of naive induction and what Kuhn sees as the preparadigmatic period, the time before which a given science has fully articulated its theory. Frye says that "a new scientific discovery manifests something that was already latent in the order of nature, and at the same time is logically related to the total structure of the existing science" (AC, 97). Kuhn would say that this is certainly true for normal scientific discoveries, that is, for those within an accepted paradigm. Yet discoveries which are revolutionary, which upset the traditional paradigm, cannot be considered as "logically related to the total structure of the existing science."

But beyond the resemblance between Frye's period of naive induction and Kuhn's preparadigmatic period, their understanding of the structure of scientific revolutions is not at all similar. Especially obvious is the absence in Frye of an awareness of the restrictive disadvantages implicit in paradigm theories, like the resistance to innovation which a particular style of thinking imposes. In fact, it is precisely the exclusiveness of paradigm theories, according to Kuhn, which sets certain scientific classics, like Aristotle's *Physica* and Newton's *Principia,* apart from the classics in other creative fields. Such classics determine not only the kinds of problems scientists are interested in but also their norms for solving those problems and their standards about the kind of fact with which their science deals. Therefore, a myopic commitment to a given paradigm, according to Kuhn, can lead simply to a "striving both for neater formulations of that paradigm and for an articulation that would bring it into closer agreement with observations of nature."[8] The necessary result is that scientists then move farther and farther away from any concern to test the principles of the paradigm. This being the case, Frye's effort to establish a structure of critical thought upon a central hypothesis analogous to that of a pure science might well be an enterprise fraught with the dangers of dogmatic exclusivism. Without showing any concern to test his own paradigm, he and his disciples may be inclined simply to further articulate the theory and bring it into closer and closer agreement with observations from literature.

If Kuhn is right, then the relationship between hypothesis and evidence in revolutionary science might well differ from their relationship in normal science; even normal sciences operating within separate paradigms may not view theory and observation in the same terms.[9] This raises large questions of the nature and function of theories, questions by no means settled by philosophers of science. But let us use the tentative definition of a theory as a set of hypotheses consistent with the facts of any given subject matter.

What procedures are involved in relating hypothesis to fact in order to arrive at a theory? For Frye it is both an inductive and a deductive procedure. "If criticism exists, it must be," he says, "an examination of literature in terms of a conceptual framework derivable from an inductive survey of the literary field" (AC, 7). There are two important claims here. One is that a thorough study of literary works is the critic's initial duty. The "first thing" he must do, Frye says, "is to read literature, to make an inductive survey of his own field and let his critical principles shape themselves solely out of his knowledge of that field" (AC, 6–7). The second important claim is that theory is arrived at by inference *from* observations about literature. "The word 'inductive,' " Frye adds, "suggests some sort of scientific procedure" (AC, 7). He does not specify what sort of procedure is involved, but the assertion that theory is derivable by inductive inference is clearly problematic. It flies in the face of the so-called hypothetico-deductive view defended vigorously by philosophers of science like Karl Popper and C.G. Hempel. Popper argues that theories are *"free* creations of our own minds, the result of an almost poetic intuition."[10] Similarly, Hempel maintains that "the transition from data to theory requires creative imagination. Scientific hypotheses are not *derived* from observed facts, but *invented* in order to account for them. They constitute guesses at the connections that might obtain between the phenomena under study, at uniformities and patterns that might underlie their occurrence."[11] These are philosophers of natural science speaking, and, of course, criticism, as Frye recognizes (AC, 7), is not a "pure" or "exact" science. The point, however, is that Frye's claim that the theoretical framework of criticism is "derivable" by inference from literature itself is not a universally accepted solution to how theories originate. While the hypothetico-deductive view itself has been questioned, a philosopher like Popper would certainly respond to Frye's position by saying that although there might be some causal explanation of how a critic derived his ideas, the kind of inference involved in scientific theory is always *from* the theory rather than *to* it. Observations from literature, that is, provide the basis for testing hypotheses rather than deriving them. We shall turn to the issue of confirmation shortly. For the moment we need only observe that Frye's proposal about how critical theory is derived is problematic.

But Frye also conceives of critical theory as deductive. In "The Archetypes of Literature" he says that the inductive and deductive methods work to "correct" each other:

> We may . . . proceed inductively from structural analysis, asso-
> ciating the data we collect and trying to see larger patterns in
> them. Or we may proceed deductively, with the consequences
> that follow from postulating the unity of criticism. It is clear, of
> course, that neither procedure will work indefinitely without
> correction from the other. Pure induction will get us lost in
> haphazard guessing; pure deduction will lead to inflexible and
> over-simplified pigeonholing. (FI, 10)

In the *Anatomy* Frye announces forthrightly which of these paths he has followed. "I have proceeded deductively, and been rigorously selective in examples and illustrations," he says. "The deductiveness does not extend further than tactical method, and so far as I know there is no principle in the book which is claimed as a perfect major premise, without exceptions or negative instances. Such expressions as 'nor-mally,' 'usually,' 'regularly,' or 'as a rule' are thickly strewn throughout" (AC, 29). This confession clearly indicates that critical hypotheses can-not be like the laws and principles of the natural sciences, which might seem an unnecessary point to make, except that Frye invites the equa-tion by comparing criticism to such disciplines as physics, astronomy, and biology. Does this mean then that critical theory, lacking the strict requirements of a pure science because it can admit occasional excep-tions to its fundamental laws, is more like that of a social science? The idea that criticism is a body of inductive knowledge presented deduc-tively from premises which are generally but not universally true sug-gests that it might be. At one point, in fact, Frye says explicitly that it is (AC, 16).

The Question of Confirmation

But what does it mean for Frye to say that he has proceeded deduc-tively? Deductive reasoning raises the issue of confirmation, and a sec-ond question we must therefore ask is whether or not Frye's conclu-sions can be tested as true. Let us consider these two issues in turn. We can assume, first of all, that Frye accepts the ordinary definition of deduction: a process of reasoning by which an unexceptionable conclu-sion is drawn from a universally accepted premise. We do not move far into the *Anatomy*, however, before realizing that Frye's method of infer-ence is not deductive at all—or at least that it is not deductive in any rigorous way. To illustrate: on the first page of the First Essay, Frye asserts four ways a fictional hero may be classified. A hero, we recall, may be either superior or inferior both to other men and to his environment, or he may be equal to either ("roughly the same" [AC, 33]). Moreover, except when these relationships involve equality, there may be differences of either degree or kind. These statements constitute Frye's premises. And there seems to be no reason for finding them objectionable, since an inductive study of literature shows that such distinctions can be made. But whereas Frye's conclusion from these premises is that there are *five* basic modes of fiction, a truly deductive argument would necessarily infer that there are twenty-five.[12] Frye gives no reason why there cannot be a mode, say, in which the hero is superior in degree to other men and in kind to his environment. But such a mode would surely follow from Frye's principles. We are left then with the question as to why he arrives at only five modes, when there are other combinations which should result from his perfectly sensible premises. John Holloway, who has specifically challenged Frye on this point, asks why it is that Frye can discover five modes, five parallel levels of meaning, four basic myths, six phases, eighteen lyric conventions, and so forth.[13] "If we were to ask," Holloway says,

> *why* these numbers, *why* these correspondences, an inductive answer would show that these and no others are what turn up if we marshall all the items of evidence and look them over. Arguing deductively would show that these and no others followed from first principles. That's what Kant did in his first *Critik,* and as far as patterns go, Mr Frye's book looks very like that one. But Kant started from what he thought could be assumed without question, the basic forms of Aristotle's logic, and then he tried to show rigorously that we find, in consequence of what Aristotle's logic lays down, certain corresponding forms of perception, understanding, knowledge, natural law, error and so on. Contrast Mr Frye at what I think is the most momentous point in his book: "a somewhat forbidding piece of symmetry *turns up* in our argument at this point, which *seems to have some literary analogy* to the circle of fifths. *I recognize* six phases of each mythos, three being parallel to the phases of a neighbouring mythos"! In fact, the book is neither inductive nor deductive. It is a series of dogmatic assertions; with illustrations to show that the kind of thing in question turns up somewhere in the whole range of written works good or bad.[14]

Holloway overstates his case, for it is clear that Frye's principles could not have been formulated without an inductive study of literature. It is no less clear that his theory results from deducing consequences, even if incomplete ones, from his principles. However, the more important issue—one implicit in Holloway's remarks—is whether or not Frye's theory can be confirmed.

A theory is overthrown when it is shown to be inadequate by some process of testing. If we operate with the classical view of testing, it is not easy to see how Frye's theory can be refuted. Such a view requires us merely to locate instances in literature of, say, Frye's Proserpine archetype. If we find a sufficiently large number of these, then there is good reason for concluding that such an archetype may be a structurally important principle in some literary works. Using this kind of confirmation procedure makes Frye's position theoretically invincible. But, as David Hume observed, no matter how many tests confirm a theory, it may still be wrong.

A more recent solution to the problem of confirmation has been advanced by Karl Popper, who has sought to discover a "criterion of demarcation" to distinguish the genuine from the false.[15] He concludes that falsifiability is the proper standard for separating the scientific from the pseudo-scientific: only those theories offering conclusions which stand an honest chance of being refuted can be called scientific. In other words, theories are never confirmed or proven true; they are only disconfirmed or proven false.[16]

From this perspective, as John Casey observed, it is easy to see how Frye's theories can continually be confirmed but difficult to see how they can be decisively refuted.[17] Meyer Abrams's review of the *Anatomy* makes the same point:

> The odd thing about evidence for an archetype is not that you cannot prove that it is present, but that you cannot help proving it, and that there is no way of disproving it. Any extended and complex literary work can, by the omission of unsuitable elements, be made to resemble almost any archetypal shape. Since there is no firm possibility of negative observations, archetypal statements are empirically incorrigible, and incorrigible statements are not good grounds for a science of criticism.[18]

To apply the falsifiability criterion to Frye's work leads to the conclusion that scientific confirmation seems impossible and that criticism is not a systematic body of knowledge in the way an empirical science is.

Perhaps Frye would respond by saying that criticism is not literally a science but only analogically so; that just as the scientist inquires into the order of nature, so the critic inquires into the order of words. But even the analogy may be misleading. Here is what Frye actually says:

It is clear that criticism cannot be a systematic study unless there is a quality in literature which enables it to be so. We have to adopt the hypothesis, then, that just as there is an order of nature behind the natural sciences, so literature is not a piled aggregate of "works," but an order of words. A belief in an order of nature, however, is an inference from the intelligibility of the natural sciences; and if the natural sciences ever completely demonstrated the order of nature they would presumably exhaust their subject. Similarly, criticism, if a science, must be totally intelligible, but literature, as the order of words which makes the science possible, is, so far as we know, an inexhaustible source of new critical discoveries, and would be even if new works of literature ceased to be written. (AC, 17)

I am not concerned here with the difference Frye sees between science and criticism (science could conceivably exhaust its subject, criticism could not) but with the similarity, for it is the analogy of "order" which may lead us astray. That all scientists possess some monolithic conception of an "order of nature" is dubious, and certainly it cannot be inferred from the fact, as Frye claims, that the natural sciences are intelligible. Perhaps a given science can, at one point in its history, be shown to possess a common body of assumptions about the physical world. But these assumptions are always changing as new discoveries are made, and, as Thomas Kuhn demonstrated, most sciences, especially in their early stages, are characterized by a continual competition among a variety of distinct views of nature.[19] An order of nature, in fact, is precisely what the sciences do not assume. What is revolutionary for one science is not necessarily revolutionary for another. "Though quantum mechanics (or Newtonian dynamics, or electromagnetic theory)," Kuhn says, "is a paradigm for many scientific groups, it is not the same paradigm for them all. Therefore, it can simultaneously determine several traditions of normal science that overlap without being coextensive. A revolution produced within one of these traditions will not necessarily extend to the others as well."[20] Frye is apparently influenced by the textbook tradition which represents scientists as having worked on the same set of problems with the same set of fixed canons and as contributing to a cumulative understanding of the order of nature. But this is a chimera, according to Kuhn.[21] Competing paradigms, he says, are incommensurate; scientists practice their trades in different worlds,[22] the effect of which is a series of discontinuous orders of nature rather than a singular ordered model of unity and consistency. The sciences, in short, do not appear to rest upon an assumption of implicit unity in some order of nature, as Frye seems to think. Anyway, the characteristics that Frye ascribes to science—progressive cumulation, coherence, and inclusiveness—are, as Meyer Abrams points out, attributes that also characterize such pseudo-sciences as astrology, physiognomy, and the theory of humours.[23]

There are two problems, then, with Frye's saying that literature is an "order of words" analogous to the "order to nature." First, it derives from a questionable assumption about the natural order which sciences actually make. And second, even if the analogy were based upon a proper understanding of scientific theory, it would suggest only in the vaguest kind of way that literature can be looked at as a whole. But we do not need the analogy between science and criticism to tell us this. The analogy, in short, is both misleading and unnecessary.

But let us return to the issue of confirmation by asking whether, if we abandon Frye's analogy between criticism and science, his theory and his conclusions can be confirmed in some other, "nonscientific" way. We can begin by assuming a hypothetical case. Suppose, after having read the classics, the Bible, and *The Golden Bough,* we are able to discover in a particular novel no less than a dozen original archetypes. Since Frye's system is based on analogy and since we are able to show similarities between our novel and each of the archetypal figures, then either Frye has to admit all twelve as legitimate descriptions, in which case the knowledge gained by systematic classification seems to dissipate, or else we must determine which of the twelve represents the "real" archetype.

The latter possibility seems to be ruled out by Frye's assumptions about the nature of criticism, for his approach is always to begin with structure in the largest sense.

> Whenever we read anything there are two mental operations we perform, which succeed one another in time. First we follow the narrative movement in the act of reading, turning over the pages and pursuing the trail from top left to bottom right. Afterwards, we can look at the work as a simultaneous unity and study its structure. This latter act is the critical response properly speaking: the ordinary reader seldom needs to bother with it. The chief material of rhetorical analysis consists of a study of the poetic "texture," and such a study plunges one into a complicated labyrinth of ambiguities, multiple meanings, recurring images, and echoes of both sound and sense. A full explication of a long and complex work which was based on the reading process could well become much longer, and more difficult to read, than the work itself. . . . It is more practicable to start with the second stage. This involves attaching the rhetorical analysis to a deduc-

tive framework derived from a study of the structure, and the context of that structure is what shows us where we should begin to look for our central images and ambiguities. (CP, 25–26)

The context of that structure, as we have seen time and again, is, first, the complete body of a writer's work and, finally, all other literature—which means that the question of how an archetype might function in a particular work is not a question Frye's method permits us easily to ask.

One conceivable way to solve the problem of confirmation would be to reduce the scope of Frye's structuralism from the context of all literature, life, and natural cycles to a context in which a work's individual structure can be examined. In other words we have to ask whether or not an archetypal pattern, a thematic mode, or a generic form can be said to serve an essential function in defining the formal nature of a particular work. And one possible way of answering this question is to determine what the intention of a work is. Archetypal themes may turn out to play an important role in such a study; yet they would be important not as they relate to other works of literature but only as they either serve the final cause of a work or are themselves the final cause. Using the intended meaning of a literary work as the problem to be solved, we can develop a method for testing the genuineness and relevance of archetypes.

To speak about a poem's intention is to deal with its emotional and structural meaning; and to discover a poem's intention is to analyze the rhetorical aspects, both affective and intellectual, which the writer uses to shape our response. This kind of analysis need not violate the autonomy of a work at all. Intentionalism does not necessarily have to refer to the motives or the psychological history of the poet, which is what Wimsatt and Beardsley have in mind in their unmasking of the "intentional fallacy." There are other meaningful ways of talking about artistic intention. Erwin Panofsky, for example, has said that an artistic work *demands* to be responded to in a particular way and that this demand is a function of the way in which the work solves an artistic problem. In this context, intention refers to rhetorical, stylistic, and structural patterns which we as readers can recognize, not as examples of archetypal categories, but as parts of a whole fitted together to achieve a certain effect—in Panofsky's words "as specific solutions of generic 'artistic problems.' "[24] In a similar manner, R.S. Crane has argued that a work of literature possesses a synthesizing idea or cause which directs whatever a poet does with his materials. This cause determines what kind of work a poet will create and what its emotional quality will be. By reasoning backward from the effect of the poem, Crane maintains, we can discover the causes which produced it. These causes would include every rhetorical and stylistic choice the author made in the process of composition.[25] And the combination of all the choices results in what we can call the intended effect, those intellectual and emotional qualities which the work "demands" that we respond to. By a careful analysis of the "causes" of individual poems, following the kind of inductive procedure Crane outlines, we can arrive at a position for making sound judgments about artistic intention. This means, of course, that we will have to abandon Frye's sharp disjunction between knowledge and experience. But it also means that we will have a method for talking about the meaning of dying-god myths and the meaning of *Lear*. And if we can show that the two intended meanings differ, then we have a falsifiability criterion which can be used to deny archetypal equations.[26]

Meyer Abrams approaches the issue of confirmation by calling for an appeal to *facts*. How do we know, he asks, whether archetypal patterns are actually in a work of literature? What is the evidence for their existence? His answer is that a genuine science of criticism "sets out from and terminates in an appeal to facts which enforce agreement from all sane, knowledgeable, and disinterested witnesses, in independent observations. It is relevant to inquire whether Frye's literary data do enforce agreement from all qualified readers. Are they discoverable by independent observations? Could even an initiate predict, in advance of publication, that Frye would discover 'displaced' forms of the dragon-killing myth in the cave episode in *Tom Sawyer* and in the hero's release from the labyrinth in Henry James's *The Sense of the Past*?" Abrams's answer is that Frye's archetypal statements are not "significant empirical propositions."[27]

Wayne Booth displays a similar skepticism. "One good way to test my misgivings," he says, "would be to take the five most respected readers of the *Anatomy* and give them a work not mentioned by Mr. Frye and ask them to decide whether it is comedy, romance, tragedy, or irony or some combination, and then to describe the archetypes they detect. The chaotic results can be predicted." "I'd like to have charge of a controlled experiment," he adds, to test the claim "that different readers working independently with Frye's categories produce identical results on a given work of art."[28] Both of these critics are appealing to literary fact. Abrams's appeal is specific; Booth's is in the context of a discussion about how critical theory relates, or should relate, to literary fact. Both critics, furthermore, want to establish a means of confirmation by appealing to independent observers.[29]

If we attend to Popper's view of confirmation, however, are not the questions raised by Abrams and Booth insufficient? On the one hand, the ability of an independent observer to locate an archetype which Frye himself has located does not confirm the theory. Nor, on the other hand, would their failure to locate it disconfirm the theory. Just because an independent observer is unable to see the relation between Newton's falling apples and the movement of the stars is no reason to conclude that the theory of gravity is not—to use Abrams's phrase—a significant empirical proposition.[30] Abrams, especially, is trying to confront Frye on his own terms by calling into question Frye's idea of a scientific criticism. But at least part of his critique rests upon an un-Popperian idea of confirmation and thus will not yield very satisfactory results if in fact Frye's theory is taken to be a scientific one. One might reply to Abrams that in science itself chaotic results could be predicted from independent observers who have not been *taught* to see the relation between falling apples and moving stars, but that once they are taught, they can understand the theory of gravity. Similarly, Frye might reply to his critics that an archetype can be recognized by independent observers once they have been taught what it is.

But even this point rests upon the assumption that scientific and critical theory are somehow the same. Would not a more fruitful approach to evaluation result from abandoning all talk of scientific and empirical confirmation? I have been trying to suggest that Frye's criticism is not "scientific" in Popper's sense of the term, but this conclusion should not in itself constitute a damaging blow to Frye's position. After all, as John Casey says, "his work could be 'unscientific' but, nevertheless of great value,"[31] which is implicit in Abrams's conclusion that in the final analysis Frye's theory is a metaphysical theory. And the important question about metaphysical theories is not whether they can be scientifically verified but whether they are meaningful and whether they produce useful knowledge. We will return to this matter below.

No literal-minded critic can read Frye without confronting a host of additional problems. Many readers have found him overly ingenious, confusing, and rhetorically high-handed. Some have claimed that his categories are badly drawn and that he distorts literary works to fit his system. Others have observed that his terms shift in meaning, that his language is imprecise, and that his propositions are not truly arguable. Many have been frustrated on being presented with some controversial premise or conclusion with little or no indication of how it was reached. There are grounds for legitimate complaint in all of these reactions. On the other hand, much of the criticism directed against Frye is senseless; it appears to stem from an unwillingness or inability to understand.

This latter, of course, varies greatly in quality. At one extreme are the willful distortions, like Pauline Kogan's mindless diatribe, *Northrop Frye: The High Priest of Clerical Obscurantism.*[32] At the other extreme are studies by serious and sophisticated critics who sometimes go wrong. Many of their anxieties about Frye, however, could be relieved by a closer attention to his work. Consider William Wimsatt's "Criticism as Myth," for example.[33]

Diagrammatic Consistency

At one point in his essay Wimsatt devotes several pages to complaining about the lack of consistency in the diagrammatic structure of the Third Essay. "Diagrammatic descriptions," he says, "ought at least to be capable of diagram. If they were not, there would seem to be a grave question as to what they are saying. Frye is really, in the long run, not very careful with his diagramming."[34] There are three parts to Wimsatt's complaint. First he is disturbed that in "The Archetypes of Literature," written a half-dozen years before the *Anatomy* and incorporated into it, the analogies between spring and comedy and between summer and romance are reversed. "Much," Wimsatt says, "turns on this analogy." Second, he is troubled by the misalignment resulting from the fact "that Frye moves from the descending *sequence* of his first essay . . . to the embarrassment of a very different sequence of 'broader categories' in the third essay." Wimsatt believes this has got "something to do with the complexities that emerge from the asserted correspondence of the first and second three of the six phases of each season with its adjacent seasons." Third, he believes the structure of Frye's framework is so confused and inconsistent that Frye himself gets lost in it:

> By a proper attention to the *terminally* climactic structure of the spring and autumn seasons and the *medially* climactic structure of the winter and summer seasons, Frye might have worked out his diagram and might have succeeded in whirling his twenty-four literary subcategories at least *consistently* around the seasonal cycle. But even that would not have paralleled the pattern of his first essay, and furthermore it would not have helped the supposedly primordial and archetypal notion of the Spenglerian four-season cycle.[35]

But in all of this is Wimsatt being fair? Has he not distorted or misunderstood Frye? The fact that the first and third essays are based on different sequences should not be disturbing if we pause long enough to realize that one essay treats the historical sequence of modes and the other, the cyclical sequence of *mythoi*. Why should we expect the two sequences to be parallel? Why should it be an "embarrassment" to have two different sequences? There is no reason for us to expect that the two essays should be based on similar sequences, disregarding altogether Wimsatt's failure to observe that the modal paradigm is also cyclical (he calls it "descending"). Furthermore, Frye explicitly points out (AC, 136–37) that a category like romance is used to mean one thing in the First Essay and another in the Third. Whether much does turn on the analogy between the seasons and the *mythoi,* as Wimsatt claims, is open to question. Frye's argument at this point seems simple enough. He wants to show that just as cyclical patterns can be observed in nature, so some of the imagery of literature—that which is not undisplaced and partakes therefore of the order of nature—can also be seen as embodying cyclic patterns. That comedy, however, is called the *mythos* of spring, romance the *mythos* of summer, and so on, is incidental to the argument. We remove these terms from the subsection titles and nothing whatsoever is lost. In brief, Frye's argument for pregeneric elements of literature does not depend on their analogy to the seasons. And although his theory of phases is complex, as we have seen, it is not inconsistent. He does not attempt to relate the *phases* to the seasonal cycle: Wimsatt seems to think that he should have and that everything would be cleared up if Frye had only paid attention to the terminal and medial climactic structure of the seasons—whatever that might mean. Although there are significant problems which the schematic nature of Frye's criticism raises, Wimsatt's example is not one of them.[36]

Semantic, Doctrinal, and Methodological Problems

Let us look at some of the genuine difficulties which Frye's criticism presents. For purposes of analysis I will divide these into three areas: semantic, doctrinal, and methodological. In practice the three areas are integrally related.

The semantic problem is chiefly a terminological one, having to do with the meaning Frye gives his various categories. Certainly a large part of his effort has been directed toward naming the objects of the literary world. "We find ourselves," he says, "in the cultural situation of savages who have words for ash and willow and no word for tree" (AC, 13). Or again: "The very word 'genre' sticks out in an English sentence as the unpronounceable and alien thing it is. Most critical efforts to handle such generic terms as 'epic' and 'novel' are chiefly interesting as examples of the psychology of rumor" (AC, 13). But the value of a new and expanded vocabulary for criticism would seem to rest on the precision of meaning which can be given its terms. This is not an expectation Frye always fulfills. Many of his terms lack precision because of their tremendous breadth of reference. Many of them are loosely defined.

Consider, for example, his use of the word "myth," a word which, it should be apparent by this point, has a myriad of meanings. This in itself need not cause concern. As Richard McKeon demonstrated, some of the best philosophers of art employ a method in which their terms undergo an almost indefinite series of gradations in meaning. Although some philosophers tend to use words univocally and take things to be variable, others see words themselves as variable in meaning and see things to be constant. McKeon cites Aristotle and Plato as classic exemplars of these differing methods, which he calls respectively the literal and the analogical forms of discourse.[37] But if one follows the analogical tradition and uses words equivocally, as Frye does, the meaning of a given term should be clear at any one point in his criticism, regardless of the meaning it might have at another point. Let us see if this is the case with regard to Frye's use of the word "myth."

In the *Anatomy* "myth" is used in three principal ways. In the First Essay it means a particular kind of story, a narrative in which some of the characters are gods whose actions have not been adjusted to the canons of plausibility or realism. In the Second Essay it refers to a verbal form of ritual and dream; it is the means for uniting and communicating those desires and aversions which exist either outside or below the level of articulation. Myth, Frye says in one of his more enigmatic statements, "gives meaning to ritual and narrative to dream: it is the identification of ritual and dream, in which the former is seen to be the latter in movement" (AC, 107). Much depends here on what Frye means by dream, ritual, and identity; in chapter 3 I attempted to specify what he means. However successful this attempt was, it should be clear at least that the word has a meaning different from that in the First Essay. There it means a kind of story, and the framework of its meaning is Frye's theory of the historical sequence of modes; but in the Second Essay it means a form of communication, and the framework of its meaning is his theory of symbolic phases, especially the last phase of this theory (see AC, 116–18). That there are two separate meanings need cause no problem, so long as we are conscious of the fact; Frye himself is careful to point out the different usages (AC, 106).

But in the Third Essay, which Frye calls his Theory of Myths, the word has still another meaning: the abstract or stylized aspect of art. This meaning is related to that of the First Essay, insofar as abstract design is most easily seen at the furthest remove from realism, namely, in stories about gods. But in the Third Essay "myth" is a much more inclusive term, for abstract structural design is to be found, according to Frye, in both *dianoia,* imagery, or theme, on the one hand, and in *mythos* or narrative, on the other. Myth, in other words, is a structural principle of literature in the widest possible sense.

This is where the real difficulty comes. Myth can mean *mythos,* and *mythos* itself has a variety of meanings. It can refer to a type of archetypal story (comic, romantic, tragic, ironic), or it can refer even more generally to narrative per se. Furthermore, when *mythos* is considered simply as the narrative of a work of literature, we are asked to keep straight *five* separate definitions of *mythos,* depending on the level of criticism we are engaged in: *mythos* as the grammar or order of words (at the literal level), as plot or "argument" (at the descriptive level), as imitation of generic and recurrent action or ritual (at the archetypal level), and as the total conceivable action (at the anagogic level). If even the most attentive of Frye's readers is able always to keep these distinctions clearly in mind, how will he respond to a statement like the following? "In literary criticism myth means ultimately *mythos,* a structural organizing principle of literary form" (AC, 341). At first glance this might seem a reasonable way for Frye to sum up his view of myth (it comes in the Conclusion), since it throws the emphasis on form rather than content; however, when we begin to substitute his definitions of myth and *mythos* into the statement, some strange combinations result. Such a substitution would yield—to take one example—this curious result: A story about a god (myth, sense number one) means ultimately grammar (*mythos* as narrative at the literal level). Or again: The identification of ritual and dream (myth, sense number two) means ultimately the imitation of ritual (*mythos* as narrative at the archetypal level). This is the kind of confusion that can result if we apply literally what Frye says. Usually, of course, the context comes to our aid. But the serious question remains whether or not the word "myth" can function properly when used in so many ways. Certainly precision of meaning tends to dissipate in the proliferation of definitions he sets forth, and we have not even considered the additional meanings which accumulate around it, like myth as a particular dramatic kind, discussed in the Fourth Essay;[38] or myth as a synonym for attitude, belief, and ideology—the kind of usage we find in an expression like "myth of concern."

There are two problems then with saying "myth means ultimately *mythos.*" First, the statement tends to obliterate the distinction between them, a distinction Frye has exerted no little effort to establish. Second, the statement can mean so many different things that its value as a definition is lost. Frye remarks in the Tentative Conclusion that the term myth obviously does have "different meanings in different subjects," but, he suggests, in literary criticism it should have one meaning (AC, 341). It is not clear, however, that he establishes finally what this one definition is. Too often his use of the word "myth" relies on innuendo, vague association, and multiple reference.

A similar kind of confusion sometimes surrounds Frye's use of the word "archetype." In his Glossary to the *Anatomy* it is defined as "a symbol, usually an image, which recurs often enough in literature to be recognizable as an element of one's literary experience as a whole" (AC, 365). Elsewhere he remarks that "the symbol in [the mythical] phase is the communicable unit, to which I give the name archetype: that is, a typical or recurring image. I mean by an archetype a symbol which connects one poem with another and thereby helps to unify and integrate our literary experience" (AC, 99). Does this broad definition, however, do justice to the special and value-laden import which Frye really wants his term to carry? "If archetypes do connect one poem with another," says John Holloway, "it's not a *mere* connection, it's a connection of some especially deep and significant kind."[39] Despite Frye's disclaimers about value judgments, one has the feeling that he would want to separate archetypes from the thousands of other things, many of which would be trifling, which connect one poem with another. But Frye's definition does not permit this distinction. It is a definition which continues to expand outward. Archetype is a term, once again, possessing multiple reference: "By an archetype I mean," he says in an essay on Blake, "an element in a work of literature, whether a character, an image, a narrative formula, or an idea, which can be assimilated to a larger unifying category."[40] But if an archetype can be a narrative formula, what are we to make of Frye's statement that the tradition of Ulysses "is an archetype in *the only sense* in which the literary critic needs the term: a *theme* which carries centuries of literary development with it, and yet in each age is as fresh as ever, and as infinitely suggestive of new modes of treatment"?[41]

And what sense are we to make of the following statement? "If archetypes are communicable symbols, and there is a center of archetypes, we should expect to find, at that center, a group of universal symbols. . . . I mean that some symbols are images of things common to all men, and therefore have a communicable power which is potentially unlimited. Such symbols include those of food and drink, of the quest or journey, of light and darkness, and of sexual fulfillment" (AC, 118). Surely this definition embraces too much. As John Holloway says, "There are hundreds of things (like toenails, sweat-glands, sensations of discomfort from very bright lights) which are common to all men. Most of them clearly have nothing whatever to do with central archetypes or universal symbols."[42] Now obviously Frye does not conceive of such things as archetypes, but his definition is not precise enough to exclude them. Even his observation that all men understand what food and drink are hardly defines and clearly does not delimit the nature of an archetype. "Noises, noses, and excretion," remarks Robert M. Adams, "are universal too."[43]

These are the kinds of semantic problems we find throughout Frye's work. In many cases he is simply not clear about the meaning of the terms he takes to be centrally important. It is not difficult to say what he means *generally* by most of his terms, but it is often exceedingly difficult to say what he means *specifically*. The acceptance of his claim, for example, that the anagogic level of both literature and criticism does in fact exist is contingent on his defining what anagogy means. But in attempting to do so, he cannot point to any kind of evidence in the nature of things which will make anagogy a universally meaningful concept. What he does do, as I have attempted to show, is to rely on a visionary language derived from the most intense moments of poetic insight. To be sure, Frye conceives of the imaginative world as a projection of man's desire, which is something rooted in the ordinary world. But the literal-minded critic is apt to respond that such expressions as the "human form divine" are meaningful only to those initiates who are already on Frye's wavelength, those who can identify with his ideal, apocalyptic reality.

This is to say that the issues of meaning and doctrine are closely aligned. When Walter Sutton protests that Frye's discussion of the symbol as monad merges into meaningless nonsense, he appears to be objecting not merely to the fuzzy definition of the doctrine but also to the doctrine itself.[44] For him the problem of meaning, however shored up by quotations from Blake and Hooker, is likely to remain a problem simply because he cannot assent to the doctrine. His position is like that of Thomas Vance, who suggests that Frye's "more imaginative flights are to be taken with a sprinkling of salt."[45] Or take this comment by Robert M. Adams:

> What does it mean to say that "Nature is now inside the mind of an infinite man who builds his cities out of the Milky Way" [AC, 119]? As an explanation of literature, this . . . seems to demand some pretty elaborate explanations of its own. I do not, by any means, think it wrong to believe in "the whole of nature as the content of an infinite and eternal living body which, if not human, is closer to being human than to being inanimate" [AC, 119]; but I think it wrong to make such a belief prerequisite to the understanding of literature. My own conviction is that the world rests on the back of a very large tortoise.[46]

Adams is saying three things: (1) he doesn't know what Frye's doctrine of anagogy means (a semantic issue); (2) he wouldn't believe it if he did know (a metaphysical issue); and (3) even if he did believe it, it's irrelevant to criticism (a methodological issue). Oppositions such as these we will simply have to let crash head-on, because they spring from a set of interests and assumptions different from Frye's. Some of Frye's doctrines, however, are much more susceptible to analysis than an idea like anagogy, and yet they are no less problematic. His controversial pronouncements on value judgments constitute one such doctrine.

For critics to remark how confused Frye is about literary evaluation has become almost a conditioned response.[47] Some have responded indignantly. John Fraser, in an article devoted ostensibly to Frye's position on value judgments, concludes that he "is probably doing more to bring discredit upon literary studies than anyone else now writing."[48] Most of Fraser's article fails to deal with what Frye has said, and thus he can slide easily into *ad hominem* diatribe by ignoring the issues. This is not to suggest that Frye has a corner on truth. But it is to suggest that Frye will not be refuted by a dogmatist who is content to twist the terms of Frye's discourse to fit his own preconceptions, proceeding thereby to dismiss the former's claims as stupid or irrelevant. The problematic nature of Frye's ideas about value judgments is more fruitfully discussed if he is met on his own terms. I shall make such an attempt by looking at one aspect of his doctrine, namely, what he says about "positive evaluations," discussed in chapter 6. My critique will suggest that there are alternative views to Frye's position.[49]

One possible alternative would be to argue that a study of formal intentions need not rely on matters of taste. What I have in mind is the kind of formal study recommended by R.S. Crane. Crane defines form by way of an analogy between the "synthesizing idea" which underlies the writing of his own essays and the essential cause of poetic structure. What actually directs him in composing an essay, he says, is a shaping cause involving the simultaneous correlation of his subject, his mode of argument or rhetoric, and his purpose. Similarly, he argues, "In the artist's intuition of a form capable of directing whatever he does with his materials in a particular work—is an essential cause of poetic structure, the most decisive, indeed, of all the causes of structure in poetry because it controls in an immediate way the act of construction itself. Without it no poetic whole; with it, a poetic whole of a certain kind and emotional quality."[50] Crane argues that if form in this sense is a necessary first principle for writers, it should be a useful principle in the analysis of their works. The mode of reasoning he recommends is a literal, *a posteriori* kind. And his starting point for analyzing poetic structure is always an individual poem, never poetry in general. We should begin, he urges, with our experience of the poem. Since the poetic effect corresponds to the formal principle of the whole—that intuition which enabled the writer to synthesize his materials—the critic begins with this effect as his hypothesis about the form of the whole and reasons backward to the causes that produced it.

Crane is aware that one can never escape from using general concepts in explaining the causes of poetic forms. But he is convinced that these concepts can be arrived at inductively. Questions about the relationship between the material and formal nature of a poem are, he says, questions of fact, the answers to which "must depend on inquiries of an *a posteriori* type which move inductively (in Aristotle's sense of induction) from the particulars to the universals they embody and from ends or forms thus defined, by hypothetical necessity to the essential conditions of their realization in poetic matter."[51] It is apparent that this process of critical reasoning moves back and forth between the particular and the universal, between the achieved formal nature of a poem and the material nature necessary to achieve the form, or between the final cause and the efficient, formal, and material causes. Crane puts it another way by saying that a critic's hypotheses "both imply and are implied by the observable traits of a work."[52] And he claims that, except analytically, there can be no separation between a hypothesis and its application, "the latter being possible only if the former already exists at least up to a certain point and the former being constantly refined as we proceed with the latter."[53]

Crane sees the process of critical reasoning, applied to mimetic works, as follows: The particulars of a work, things like a series of moral actions, lead us to an assumption about the universal or generic principle which the particulars must embody—say, a tragic or comic form. These universals are hypothetical, specific powers which in our experience of a work are apprehended through the way a writer shapes our expectations and desires. On the other hand, the uniqueness of a given poem's form, as compared to its generic quality, derives from the synthesizing principle, or from what Aristotle calls *dynamis*. Crane, like Aristotle, is most interested in discovering the synthesizing principles of various poetic species.

Now this kind of procedure would seem to offer a reasonably sound basis for making judgments about the "goodness" of a poem (or what Frye calls "positive evaluation"), provided we have done a careful analysis. In other words, we should be able to determine whether or not a given work has fulfilled the necessities demanded by its "intention," using this word in Crane's sense of final cause. Crane, in fact, says that "a kind of judgment of value will . . . emerge in the very process of our analysis: if a writer has indeed done, somehow, all the essential things he would need to do on the assumption that he is actually writing the kind of work we have defined [in our description of the work's form], then to that extent the work is good or at least not artistically bad."[54] This, we might say, is the criterion of the necessary. A second standard is the criterion of the possible. Here the question becomes, in Crane's words, "What is it that the writer might have done, over and above the minimum requirements of his task, which he has not done, or what is it we have not expected him to do which he has yet triumphantly accomplished?"[55] Answers to these questions will, of course, depend on relative rather than absolute criteria, since they would be different for each literary work. And such criteria would not be infallible, since human reason can err. But they need not depend on matters of social, moral, or political taste.

How might Frye respond to this proposal? His method, of course, is ill-equipped to handle the kind of formal analysis Crane recommends. Moreover, he is not really interested in looking at specific literary works in this way. He would probably reject all talk of intention and affective response, saying that one is external to the critic's true function and that the other has to do with direct experience rather than knowledge. In fact, the absolute disjunction between knowledge and taste Frye makes in the Polemical Introduction would seem to rule out the kind of judgment I am suggesting: he does clearly equate positive evaluations—those that treat the goodness of a poem—with taste, and taste is always suspect. But perhaps Frye's disjunction is too absolute, since there does seem to be at least one method which can give us knowledge about how well literary works are made.[56]

A second alternative might begin by asking what kind of reasons can be given for the adequacy of evaluative criteria. Frye rejects all such reasons out of hand, seeing them as rationalizations for subjective preferences. To escape from this relativism we could maintain that some reasons, although neither necessary nor sufficient properties for literary greatness, are valid justifications for the criteria used in making value judgments. This is the position Morris Weitz takes in his book on *Hamlet* criticism.

Weitz argues that "some evaluative utterances can be supported by good reasons," that is, by criteria or principles which cannot be sensibly questioned. "If this contention is correct," he says, "it refutes two opposing views: The traditional one, shared by evaluative critics of Shakespeare and many philosophers, that *all* critical evaluative utterances can be supported by reasons which can be defended by further reasons about necessary or sufficient properties of dramatic greatness; as well as the contemporary view that *no* critical evaluative utterance can be supported by good reasons."[57] Weitz believes that these opposing views misconstrue the nature of evaluative statements by equating them with descriptive utterances. In other words, both views have assumed that value judgments *describe* how a given work meets a criterion which has been posited as the major premise of a deductive argument. If one claims, for example, that *The Sound and the Fury* is a great novel because it possesses a given property, then evaluation, according to Weitz, is essentially a procedure for showing how the novel possesses that property. But Weitz contends that to consider the conclusions of such evaluative arguments as either true or false statements drawn from either true or false premises is to misconceive the nature of critical evaluation:

> "*Hamlet* is great" and "*Hamlet* is great because it has P" are not true (or false) statements. Dramatic greatness is not a property because if it were[,] praising (or condemning) *Hamlet* would be describing *Hamlet*. How, then, can the perennial critical disagreement about whether *Hamlet* is great be resolved by a true answer? *It cannot.* There is nothing in this disagreement—no self-evident intuition, metaphysical essence, or empirical property—about which an answer could be true (or false).[58]

Instead of being a statement of fact, "*Hamlet* is a great drama because it has P" is rather an "expression of praise that is joined by a reason in support of the praise." And Weitz believes that such reasons can be made more or less satisfactory. Several tests for their adequacy he suggests are clarity, concrete application, consistency, unchallengeability. In sum, Weitz believes that good reasons for evaluative criteria can be given, once the truth or falsity of evaluative statements is rejected.

How might this position be an important corrective to Frye's idea of positive evaluations? He gives a number of examples of evaluative criteria based on critical taste. But following Weitz's view, we could consider these criteria not as statements about the necessary or sufficient properties of greatness but rather as reasons for expressions of praise. Whether we could convince Frye of our reasons is open to question. But at least we would not get caught up in the dilemma of empirically proving premises about greatness, because we would not have reduced, as Frye implicitly does, all statements to the same level. Statements of praise, he says, are either infallible or else they are meaningless. This seems to be too simple a disjunction and too easy an escape from questions which many critics feel are worth asking. It is too simple a disjunction because it does not account for the wide variety of reasons which can be given for how well a poem is made. It is too easy an escape because it equates all reasons for poetic greatness with subjective taste.

This is not intended to be a refutation of Frye's position. I have not even confronted some of the central claims about knowledge and value which he makes and which were documented in chapter 5. My aim has been simply to suggest that some aspects of Frye's thought—I have called this one doctrinal—are limited. The limitations pertain both to his assumptions and to the conclusions he draws from them. His doctrine of "positive evaluation" is problematic since reasonable alternative solutions can be proposed.[59]

Frye's method of argument constitutes a third problematic area. Sometimes his arguments progress by what can only be taken as arbitrary assertion. Since we have considered his book on Milton, let us turn to it for several examples. We recall that in the first chapter of that book Frye divides *Paradise Lost* into a sequence of twelve sections, the first four of which represent the four main events in Raphael's speech and the last four, the main events in Michael's (RE, 18–19). Now some readers of Milton would be concerned to know whether he actually used, intentionally or not, this twelvefold symmetrical pattern. In his first reference to the duodecimal schema, Frye says, in anticipation of some readers' objections, "we shall try to suggest in a moment that the association of Milton's epic with this sacred and zodiacal number may be less arbitrary than it looks" (RE, 13). But when he gets to the point of showing that it *is* less than arbitrary, his argument depends more on assertion than on demonstration. The skeptical reader will require more evidence than Frye provides. Consider this statement: "Some of the [twelve] divisions take up several books and others only a few lines, but that is of no importance. Most of the shorter ones are from the Bible, and Milton expected his reader to be able to give them their due importance" (RE, 18). But if Milton did depend upon the symmetrical model to the degree Frye suggests, it is certainly not clear why it is "of no importance" that he devotes several books to some phases and only several lines to others. How are we to know that what Milton presents in a few lines is structurally as important as what he presents in several books? Frye says that Milton *expects* us to see the importance. If so, it seems that this expectation would appear somewhere, either internally or externally. Some Miltonists think that it appears nowhere, that *Paradise Lost* simply does not possess the kind of formal symmetry Frye attributes to it.[60] Frye assumes that poetic thinking is by definition schematic. But this assumption, coupled with the fact that epics have traditionally been divided into twelve parts, provides little reason for Frye's own outline. To be convincing, he needs more particular evidence than he provides.

Part of his argument for the symmetrical design depends on our seeing the events of Raphael's speech as corresponding in reverse order to those of Michael's. This is by no means a clinching argument, but it would appear to be a more than accidental kind of correspondence. A close inspection of Frye's twelve phases (RE, 20–21), however, will show that they are not in reverse order after all. For Milton's plan to be symmetrical, phase 8 should parallel phase 3 rather than phase 4, and 9 should parallel 4 rather than 3 (see p. 163 above). Frye qualifies this by saying that the two groups are "roughly" in reverse order. But if half of the events do not fit the pattern, they cannot be in reverse order, roughly or otherwise. It is this kind of argument which leads us to suspect that Frye's symmetrical scheme is his own creation, imposed upon rather than derived from *Paradise Lost*. The pattern, to be sure, is ingeniously constructed, and no one, after having read Frye's book, is likely to read Milton again without this pattern influencing the way he sees the poem. Undoubtedly it can provide insights. But Frye does not demonstrate that Milton intended such a pattern, which is a crucial point in interpretation. We must conclude, then, that if the principles of criticism do, as Frye claims, shape themselves out of the literature we read, this example is not an adequate demonstration of the claim.

If the method of Frye's argument proceeds sometimes by assertion, at other times it progresses by analogy. In fact, there is no single methodological principle so important in Frye's work as analogical association. We have already seen dozens of instances of the method at work. The method itself is a logical consequence of one of Frye's chief aims, the relating of literature to other literature. The discovery of similarities permeates everything he has written simply because, we might say, of the way his mind operates. It is a precritical aspect of his method.

Richard McKeon draws a useful distinction between literal and analogical methods. Philosophical critics like Aristotle, Bacon, and Horace, while basing their views of art on different philosophic principles, nevertheless agree methodologically, according to McKeon, since they are concerned to discover the peculiar causes of art viewed as a human product. Plato, Kant, and Tolstoy, on the other hand, agree methodologically insofar as they seek their principles in something which conditions all things (Plato), or all imaginations (Kant), or all actions (Tolstoy). They aim not to isolate poetry in its essential nature but to analogize it to something else.[61] Despite some obvious differences between Frye and this latter group of critics, we can include him in their company on two counts. He is concerned ultimately with the imagination, something outside the specifically human product of art. He is not concerned with a causal analysis which defines the unique qualities and character of individual works of art. In these respects he is an analogical, rather than a literal, critic.

The analogical method manifests itself in Frye's system in two chief ways. One, he analogizes literature to other literature by way of myth and archetype, convention and genre. Two, the categories he uses to do this are frequently themselves derived by analogy. As a method of criticism, analogy itself is "immune to theoretical questioning," to use Crane's phrase again. We cannot fault Plato for not having used a literal method, nor Aristotle for not having used an analogical one. But the application of the method is not immune to such questioning. We can require of a critic that his method be sound, sensible, tactfully applied, consistent with commonsense apprehension, and the like. And it is in this respect that Frye's analogizing does not always measure up to what we can rightfully require of critical theory. Let us take three examples to illustrate how the method can sometimes issue in arbitrary and facile principles.

In the Second Essay Frye devotes a number of pages to expounding what the meaning (or *dianoia*) and the narrative (or *mythos*) are for each of his phases of symbolism. These broad concepts shape his discussion at a number of points, but the way he uses them here is to analogize them to a dialectical pair of opposites for each symbolic level. At the literal level, for example, he understands *mythos* to be the rhythm or movement of words and *dianoia* to be the structural unity formed by a pattern of words. At the descriptive level *mythos* is the imitation of real events and *dianoia* the imitation of objects or propositions—and so on, through each of the five phases. In each case there is a broad analogy established, on the one hand, between *mythos* and some aspect of time, movement, or recurrence, and on the other hand, between *dianoia* and some aspect of space, stasis, or simultaneity.

A close look at these analogies will reveal the kinds of problems they create. In the fourth phase Frye's dialectical opposites are recurrence and desire, and ritual and myth. The question is, how do these terms derive from *mythos* and *dianoia*? Here is the passage where the analogical leap takes place: "The narrative aspect of literature is a recurrent act of symbolic communication: in other words a ritual. . . . [And] the significant content is the conflict of desire and reality which has for its passage the work of the dream. Ritual and dream, therefore, are the narrative [*mythos*] and significant content [*dianoia*] respectively of literature in its archetypal aspect," that is, in the fourth phase of symbolism (AC, 104–5). What lies behind the "therefore" in this last sentence? That ritual is the *mythos* of the archetypal phase follows only because Frye defines ritual as a recurrent act of symbolic communication. That is, the analogy between narrative and ritual—or what they have in common—is the quality of recurrence. In a vague way, this quality is present in Frye's initial definition of narrative (in the literal phase) as rhythm, the recurring movement of words. Now it is clear that Frye wants to maintain "recurrence" as a principle of narrative throughout his analysis of each of the phases. But it disappears altogether in his discussion of the formal phase, where the typical event and the typical precept are his dialectical opposites. Thus, to keep his categories consistent, he must find a way of introducing it into the formal phase, for then he can make an easy transition to the category of ritual. And he does this simply by asserting that in "the exemplary event there is an element of recurrence" (AC, 104). Similarly, he moves from the precept of the formal phase to the dream of the mythical phase, simply by asserting that there is a strong element of desire associated with precept.[62]

Stating these relations in a simpler form, we get the following kinds of argument. Recurrence is related to event; the typical event is the *mythos* of formal criticism. Recurrence is related to ritual; ritual is the *mythos* of archetypal criticism. Or to take the second series of analogies: Desire is related to precept; the typical precept is the *dianoia* of formal criticism. Desire is related to dream; dream is the *dianoia* of archetypal criticism.

Now in all of this the analogies are tenuous and somewhat arbitrary. It is perhaps true that there is an element of recurrence in the exemplary event, insofar as we desire it to be repeated again and again. But there are many aspects of a typical event which are not exemplary; it appears, then, that Frye arbitrarily arrives at recurrence as the principle for defining the *mythos* of the formal phase. Or take the second example, where the middle term is desire. In what way is desire related to precept? It is related only by associating precept with dream and by then associating dream with desire. But there are countless other aspects of desire and countless other mediating categories which one could select as a middle term. What if we wanted to argue, for example, that the *dianoia* of the mythical phase is a moral imperative of some sort? Within Frye's analogical framework the solution would be simply to assert that in the precept there is a strong element of the commandment or the law; and that the archetypal content in this phase is therefore always morally significant. Or what if Frye were a Freudian? It would be easy for him to assert that poetic content always contains a latent expression of sexual desire or aversion and that archetypal *dianoia* is therefore always sexually significant.

John Holloway remarks that the word "recurrence" functions like a grappling hook. "With it," he says, "Mr Frye straightway hooks the 'cyclical process' of nature: sun and moon and all. Then he flips his hook deftly back again, and catches art as ritual. It's brilliant in a way, and exciting, but—laying the foundations for criticism as a science? It's got nothing to do with *that*."[63] This is precisely the point. Frye's method of analogy shows only the possible, rather than the necessary, relations among things. His categories in this case are not a logical inference from his principles but a consequence of what he has already determined to find, things like dream and ritual. While the complex relations he establishes are creative and ingenious, the literal-minded critic will see them as too facile, for what Frye does is first to decide *a priori* what his categories for the third and fourth phases are going to be, and then to search for a middle term which will relate them to his principles of *mythos* and *dianoia*. This means, of course, that the content of words like "narrative" and "meaning" constantly changes, which is one of the reasons it is so difficult sometimes to follow the intricacies of Frye's arguments. The difficulty can be traced back to the kind of freewheeling analogical process just outlined.

Because the method of analogy does not sharply differentiate among things, it also leads to problems when Frye actually begins to classify literary works. The categorizing of the First Essay has been criticized on the grounds that it tells us very little about individual poetic species and provides no easy way for preventing (say) a given novel from falling into a number of different categories.[64] Since the orientation of the First Essay is "ethical" rather than "specific," this criticism is largely irrelevant to Frye's purpose: he is classifying character types and relationships, not novels. But the critique does point up a difficulty regarding the descriptive value of the categories, for it *is* true that tragic fictional characters can—and in Frye's treatment do— find their way into more than one mode. Hardy's Tess, for example, is seen by Frye both as a *pharmakos* of tragic irony and as a heroine of low-mimetic tragedy (AC, 38, 41). Tess can serve two roles, of course, because she is *similar* in some respects to one kind of mode and similar in some respects to another. The problem here is not so much that a given hero cannot be characterized by attributes belonging to two different modes. The problem relates rather to Frye's method of definition, which relies heavily on specific examples. If the example of Tess is used to help *define* a given mode, the fact that she is an "ethical" type for two of the modes does less than adequate service as a means for differentiating them. It is a difficulty which can be traced back to Frye's penchant for locating similarities.

A final example of the arbitrariness which can result from this method comes from that section of the Fourth Essay which treats the thematic forms of the lyric. I have provided a fairly complete account of this section already, along with a diagram of the chief lyric forms or conventions Frye is able to locate; and my critique of this section is implicit in what I have already said, especially in the analysis of the method he uses to arrive at the cycle of forms. In this sequence a

Hopkins-type lyric is followed by the public religious lyric, the thing they have in common being their religious content. This latter form is related to the hymn, which, because it is a lyric of praise, is related in turn to the panegyric. Panegyrics, subsequently, are related to poems of community, like patriotic verse, because they both invite the reader to gaze at "something else"—and so on around the cycle, through about two dozen different forms. This kind of schema clearly rests on analogy, but it is somewhat arbitrary since the *basis* of similarity changes with each succeeding form. If a bioligist classifying forms of animal life were to follow the same procedure, he would be able to rationalize a schema like the following: Men are related to birds because they both have eyes; birds are related to bats because they both fly; bats are similar to giraffes because they are both warm-blooded; and so on.[65] This is perhaps too much of a caricature of Frye's method, but it does illustrate how, with only a little ingenuity, one can establish two cardinal points and locate any number of forms between them on the basis of analogies. The only rule to be followed is that the basis of comparison can never remain constant.

The point is that Frye's sequence of lyric forms represents no necessary schema of classification. To be sure, it follows in a general way from his cyclical model and his selection of four cardinal points. It is likewise dependent on his innocence-experience and his *melos-opsis* dichotomies and on his fourfold division of the pregeneric literary elements. But if one were to start with four different cardinal points he would arrive at an altogether different sequence. And even if he were to start with the same points, there are no principles which would guarantee his arriving at the same sequence of conventions as Frye. This is not to deny that Frye's categories can be usefully applied to illuminate the lyric. It is rather to suggest that his particular lyric conventions are not necessary inferences from his principles. In this case there is a certain arbitrariness in the method of analogy which works against the rational and systematic theory he wants to establish.

My discussion has been focusing on several aspects of Frye's thought which are problematic. He himself has always insisted on critics being coherent and consistent; and the study of the humanities in general, he says, requires "accuracy of statement, objectivity and dispassionate weighing of evidence, including the weighing of negative evidence" (SS, 42). If Frye does not always completely satisfy these demands, neither does any other critic who has dared to ask so many large questions about so much. But while Frye's criticism does raise legitimate problems, pointing them out and suggesting alternative solutions does not constitute a refutation of his views. Genuine critical theories cannot be refuted anyway, in the sense of being proven wrong.

They may be dismissed, ignored, questioned, and rejected, but not refuted. Aristotle does not prove Plato wrong; nor Kant, Aristotle—though the critic can, I think, provide good reasons for preferring one system over another.

Instrumental and Final Values in Frye's Criticism

The spirit in which Frye's work should be assessed is suggested in his own "Letter to the English Institute," written on the occasion of the conference devoted to his work.

> I should want the discussion, in particular, to be as uninhibited as possible. . . . I have no itch to demonstrate that my views are "right" and that those who disagree with me are "wrong." . . . Nor do I wish to correct others for "misunderstanding my position": I dislike and distrust what is generally implied by the word "position." Language is the dwelling-house of being, according to Heidegger, but no writer who is not completely paranoid wants his house to be either a fortress or a prison.[66]

This is more than a politeness demanded by the occasion, for in the house that Frye has built there is indeed room for all manner of critical views. I have spoken of his reconciliatory aim, an aim which assumes that critical systems are judged neither right nor wrong but complementary. They interpenetrate, to use a spatial metaphor from the letter just quoted. "Literature itself is not a field of conflicting arguments," he says, "but of interpenetrating visions. I suspect that this is true even of philosophy, where the place of argument seems more functional. The irrefutable philosopher is not the one who cannot be refuted, but the one who is still there after he has been refuted."[67]

What Frye says here about literature and philosophy can be applied to criticism as well. His own work "is still there" after all the objections have been raised. The farther back from the whole of his work we stand, the less important these objections tend to become. Standing back also reveals the continuous vision that informs everything that Frye has written. "The decline in the admiration for continuity," he remarks, "is one of the most striking differences between the Romantic and the modern feeling" (MC, 65), and in one of the few places where he reflects on the sources and development of his intellectual life, he says that "the sense of continuity in memory" was necessary for the growth of his own creative and critical work. Like his preceptor Blake, Frye observes, he unconsciously arranged his life to be without incident, adding that "no biographer could possibly take the smallest interest in me" (SM, 16). While some future biographer might look upon Frye's life differently, no one can dispute the sense of continuity that pervades his work. It is especially apparent in what he has written since *Fearful Symmetry*. But even in his earliest essays, which were on music, opera, ballet, and film, we discover the roots of many ideas which were to be developed in the *Anatomy* and in the fifteen books which followed.

In his first published essay Frye refers to the opposition between realism and convention, the two poles which were to figure importantly in many of his later mental diagrams. He speaks here also of the *mythological* framework of Wagner, thus using the word which points toward what was to become a central interest.[68] In his second published work we discover in a discussion of music—the structural principles of which were to provide some of Frye's chief metaphors for explaining literary structure—an analysis of melody and harmony, rhythm and pattern. Tucked away here unobtrusively, then, are the two principles which, translated into *mythos* and *dianoia* almost twenty years later, were to stand as the backbone of the *Anatomy*.[69] Frye's first piece of literary criticism was a defense of Spengler against the attacks of Wyndham Lewis.[70] The formative influence of Spengler on Frye's thought began early, and, as if imitating the rhythm of Spengler's vision itself, he has returned to *The Decline of the West* at least once each decade since the publication of this defense. Many such evidences of continuity are apparent when we look at Frye's work as a whole, placing the essays of the 1930s and 40s alongside his most recent work and considering the issues and themes which have occupied him over the years.

The continuous vision gives Frye's work a continuous form, stretching before us like those encyclopaedic works which have captured his own imagination. In *A Map of Misreading* Harold Bloom remarks that Frye's myths of freedom and concern are a Low Church version of Eliot's Anglo-Catholic myth of tradition and the individual talent, but that such an understanding of the relation of the individual to tradition is a fiction. Bloom says:

> This fiction is a noble idealization, and as a lie against time will go the way of every noble idealization. Such positive thinking served many purposes in the sixties, when continuities, of any kind, badly required to be summoned, even if they did not come to our call. Wherever we are bound, our dialectical development now seems invested in the interplay of repetition and discontinuity, and needs a very different sense of what our stance is in regard to literary tradition.[71]

This remark contains more than a hint of the anxiety of influence. But regardless of whether one agrees with Bloom's projection about what our development "seems" to involve, it is mistaken to suggest that Frye has failed to observe the "interplay between repetition and discontinuity." In words that could stand as a motto for theories of misprision, he says that "the recreating of the literary tradition often has to proceed . . . through a process of absorption followed by misunderstanding."[72] Even if Frye's ultimate allegiances are to a continuous intellectual and imaginative universe, to order rather than chaos, to romance rather than irony, he cannot be accused of having turned his back upon the discontinuities in either literature or life. We should not let Bloom's remark deceive us into thinking that in the 1960s Frye began suddenly to summon continuities as a bulwark against the changing social order. The central principles in Frye's critical universe have remained constant over the years. Reflecting on his own work since the mid-fifties, he says that it

> has assumed the shape of what Professor Jerome Bruner would call a spiral curriculum, circling around the same issues, though trying to keep them open-ended. . . . Emerson, as we know, deprecated what he called a foolish consistency, but there is always one form of consistency which is not foolish, and that is continuity. With some people continuity takes a revolutionary and metaphoric direction: a philosopher may repudiate everything he has written up to a certain time and start afresh. Even so, I doubt if he can start afresh until he discovers the real point of contact with his earlier work. With me, continuity has taken a more gradual direction, not because I insist that everything I have said earlier, in *Anatomy of Criticism* or elsewhere, must be "right," but because the principles I have already formulated are still working as heuristic assumptions, and they are the only ones available to me. (SM, 100–101)

The gradual direction of Frye's continuity can best be observed if we distance ourselves from the local complaint and the particular debatable issue.[73] From this perspective we can turn back to the precritical issue raised at the beginning of this chapter, which has to do with Frye's conception of criticism as a whole. My final assessment is made from this perspective. It rests upon three particular claims. First, Frye's work is of practical value, a system of terms and doctrines and a method which can be used to answer one kind of critical question. Second, his criticism is a creative and aesthetic achievement in itself: it has final as well as instrumental value. And third, his writings taken together form what might be called a metacriticism, reaching far beyond literature itself in an effort to account for and defend all the products of human culture. In this respect Frye provides a meaningful apology for the humanities and a way of doing criticism on a grand scale.

Practical Value To say that Frye's criticism is practically valuable is to say that the theory can be applied to good advantage in interpreting literature. But we must recognize what his system can and cannot do. It is clearly of limited value in helping to determine all the formal relations which combine to produce *particular* literary works. He offers guidance in rhetorical analysis only at the median level of generality. In discussing a comic work, for example, the total form of comic action is more important for him than whether or not a given work manifests every phase of the total form. Thus his concern is not to determine what makes an individual comedy a special kind of poetic whole but to see how it relates both to other comedies and to an ideal comic form. He characteristically moves away from, rather than into, the literary work, and thus he emphasizes the thematic, narrative, and archetypal similarities among literary works rather than the explication of single texts. The question is not whether one approach is better than the other. They are simply different. And for his own kind of critical study Frye has provided a powerful set of analytical tools. The evidence for this is not only his own work but the growing number of critics who have found his general approach, his special categories, and his method of doing criticism genuinely useful. As Meyer Abrams puts it:

> The test of the validity of a theory is what it proves capable of doing when it is put to work. And each good (that is, serviceable) theory, as the history of critical theory amply demonstrates, is capable of providing insights into hitherto overlooked or neglected features and structural relations of works of art, of grouping works of art in new and interesting ways, and also of revealing new distinctions and relations between things that (from its special point of view) are art and things that are not art.[74]

Frye's critical theory is valid on all three counts.

Those who have found Frye's work to be the New Criticism writ large, while correctly discovering some important influences, have committed, I think, the error of misplaced emphasis.[75] My own view is that Frye will be seen historically as having moved far beyond the New Critical assumptions because he is primarily interested in asking questions different from those of the New Critics. There is value in this very fact, insofar as Frye's universalism has helped to deflect criticism from a myopic organicism to a wider view of literature. It is frequently said that the New Criticism, for all its contributions to formal analysis, reduced criticism to explication or at least tended to see close analysis as the preeminent critical task. Despite a degree of caricature in this judgment, it is true, nevertheless, that Frye has helped us to see that there are other ways of talking meaningfully about literature. This is to say not only that a pluralism of critical methods should prevail but also that Frye's work, as a healthy corrective to the New Critical emphasis, helps insure that a pluralism will prevail.

Pluralism is not the same thing as Frye's vision of complementary critical methods. He talks too often about the archetypal approach as the one way for breaking down barriers among critics and about a syncretism of interpenetrating views for us to label him a critical pluralist. But he has attacked provincialism on many fronts and thus has helped to extend the range of critical questions that may be legitimately asked. At a time when realism and irony dominate the literary world he has reminded us that a complete "iconography of the imagination" must account for myth and romance as well, that comedy is as deserving of critical attention as tragedy. A large measure of Frye's practical value depends finally on his opening up the critical world to questions previously slighted and to literary works frequently neglected and on his providing us with some excellent analytical tools and an extensive glossary of concepts to better accomplish one kind of critical task.

Frye's ideas have had far-ranging consequences. An entire generation of literary critics has found his work to be useful and challenging. The practical effect of his criticism, however, extends far beyond its application to individual literary texts, having influenced the nature of the curriculum and provided models for entire educational programs in the humanities.[76] Moreover, his work has helped determine the kinds of material—both literary and critical—that gets anthologized in textbooks, and his presence has even been felt by a group of Canadian writers, sometimes called the "Northrop Frye school" of poets.[77]

Aesthetic Value   Earlier I suggested that Frye's criticism is an aesthetic achievement. This refers not merely to the wit and stylistic charm that grace his pages but to the fact that his *oeuvre* is an object for aesthetic contemplation itself. The complex conceptual structures we have looked at are as intricately designed and as resonant with allusive meaning as many literary works. George Woodcock remarks that *Anatomy of Criticism* is

> a great and intricate edifice of theory and myth whose true purpose is its own existence; it has the same ultimate effect as buildings like the Angkor Wat or the Sainte Chapelle, which were built to exemplify religious truths and which survive, when

their message is forgotten or derided, as objects whose sole meaning to modern man lies in their beauty.... [Frye] has exemplified more effectively than Wilde himself the latter's argument that criticism is primarily a creative process, leaving its masterpieces to impress and move by their skill and grandeur long after their subjects have ceased to interest us.[78]

Woodcock dismisses too easily the practical value which a whole generation of critics and teachers have found in Frye's work, and he overstates his case by using such expressions as *true* purpose and *sole* meaning.[79] But he is surely correct in calling attention to the creative genius in Frye, a genius we associate more closely with artistic accomplishment than with discursive judgment.

It is significant that Frye labels one of his forms of prose fiction the "anatomy." This extroverted, intellectual, and often satiric form is born of a thematic interest, replete with catalogues and diagrams, encyclopaedic in scope and reliant on the free play of intellectual fancy; like its forerunner, the Menippean satire, it "presents us with a vision of the world in terms of a single intellectual pattern" (AC, 310). All of which seems to describe quite well Frye's magnum opus itself, even without his title calling it to our attention. Many readers have felt that the *Anatomy*—with its own oracular rhythm, aphoristic manner, associational logic, with its cyclical and epicyclical designs—is, in part at least, a narrative to be unraveled or a design to be contemplated. "I should call *Anatomy of Criticism*," says Frank Kermode, "a work of sixth-phase Symbolism.... Certainly it would be reasonable to treat this as a work of criticism that has turned into literature.... As literature it has, if I may be permitted to say so, great value."[80] Other readers have made similar claims. Graham Hough maintains that the *Anatomy* is not so much a treatise providing us with usable critical tools as it is a work of literature in its own right: "Frye has written his own compendious *Golden Bough*.... It is itself poetry." Harry Levin sees the *Anatomy* as a book we may set on our shelves beside Yeats's *A Vision*. And René Wellek remarks that Frye's work is "an elaborate fiction."[81] While each of these readers commits the fallacy of misplaced emphasis (reducing Frye's work to something less than it is), there is nevertheless a strong aesthetic interest that radiates from all his writing.

The clearest expression of this interest is in the schematic structures Frye erects and upon which he builds his elaborate taxonomies. He says that criticism must be schematic because the nature of poetic thinking itself is schematic.[82] Whether the patterns Frye observes—his five modes of fiction and five levels of symbolism, his four *mythoi* and twenty-four phases, and so on—actually exist in literature or whether they exist in the mind of their beholder is, as we have seen, not an easy question to answer. But let us seek a tentative solution by asking another question: What is the purpose of classification anyway?

Attempts at a taxonomy of literature would seem to be pointless if the aim is merely to attach labels, but the desire to know and to name literary differences and similarities is another matter. Frye's schematic taxonomy is in part a method for ordering recognized doctrines, the best example of which is the Second Essay. But he also sees classification as a necessary propaedeutic for inquiry. It is a method for isolating a subject of discussion so that inquiry may proceed. Moreover, there is in Frye's taxonomies a peculiarly inventive quality which seems to spring from a rage for order that is aesthetically rather than instrumentally motivated. The words of a scientist may help us make the point. Claude Lévi-Strauss quotes a biological taxonomist as saying:

> Scientists do tolerate uncertainty and frustration, because they must. The one thing they do not and must not tolerate is disorder. The whole aim of theoretical science is to carry to the highest possible and conscious degree the perceptual reduction of chaos that began in so lowly and (in all probability) unconscious a way with the origin of life. In specific instances it can well be questioned whether the order so achieved is an objective characteristic of the phenomena or is an artifact constructed by the scientist. That question comes up time and again in animal taxonomy. . . . Nevertheless, the most basic postulate of science is that nature itself is orderly. . . . All theoretical science is ordering and, if systematics is equated with ordering, then systematics is synonymous with theoretical science. . . . Taxonomy, which is ordering par excellence, has eminent aesthetic value.[83]

"Given this," concludes Lévi-Strauss, "it seems less surprising that the aesthetic sense can by itself open the way to taxonomy and even anticipate some of its results."[84]

There is a good deal of evidence that Frye's aesthetic sense does anticipate his own results. In fact, some of his categories seem to spring directly from an urge to construct an ordered artifact. Why are there four aspects to his central unifying myth (*agon, pathos, sparagmos,* and *anagnorisis*)? Partially, at least, because there are four *mythoi* by prior definition, and Frye's sense of order demands that they be made to correspond. Why are there six phases for each *mythos*? Because Frye says he recognizes them (AC, 177). Or why are there four forms of prose fiction? Because Frye's sense of order seems to require four: after defining three of the forms on the basis of the extroverted-introverted and the personal-intellectual dichotomies, he says "our next step is evidently to discover a fourth form of fiction which is extroverted and intellectual" (AC, 308). That this is Frye's "next step" is at least partially a result of his compulsion for symmetrically ordering his categories.

In fact, sometimes Frye seems to offer literature as an explanation for his categories rather than vice versa: literary works become exemplary explanations for the schema itself. William Righter believes that Frye's work

> turns away from the traditional Anglo-Saxon commitment to interpretation. It has been an almost unchallenged presupposition of our critical thought that criticism is some sort of second-order language which comments on, explicates, or explains something quite distinct from itself: a literary work which is assumed to be an imaginative creation of the first order. Frye violates this presupposition in two important ways. First, in spite of individual insights of the greatest interest he is hardly concerned, especially in the *Anatomy,* with particular literary works and their interpretation. He almost reverses the process. . . . The literary work acts as the "explanation" of a symbolic scheme, making the critical work the first order language on which the example acts as a commentary. . . . Secondly, his lack of concern with particular literary works and his breadth of concern with literature as a whole have created his own intensely personal form of metacritical language, perhaps of a third order, working at a higher level of abstraction than we normally expect of critical thought.[85]

Righter is correct, I think, in underlining the impression we often have that Frye's critical order itself is an imaginative construct which needs no justification other than its own existence. Perhaps this should not be surprising, considering the fact that Frye practically equates poetry and criticism at the anagogic level. In *Fearful Symmetry* Blake as poet and Frye as critic tend to merge into one: it is often difficult to determine whether we have Blake's ideas, or Blake as interpreted by Frye, or simply Frye's ideas themselves. It is almost as if the critic has become artist, forging his own myths out of the uncreated conscience of his race.

In fact, because Frye sees criticism as creative, he has frequently emphasized the necessity of breaking down the barriers that separate the artist from the critic. He says that he learned from E.J. Pratt—his teacher and Canada's most important English-language poet—"to become more detached from the romantic mystique that opposes creative writers to critical ones" (SM, 24). The same note is sounded on both the first and last pages of the *Anatomy*:

The conception of the critic as a parasite or artist *manqué* is still very popular, especially among artists. It is sometimes reinforced by a dubious analogy between the creative and the procreative functions, so that we hear about the "impotence" and "dryness" of the critic, of his hatred for genuinely creative people, and so on. The golden age of anti-critical criticism was the latter part of the nineteenth century, but some of its prejudices are still around. (AC, 3)

If I have read the last chapter of *Finnegans Wake* correctly, what happens there is that the dreamer, after spending the night in communion with a vast body of metaphorical identifications, wakens and goes about his business forgetting his dream, like Nebuchadnezzar, failing to use, or even to realize that he can use, the "keys to dreamland." What he fails to do is therefore left for the reader to do, the "ideal reader suffering from an ideal insomnia," as Joyce calls him, in other words the critic. Some such activity as this of reforging the broken links between creation and knowledge, art and science, myth and concept, is what I envisage for criticism. (AC, 354)

Frye does not want us to think of criticism "as somehow sub-creative, in contrast to the 'creative' writing of poems and novels" (SM, 105). His own work illustrates the kind of creativity Wilde describes in "The Critic as Artist."

How are we to respond to this creative aspect of Frye's work, to his intricate schematic designs and his rage for order, what I have labeled an aesthetic achievement? Are we to lament the fact that it obliterates the traditional distinction between the first-order language of poetry and the second-order language of criticism and thus conclude, with William Righter, that Frye's work is a "perversity of invention," an "eccentric episode in literary history"?[86] Are we to look upon Frye with suspicion because the total form of his criticism is a source of pleasure in itself? I think not. There is no good reason why criticism cannot both instruct and delight at the same time.

This is to say that Frye's criticism goes beyond a strict functionalism where practical and utilitarian values reign supreme. Readers like myself who find a special fascination in the creative intellectual structures Frye builds must make their appeal finally to taste and sensibility. But there is no need to apologize for the aesthetic interest or to consider Frye's criticism less valid because of it. Meyer Abrams, though commenting on only a part of Frye's artistry, namely, his extraordinary ability for combining dissimilars and for discovering resemblances in apparently unlike things, makes a sound assessment:

When we are shown that the circumstances of Pope's giddy and glittering Augustan belle have something in common with the ritual assault on a nature goddess, that Henry James's most elaborate and sophisticated social novels share attributes with barbaric folk tales, and that the ritual expulsion of the *pharmakos,* or scapegoat, is manifested alike in Plato's *Apology,* in *The Mikado,* and in the treatment of an umpire in a baseball game, we feel that shock of delighted surprise which is the effect and index of wit. Such criticism is animating; though only so, it should be added, when conducted with Frye's special *brio,* and when it manifests a mind which, like his, is deft, resourceful, and richly stored. An intuitive perception of similars in dissimilars, Aristotle noted, is a sign of genius and cannot be learned from others. Wit-criticism, like poetic wit, is dangerous, because to fall short of the highest is to fail dismally, and to succeed, it must be managed by a Truewit and not by a Witwoud.[87]

The fact that Frye is a Truewit will not provide the ultimate justification for his work. But it does provide one good reason for reading him, especially for those of us who believe that criticism need not exalt instruction at the expense of delight.

There is finally, however, more to be said of Frye's intricate formal structure than simply that it delights: it contains a kind of truth which, although not literally corrigible in the way a philosopher such as Popper would like, is nonetheless real. The structure itself teaches us by explaining. It tells us much about the world of literature that we did not previously know and that we could not have said in any other, more literal form. To say that the formal structure itself has explanatory power is to point back to my first claim, that Frye's criticism has instrumental value. To say that the formal structure embodies one kind of truth is to point forward to my final claim, that Frye's critical theory is similar to metaphysics.

Metacritical Value   Two of Frye's more sensitive readers have, in fact, likened his work to metaphysics.[88] The parallel has broad and ambiguous connotations, but perhaps we can explore it briefly as a final way of suggesting the nature of Frye's achievement. It we define metaphysics as speculative (rather than empirical) inquiry, which asks questions about first principles and the nature of reality, then Frye in some respects is not unlike a metaphysician. He has his own solution to the problem of the One and the Many and to the materialist-idealist dilemma. The most crucial points of his theory depend on premises about the relation between mind and body, space and time, being and becoming. He has developed his own expansive, conceptual universe in which all forms of thought, action, and passion are assigned their appropriate places. In fact, there is a parallel between Frye's work and what Richard McKeon calls the "transcendental" form of metaphysics. This form of metaphysics, says McKeon,

> seeks being and intelligibility in a reality and intelligence which transcends becoming and opinion, [and it] has always had an affinity with the assimilations of dialectic and the construction of systems based on hierarchies of value. The emphasis in transcendental or systematic traditions is appropriately (since "*systema*" means "a whole," "a constitution," "a flock," "a company," "a musical scale") on organic wholes, on syntheses and systems in which wholes and parts mutually influence each other.... We have gained confidence in the discovery and institution of a system of communication and a system of communities by which to order what we say and do, and even what we think and know about the order of things. We hope to transform partial discussions with their divisions, oppositions, and polarizations by providing an originative principle of discussion in what we like to call "dialogue," and to transform partial economic, social, and political communities by reordering them in the inclusive cultural community of mankind. The ordering of the new architectonic principle of culture will be an open-ended use and advancement of freedom and universality.... Systems of culture and communication are generative constructions used to open up meaning and values and to remove limitations to action and insight. Culture and communication depend on ordering principles and systems, and metaphysics has been, and must continue to be, a systematic ordering of parts in wholes holoscopically and systematic constructing of wholes from parts meroscopically.[89]

There is an interesting affinity between McKeon's description of transcendental metaphysics and the whole of Frye's work, with its transcendence of becoming, its dialectical systematizing, its opposition to partial views, its emphasis on inclusiveness and dialogue, and its holoscopic and meroscopic ordering of reality. Frye, of course, is not actually constructing a metaphysical system, but what he does construct has its roots in the grandeur of conception and the subtlety of thought that distinguishes metaphysics.

The great metaphysical systems, like Plato's or Spinoza's, have a range and variety and power which makes them survive critique and "refutation." The eminence of the mind behind them has something to do with this resiliency and vitality. Another reason, as John Holloway remarks, is "that metaphysical systems are often generated from some hitherto neglected great idea of which the writer has taken possession: some radically new point of view from which life may be seen—from which the whole of it, or great parts of it, take on a new appearance from which the lines of force, as it were, may be seen running in new directions."[90] Although Frye is not doing metaphysics, he does invite us to consider a broad point of view from which things take on a new appearance. And behind it all we see a distinguished intellect thinking and writing. With the analogy in mind, we might say that Frye constructs a "metacritical" universe.

It is a universe in which art stands at the center, flanked by history, action, and event on one side and by philosophy, thought, and idea on the other. Art for Frye is the preeminent creation of man because it figures forth the imaginative world most fully and most obviously, and the imaginative world is the locus of Frye's ultimate values. But criticism is not restricted merely to literature and the arts. "Is it true," Frye asks, "that the verbal structures of psychology, anthropology, theology, history, law, and everything else built out of words have been informed or constructed by the same kind of myths and metaphors that we find, in their original hypothetical form, in literature?" (AC, 352). And his answer is—indirectly in the *Anatomy* and directly in much of his later work—that it *is* true. This is the hypothesis upon which Frye builds his theory of culture and which permits him, because criticism is the unifying principle of culture, to practice his craft upon such a grand scale. One of Frye's ardent apologists over the years, E.W. Mandel, argues that the relationship of criticism to culture is the "informing principle" of Frye's work.[91] The more Frye writes, the more accurate Mandel's claim seems to be. Certainly a part of Frye's power as a critic derives from the catholicity of perspective which permits him to apply to the nonliterary aspects of culture the principles he has learned from literature. Similarly, both fictional and nonfictional discourse are subjected to his centrifugal gaze, because they are both forms of imaginative projection. The keystone of Frye's metacriticism, we keep discovering, is his doctrine of the imagination.

In *The Secular Scripture* Frye remarks that "not all of us will be satisfied with calling the central part of our mythological inheritance a revelation from God, and, though each chapter in this book closes on much the same cadence, I cannot claim to have found a more acceptable formulation" (SeS, 60). The context of this observation is still another of Frye's many efforts to name the imagination's sense of otherness, but what is perhaps most revealing about the passage is the dependent clause tucked away in the middle. To speak of the cadence of closure calls our attention to the close relationship between the rhythm of Frye's ideas and his sense of an ending. Like the reversible motto of Eliot's "East Coker," Frye's endings are also his beginnings. The conclusions to many of his books, even to chapters within books, frequently return to his own sense of the fundamental—glimpses of that "third order of experience" which only the imagination can provide. The return of endings to beginnings is still another example of the continuity which characterizes Frye's work.

The metacritic engages in a bold enterprise, and he cannot help but be haunted by the many fallen structures which lie along the road to the eternal city of man's dreams, both intellectual and imaginative. Much is risked because much is attempted. The ambition to write on such a broad front, as Frye himself points out, makes a critic particularly vulnerable to objections.[92] But in Frye's case the risk has been worth taking: a great mind has produced a great body of knowledge which will continue to instruct and delight so long as critics ask questions and dream dreams.

Notes

Preface

1. *Criticism: The Major Texts* (enlarged ed.; New York: Harcourt Brace Jovanovich, 1970), pp. 597, xiv–xv.

2. "Northrop Frye and Contemporary Criticism," in *Northrop Frye in Modern Criticism,* ed. Murray Krieger (New York: Columbia University Press, 1966), p. 1.

3. *American Scholar* 34 (1965): 484.

4. "Northrop Frye Exalting the Designs of Romance," *New York Times Book Review,* 18 April 1976, p. 21. Bloom's opinion is echoed by Gregory T. Poletta, *Issues in Contemporary Criticism* (Boston: Little Brown, 1973): "Northrop Frye . . . is the foremost theorist of literature writing in English since the 1950's" (p. 6). While Frye's work is of course best known among English and American readers, the *Anatomy* has been translated into German, French, Italian, and Spanish, and there have been ten translations of his other books into these languages as well as Japanese.

5. Lawrence I. Lipking and A. Walton Litz, eds., *Modern Literary Criticism: 1900–1970* (New York: Atheneum, 1972), pp. viii, 180.

6. A complete listing of these through June 1973 can be found in my *Northrop Frye: An Enumerative Bibliography* (Metuchen, N.J.: Scarecrow Press, 1974). This volume includes a list of Frye's writings, an annotated account of writings about his work, and a list of the reviews of his books. A supplement to the bibliography is in the *Canadian Library Journal* 34 (June 1977): 181–97, and (August 1977): 301–2.

7. These "four causes" of criticism derive from the observations underlying R.S. Crane's argument for a pluralism of critical methods, an argument which provides an analytically powerful framework for the understanding and critique of critical systems. See my "R.S. Crane's Critical Method and Theory of Poetic Form," *Connecticut Review* 5 (April 1972): 46–55.

8. "Anatomy of Criticism," *University of Toronto Quarterly* 28 (1959): 191.

9. See Mary C. Tucker, "Toward a Theory of Shakespearean Comedy: A Study of the Contributions of Northrop Frye" (Ph.D. dissertation, Emory University, 1963), p. 42.

10. "Expanding Eyes," *Critical Inquiry* 2 (Winter 1975): 212; reprinted in *Spiritus Mundi* (Bloomington: Indiana University Press, 1976), p. 117. Hereafter cited as SM. In *Anatomy of Criticism* Frye observes that "very often a 'structure' or 'system' of thought can be reduced to a diagrammatic pattern. . . . We cannot go very far in any argument without realizing there is some kind of graphic formula involved" (pp. 335–36).

Chapter 1

1. *Anatomy of Criticism* (Princeton, N.J.: Princeton University Press, 1957), pp. 365, 367, 365, 366. Hereafter cited as AC.

2. R.S. Crane, for example, although he offers no criteria for defining all poetry, does maintain that literature can be generally classified into mimetic and didactic kinds, or into what he sometimes refers to as representational and discursive forms. The distinction is based on differences of a formal nature, which are, in turn, determined by the respective final causes of the two types. See *The Languages of Criticism and the Structure of Poetry* (Toronto: University of Toronto Press, 1953), pp. 47–49, 156; *Critics and Criticism,* ed. R.S. Crane (Chicago: University of Chicago Press, 1952), pp. 18, 21; *The Idea of the Humanities,* 2 vols. (Chicago: University of Chicago Press, 1967), 1: 183–89; 2: 59–60. Elder Olson makes the same mimetic-didactic distinction in *Critics and Criticism,* pp. 65–70, 588–92. For Frye's views on the Chicago neo-Aristotelians see "Content with the Form," *University of Toronto Quarterly* 24 (1954): 92–97, and *Shakespeare Quarterly* 5 (1954): 78–81.

3. This observation needs underlining, for much of the recent discussion of the theory of modes, which has centered on Frye's failure to represent all the modal possibilities which would seem to follow from his premises, simply ignores nine-tenths of the modal theory. The objection has been that Frye is highly selective in deducing the number of modes which logically follow from his categories of superiority, inferiority, and equality. John Holloway was the first to lodge a complaint, saying that Frye's theory of modes "ought to yield several hundreds of sensible and consistent combinations" (*The Colours of Clarity* [London: Routledge & Kegan Paul, 1964], p. 155). Tzvetan Todorov, less given to overstatement, guesses that there are thirteen theoretical possibilities (*The Fantastic* [Cleveland: Press of Case Western Reserve University, 1973], p. 13). Robert Scholes, whose critique of Frye derives from Todorov, cannot settle upon the exact number but thinks there is "a minimum of nine modal categories and a maximum a good deal higher" (*Structuralism in Literature: An Introduction* [New Haven: Yale University Press, 1974], p. 119). And Christine Brooke-Rose, agreeing with Todorov that thirteen is the proper number, charts the possibilities for us in binary code ("Historical Genres/Theoretical Genres," *New Literary History* 8 [Autumn 1976]: 147). The failure of these readers to agree comes from the fact that the way Frye's categories can be applied is open to interpretation. Yet the entire discussion, by fastening upon only one of at least a half-dozen principles Frye uses to define the literary modes, seems rather insignificant when we look closely at what comes after the opening pages of the First Essay. (My own reckoning of the logical possibilities is that the six relationships among Frye's categories, with their differences of degree and kind, actually yield twenty-five possible modes: the superior and inferior relationships produce sixteen combinations; the relationships of equality, nine more.)

4. "The Encyclopaedic, Two Kinds of," *Poetry* 91 (1958): 325.

5. Todorov, for example, makes Frye appear to have introduced no distinctions other than those of superiority and inferiority (*The Fantastic,* p. 15), and Brooke-Rose makes the curious statement that "Frye abandons the principle [of naive and sophisticated forms] for modes other than romance, presumably because there happened to be naive romances in his corpus, but not naive tragedies, etc." ("Historical Genres/Theoretical Genres," p. 148). The fact is, however, that Frye gives naive and sentimental examples for each of the ten modes (see Figure 1). Cf. Bruce Bashford, "Literary History in Northrop Frye's *Anatomy of Criticism,*" *Connecticut Review* 8 (October 1974): 48–55. One of the few readers who have analyzed closely the argument of the First Essay, Bashford shows how Frye's initial distinction of heroic powers of action is related to emotional qualities.

6. This is a schematic correspondence, relating to the bipolar structure of Frye's argument and not to any common principles underlying the two pairs of categories.

7. As early as 1936 Frye declares that the theses of *The Decline of the West* "have become inseparable from our present modes of thinking" ("Wyndham Lewis: Anti-

Spenglerian," *Canadian Forum* 16 [1936]: 21). And four years later he refers to "Spengler's irrefutable proof of the existence of organic culture growths" ("War on the Cultural Front," *Canadian Forum* 20 [1940]: 144). See also "Oswald Spengler," in *Architects of Modern Thought* [1st series] (Toronto: Canadian Broadcasting Corporation, 1955), pp. 83–90; "Toynbee and Spengler," *Canadian Forum* 27 (1947): 111–12; reprinted as "The Shapes of History" in *Northrop Frye on Culture and Literature: A Collection of Review Essays*, ed. Robert D. Denham (Chicago: University of Chicago Press, 1978), pp. 76–83, hereafter cited as CL; "New Directions from Old," in *Myth and Mythmaking*, ed. Henry A. Murray (New York: George Braziller, 1960), pp. 117–18, reprinted in *Fables of Identity* (New York: Harcourt, Brace, 1963), pp. 53–54, hereafter cited as FI; and *The Modern Century* (London: Oxford University Press, 1967), p. 42, hereafter cited as MC. Frye's most recent treatment of Spengler, which he describes as "an effort to lay the ghost to rest," is *"The Decline of the West* by Oswald Spengler," *Daedalus* ˙103 (Winter 1974): 1–13, reprinted as "Spengler Revisited" in SM, 179–98.

8. CL, 77. The other obvious debt which Frye owes to Spengler, seen also in this passage, is the metaphor of the four seasons, each referring to one part or "culture" of the historical cycle.

9. "Letter to the English Institute," in *Northrop Frye in Modern Criticism*, p. 142.

10. "Oswald Spengler," p. 86. See also SM, 113, 185. Frye, however, does use the word "cycle" to refer to Spengler's theory of history in "The Rising of the Moon: A Study of 'A Vision,' " in *An Honoured Guest: Essays on W.B. Yeats*, ed. Denis Donoghue and J.L. Mulryne (London: Edward Arnold, 1965), p. 15; reprinted in SM, 254.

11. "Towards a Theory of Cultural History," *University of Toronto Quarterly* 22 (July 1953): 341. Frye does not use the word *cycle* in the First Essay to refer to his own theory, though he does observe that as ironic literature moves toward myth, it is often accompanied by cyclical theories of history, as in Nietzsche, Joyce, and Yeats. See also SM, 113.

12. Frye also appeals to Vico's *ricorso* view of history to illustrate his understanding of cultural movement. See SM, 113. On the influence of Vico, see also *The Critical Path* (Bloomington: Indiana University Press, 1971), p. 34. Hereafter cited as CP.

13. Robert Scholes and Robert Kellogg, owing a clear debt to Frye, have developed this idea in some detail in *The Nature of Narrative* (New York: Oxford University Press, 1966).

14. Displacement can move in the direction of the moral as well as the plausible. See below, pp. 64–66.

15. "Generic Criticism: The Approach Through Type, Mode and Kind," in *Contemporary Criticism*, ed. Malcolm Bradbury and David Palmer (London: Edward Arnold, 1970), pp. 94, 95, 92. Rodway remarks that Frye "tries to define mode solely in terms of character status" (p. 92), and he suggests that "we need to give Frye's technical definition of mode a psychological dimension" (p. 94); this latter refers apparently to literary effect—how a work "will strike the reader" (p. 95). Frye's classification of modes, however, does not at all rely *solely* on character status; and since literary effect is one of the central principles he uses to differentiate the modes, he does not deny the "psychological dimension."

16. "Utopian History and the Anatomy," in *Northrop Frye in Modern Criticism*, pp. 34–35.

17. *The Nature of Narrative*, pp. 13–15, 242–45. See also *The Elements of Fiction* (New York: Oxford University Press, 1968), pp. 1–14; and "Towards a Poetics of Fiction: An Approach through Genre," *Novel* 2 (1969): 101–11. This last essay appears in an expanded form in Scholes's *Structuralism in Literature*, pp. 117–41.

18. *Structuralism in Literature*, p. 132.

19. Ibid., pp. 133, 118.

20. Ibid., pp. 118, 119–22. Scholes's critique depends heavily on Tzvetan Todorov's chapter on Frye in *The Fantastic.*

21. "Towards a Poetics of Fiction," p. 109.

22. *Structuralism in Literature,* pp. 138, 139.

23. *The Fantastic,* pp. 13–15, 21.

24. Todorov complains that it is impossible for Frye to combine the systems of classification in his First and Third Essays, and Brooke-Rose echoes the complaint in "Historical Genres/Theoretical Genres," p. 148. There is no reason, however, that the taxonomies here should be or need to be combined: Frye is simply treating two different kinds of literary conventions. For an analysis and critique of Todorov's own theory of literary types, see David H. Richter, "Pandora's Box Revisited," *Critical Inquiry* 1 (December 1974): 471–74. See also Jonathan Culler, *Structuralist Poetics* (Ithaca: Cornell University Press, 1975), pp. 136–37.

25. Historical Genres/Theoretical Genres," p. 148.

26. "Literary History in Northrop Frye's *Anatomy of Criticism,*" p. 53.

27. *Validity in Interpretation* (New Haven: Yale University Press, 1967), pp. 78, 265–74.

28. New York: Harcourt Brace Jovanovich, 1972. See also Paul Smith, "Criticism and the Curriculum: Part I," *College English* 26 (1964): 23–30, an essay on curricular revision based on principles similar to Frye's; and Robert D. Foulke, "Criticism and the Curriculum: Part II," *College English* 26 (1964): 30–37, an outline of four critical approaches to teaching literature, each of which has a parallel in Frye's work.

29. *An Anatomy of Literature,* p. 14.

30. Ibid., p. 15.

31. Ibid., p. 18.

32. *Structuralism in Literature,* p. 138.

33. *An Anatomy of Literature,* pp. 14, 19.

34. Ibid., p. 19.

35. *The Fantastic,* p. 14.

36. "Utopian History and the *Anatomy,*" in *Northrop Frye in Modern Criticism,* pp. 32, 34, 56.

37. Ibid., pp. 34 (see also p. 43), 53.

38. *Historical Inevitability* (London: Oxford University Press, 1955), p. 14, as quoted by Angus Fletcher in "Utopian History and the *Anatomy,*" p. 52. In "Northrop Frye: The Critical Passion," *Critical Inquiry* 1 (1975): 741–56, Fletcher reexamines Frye's understanding of history, qualifying his earlier judgment about its utopian character but still maintaining that the First Essay is "based on a theory of literary history. Essay I is not a history of literature: it is a theoretical history of literature, that is, it presents the past of our literature under the guise of a hypothetical formation of series of eventualities" (p. 753). The view that the First Essay *"gives a shape to history,* rather than discovering one in a wholly empirical manner" is also argued by Bruce Bashford in "Literary History in Northrop Frye's *Anatomy of Criticism,*" pp. 48–55.

39. "Literary Criticism and History: The Endless Dialectic," *New Literary History* 6 (Spring 1975): 507.

40. "New Directions from Old," in FI, 55.

41. "Interpretation in History," *New Literary History* 4 (1973): 287, 291, 295. See also *Metahistory* (Baltimore: Johns Hopkins University Press, 1973), pp. 7–11, 231–33, where White draws upon Frye's theory of myths to identify four different modes of plotting which he then uses as a part of his framework for analyzing nineteenth-century historians. Cf. Frye's remark in "Reflections in a Mirror": "The only shaping principles of history in literature itself I have dealt with . . . are those of displacement, the oscillating

of technique from the stylizing of form to the manifesting of content and back again, and of what I call existential projection, the attributing of poetic schematism to the objective world, which takes different forms in different historical epochs" *(Northrop Frye in Modern Criticism*, pp. 142–43).

42. *Fearful Symmetry: A Study of William Blake* (Princeton, N.J.: Princeton University Press, 1947), p. 29. Hereafter cited as FS.

43. *Critics and Criticism*, ed. R.S. Crane, abridged ed. (Chicago: University of Chicago Press, 1957), p. iv.

44. *Critics and Criticism*, ed. R.S. Crane (Chicago: University of Chicago Press, 1952), p. 9, and *The Languages of Criticism and the Structure of Poetry*, p. 31. For Frye's reviews of these two books, see note 2 above.

45. P. 13. The chief source of Crane's formulation of pluralism is Richard McKeon, "The Philosophic Bases of Art and Criticism," in *Critics and Criticism*, ed. R.S. Crane (Chicago: University of Chicago Press, 1952), pp. 463–545. On pluralism, see also Wayne C. Booth, *Now Don't Try To Reason with Me* (Chicago: University of Chicago Press, 1961), pp. 103–49, and Elder Olson, "The Dialectical Foundations of Critical Pluralism," in *"On Value Judgments in the Arts" and Other Essays* (Chicago: University of Chicago Press, 1976), pp. 327–59. There is a lively discussion of critical pluralism by Booth, M.H. Abrams, and J. Hillis Miller in *Critical Inquiry* 2 (Spring 1976): 411–64, and 3 (Spring 1977): 407–47. The most complete account of pluralism is in Booth's forthcoming book, *Critical Understanding* (Chicago: University of Chicago Press).

46. But compare this remark: "Aristotle is the only philosopher known to me who not only talks specifically about poetics when he is aware of larger aesthetic problems, but who assumes that such poetics would be the organon of an independent discipline. Consequently a critic can use the *Poetics* without involving himself in Aristotelianism (though I know that some Aristotelian critics do not think so.") (AC, 357).

47. See Leon Golden, "Aristotle, Frye, and the Theory of Tragedy," *Comparative Literature* 27 (1975): 47–58. Golden observes that in comparing the approaches of Frye and Aristotle "we are struck by their wide divergence in method and conclusion," yet he wants to argue, like the syncretist, that the strengths of Frye's observations about the range of tragic works can be combined with Aristotle's definition of the genre to produce a more adequate theory of tragedy.

Chapter 2

1. AC, 72. Frye equates pluralism here with relativism. And yet, although pluralism would also affirm that there is a finite number of valid critical methods, it would certainly deny that they can all be contained in a single theory. Pluralism and relativism need not be the same thing. Even if there are several valid critical methods, it does not necessarily follow that they can be, or even need to be, contained within a single theory. But Frye's synoptic goal and his approach to the problem of meaning require that he attempt to include in one theoretical scheme all the different methods found in the history of criticism and the theories of meaning they produce.

2. AC, 82. Frye's account of literal meaning derives in particular from Richards, Blackmur, Empson, Brooks, and Ransom; see AC, 358. The conception of *mythos* and *dianoia* assumed by the literal phase figures importantly in the Fourth Essay of the *Anatomy*.

3. See *The Languages of Criticism and the Structure of Poetry*, pp. 100–102.

4. It can be argued that in attempting to refute the logical positivists, Frye has let his opposition dictate the terms of his argument. Meyer Abrams makes the same point

with regard to Philip Wheelwright's *The Burning Fountain* ("The Newer Criticism: Prisoner of Logical Positivism?" *Kenyon Review* 17 [1955]: 139–43). An opposing assessment of Frye's position on this issue has been stated, though not argued, by Walter Sutton: "By asserting in his discussion of the descriptive and literal phases that the literary symbol has both outward, or centrifugal, and inward, or centripetal, meaning—that it functions both as a *sign* and as a *motif*—Professor Frye avoids the *referential-syntactical* dilemma that has plagued modern contextualist criticism since the formulation, in the mid-Twenties, of I.A. Richards' distinction between the emotive pseudo-statements of poetry and the referential language of science" (*Symposium* 12 [1958]: 212). Homer Goldberg, on the other hand, has argued that the New Critical assumptions about discourse underlie not simply Frye's discussion of the first two phases but the entire Second Essay ("Center and Periphery: Implications of Frye's 'Order of Words.'" Paper read at the Modern Language Association Meeting, 27 December 1971, pp. 3–6. Photoduplicated copy). On Frye's relationship to the New Criticism, see also Robert Weimann, "Northrop Frye und das Ende des New Criticism," *Sinn und Form* 17 (1965): 621–30; Pierre Dommergues, "Northrop Frye et le critique américaine," *Le Monde* (Supplement au numéro 7086), 25 Octobre 1967, pp. iv–v; Richard Poirier, "What Is English Studies, and If You Know What That Is, What Is English Literature?" *Partisan Review* 37 (1970): 52–53; Monroe K. Spears, "The Newer Criticism," *Shenandoah* 21 (1970): 110–37; Edward Wasiolek, "Wanted: A New Contextualism," *Critical Inquiry* 1 (March 1975): 623–29. In *The Critical Path*, Frye remarks that the great value of the New Criticism "was that it accepted poetic language and form as the basis for poetic meaning" and thus resisted all forms of determinism. "At the same time, it deprived itself of the great strength of documentary criticism: the sense of context. It simply explicated one poem after another, paying little attention to genre or any larger structural principles connecting the different works explicated" (CP, 20).

5. *Freistimmige,* a term Frye borrows from music, refers to the pseudocontrapuntal style where strict adherence to a given number of parts is abandoned, voices being free to enter and drop out at will.

6. AC, 89, 91. See also Frye's article on "Allegory" in *Princeton Encyclopedia of Poetry and Poetics,* ed. Alex Preminger (Princeton, N.J.: Princeton University Press, 1965), pp. 12–15. On "commentary," see also his essay "Literary Criticism," in *The Aims and Methods of Scholarship in Modern Languages and Literatures,* ed. James Thorpe (New York: Modern Language Association, 1963), pp. 65–66.

7. Perhaps as much as any other contemporary critic, Frye has tried to collapse the distinction between high and low culture, between sophisticated and naive forms of art. This is one of the chief reasons for his wanting to remove value judgments from the proper scope of criticism. For Frye's ideas on popular literature, see *The Secular Scripture* (Cambridge: Harvard University Press, 1976), pp. 21–29. Hereafter cited as SeS.

8. Frye uses the word "ritual" more or less conventionally. "Dream," however, as evident from our discussion already, refers not simply to the subconscious activities of sleep but to the entire interrelationship between desire and repugnance in shaping thought. See AC, 359. For a more extensive discussion of ritual as a socially symbolic act, see SeS, 55–58.

9. See also *A Natural Perspective* (New York: Columbia University Press, 1965), p. 73, hereafter cited as NP; and Theodore Gaster's notes to *The Golden Bough* (New York: Criterion Books, 1959), pp. 391–92.

10. "Three Meanings of Symbolism," *Yale French Studies,* no. 9 (1952), p. 18.

11. Quoted and endorsed as aptly characterizing Frye's definition of the anagogic symbol by Walter Sutton, *Modern American Criticism* (Englewood Cliffs, N.J.: Prentice-Hall, 1963), p. 255. See also Warren Shibles, "Northrop Frye on Metaphor," in *An*

Analysis of Metaphor in Light of W.M. Urban's Theories (The Hague: Mouton, 1971), pp. 145–50.

12. The word comes from the Greek, meaning "mystical" or "elevation" (literally "a leading up"). As a medieval level of interpretation, it signified ultimate truth, belonging outside both space and time. Dante refers to it as "beyond the senses" and as concerned with "higher matters belonging to the eternal glory" (*Convivio*, vol. 2, 1, trans. W.W. Jackson [Oxford: Clarendon Press, 1909]: 73–74); see also Dante's "Epistola X" (to Can Grande) in *The Great Critics*, 3d ed., ed. James H. Smith and Edd W. Parks [New York: Norton, 1951], p. 146. Before him Aquinas had defined the "anagogical sense" in similar terms (see *Summa Theologica*, Part I, Q1, Art. 10, in *Basic Writings*, ed. Anton C. Pegis [New York: Random House, 1945], 1: 16–17). The word generally seems to have meant spiritual or otherworldly. Frye's term "universal" appears more accurately to parallel the second medieval level, the allegorical, which referred to truth in relation to humanity as a whole, or universal truth. See Helen F. Dunbar, *Symbolism in Medieval Thought* (New Haven: Yale University Press, 1929), pp. 19, 95–98, 270–71, 468–69.

13. AC, 116. Frye calls attention to the fact that he uses the word "myth" in two senses in the Third Essay, myth as a form of communication combining ritual and dream (in his discussion of the fourth phase), and myth as a story about the gods (in his discussion of the fifth phase, as well as in the First Essay). See AC, 106, 116. Frye would prefer the epithet "visionary" to "mystical." See FS, pp. 7–8, for Frye's distinction between the two terms as they relate to Blake, and pp. 431–32 for his qualifying note on Blake's mysticism.

14. For Frye's description of the same kind of profound experiences in music, see SM, 118.

15. A classic study of this aspect of criticism is Richard McKeon's "The Philosophic Bases of Art and Criticism." Some influential critics have, of course, been poets at the same time—writers like Jonson, Dryden, Coleridge, Shelley, Arnold, and Eliot; but their influence on other critics has not come primarily from their poetry.

16. *Fearful Symmetry* (Boston: Beacon Press, 1962), p. ii. Frye's remarks on the Blakean influence are scattered throughout his work. See especially CP, Part One, and SM, 14–18, 108–15. For a personal account of his early attraction to Blake, see his letter in Pelham Edgar, *Across My Path*, ed. Northrop Frye (Toronto: Ryerson Press, 1952), pp. 85–87.

17. "Notes for a Commentary on *Milton*," in *The Divine Vision: Studies in the Poetry and Art of William Blake*, ed. Vivian de Sola Pinto (London: Gollancz, 1957), p. 107.

18. Ibid., pp. 106–7.

19. See, for example, CL, 98–99, and FI, 141–42.

20. "Notes for a Commentary on *Milton*," p. 108.

21. "Blake's Treatment of the Archetype," in *Discussions of William Blake*, ed. John E. Grant (Boston: Heath, 1961), p. 8. On "apocalypse," see also FS, *passim*, and FI, 143.

22. See SeS, especially chapters 4–6. On "Identity," see also FS, 116–17, 122–23, 249; *The Educated Imagination* (Bloomington: Indiana University Press, 1964), pp. 32–33; "The Rising of the Moon: A Study of 'A Vision,'" especially pp. 8–15; *The Stubborn Structure* (Ithaca, N.Y.: Cornell University Press, 1970), pp. 98–100; FI, pp. 32, 35; NP, 60; and *A Study of English Romanticism* (New York: Random House, 1968), especially chapter 4. *The Educated Imagination* hereafter cited as EI; *The Stubborn Structure* as SS; and *A Study of English Romanticism* as SER.

23. An excellent treatment of Frye's theory of symbols is Alvin A. Lee, "Old English Poetry, Mediaeval Exegesis and Modern Criticism," *Studies in the Literary Imagination* 7 (Spring 1975): 47–73. Lee compares Frye's levels of meaning with the four medieval levels and then applies both to Old English poetry.

Chapter 3

1. "One of the central principles in *Anatomy of Criticism*," Frye remarks almost twenty years later, "is founded on an analogy with music. . . . I am by no means the first critic to regard music as the typical art, the one where the impact of structure is not weakened, as it has been in painting and still is in literature, by false issues derived from representation" (SM, 117–18).

2. AC, 140. On the metaphor of "standing back" as it relates to Blake's poetry, see "Poetry and Design in William Blake," in *Discussions of William Blake*, p. 48. The metaphor is also discussed in "Reflections in a Mirror," in *Northrop Frye in Modern Criticism*, p. 139.

3. The influence of Blake on Frye's entire conception of archetypal imagery should be noted. His essay on Blake's *Milton* is strikingly similar to the first section of the Third Essay. In charting the structure of Blake's symbolism, Frye relies on the same matrix of categories as in the *Anatomy*. The one difference is that Blake conceives of only four levels of vision (Eden or Paradise, Beulah or Innocence, Generation or Experience, and Ulro or Hell), whereas in the *Anatomy* there are five. It is perhaps significant that Frye attaches no name to his additional category. He says, in fact, that he will devote little attention to it "in order to preserve the simpler undisplaced structures," that is, the apocalyptic and demonic ones (AC, 151). The inference seems to be that in Blake's conception of the four levels of vision we have the source for the horizontal categories of Frye's archetypal matrix. Certainly the seven vertical categories do not derive from Blake; they are much older than that. But Frye puts them to extensive use in outlining the symbolism in each of Blake's four "worlds." See "Notes for a Commentary on *Milton*," pp. 108–29.

4. In the Second Essay "phase" is used to describe the different kinds of symbolic interpretation. Frye also uses the word to refer to the fourfold division of cyclical symbols. See AC, 160.

5. There is a slight variation on this pattern in Frye's treatment of the fourth *mythos*.

6. Frye's earliest account of the dragon-killing theme is his discussion of Blake's Orc symbolism in FS, 207–26.

7. Twenty years after the *Anatomy*, Frye says: "Romance is the structural core of all fiction: being directly descended from folktale, it brings us closer than any other aspect of literature to the sense of fiction, considered as a whole, as the epic of the creature, man's vision of his own life as a quest" (SeS, 15).

8. The contexts and themes of romance are given much fuller treatment in SeS, chapters 2, 4, and 5.

9. The fact that there can be tragic or ironic *alazons* has already been anticipated in the First Essay (AC, 39–40).

10. The name comes from those tricksters, like Matthew Merrygreek of *Ralph Roister Doister,* who are "generally said to be developed from the vice or iniquity of the morality plays" (AC, 173).

11. The *Tractatus Coislinianus,* in fact, has but one brief sentence about character: "The characters [*ethe*] of comedy are (1) the buffoonish, (2) the ironical, and (3) those of the imposters." From Lane Cooper's translation in his *An Aristotelian Theory of Comedy* (New York: Harcourt, Brace, 1922), p. 226.

12. This is not to say, however, that within a *mythos* some literary kinds are not more likely to be found in one phase than in another.

13. William Righter maintains that the criteria for Frye's definition of the comic phases "differ considerably from one phase to another." He observes that "some phases are distinguished by the relational elements of plot, others by character type, others (perhaps especially the fifth) by a quality of tone, others such as the sixth by special psychological criteria as 'oracular solemnity' (or is this tone?) and the desire to return to

the womb" ("Myth and Interpretation," *New Literary History* 3 [1972]: 336). Although what Righter says is surely correct, he neglects to point out the one constant principle Frye uses throughout the discussion of comic phases, the nature of the comic society.

14. "Reflections in a Mirror," in *Northrop Frye in Modern Criticism*, pp. 136–37.

15. "The Structural Study of Myth," in *Structural Anthropology* (Garden City, N.Y.: Doubleday, 1967), pp. 202–28.

16. The best account of Frye's relationship to the Structuralist movement is Geoffrey Hartman, "Structuralism: The Anglo-American Adventure," *Yale French Studies,* nos. 36–37 (1966), pp. 148–68, reprinted in *Beyond Formalism* (New Haven: Yale University Press, 1970), pp. 3–23. Hartman, like Harold Bloom in *A Map of Misreading* (New York: Oxford University Press, 1975, p. 30), finds that Frye's theory of recurrence does not properly emphasize a theory of discontinuity. On Frye's work in the context of structuralism, see also Ewa M. Thompson, "Structuralism: Some Possibilities and Limitations," *Southern Humanities Review* 7 (Summer 1973): 247–60; and Evan Watkins, "Criticism and Method: Hirsch, Frye, Barthes," *Soundings* 57 (Summer 1975): 257–80. Frye himself remarks that structuralism has made "a rather disappointing contribution" to our understanding of literature (SM, 106).

Chapter 4

1. In discussing the *mythos* and *dianoia* of the literal phase, Frye says that literary works "move in time like music and spread out in images like painting. The word narrative or *mythos* conveys the sense of movement caught by the ear, and the word meaning or *dianoia* conveys, or at least preserves, the sense of simultaneity caught by the eye. We *listen to* the poem as it moves from beginning to end, but as soon as the whole of it is in our minds at once we 'see' what it means" (AC, 77). See also "Lexis and Melos," Frye's introduction to *Sound and Poetry,* ed. Northrop Frye (New York: Columbia University Press, 1957), ix–xxvii.

2. AC, 245–46. "I do not claim," Frye adds in a note, "that I am correctly interpreting Coleridge's term, but the necessity of being a terminological buccaneer should be clear enough by now" (AC, 362).

3. Frye's "radical of presentation" could be used to argue (against critics such as Croce) that genuine classification is intrinsic to literary understanding. See Richard Wollheim, *Art and Its Objects* (New York: Harper & Row, 1968), pp. 59–61.

4. "Utopian History and the *Anatomy,"* in *Northrop Frye in Modern Criticism*, pp. 39–42.

5. As some of the quotations I have used indicate, Frye also draws upon qualitative or phonetic features of recurrence in his illustrations of musical and nonmusical poetry. The pararhythmic features, however, are secondary to stress or accent.

6. Frye speaks of prose as well as verse *epos.* See AC, 263.

7. For a critique of Frye's musical theory of metrics, see William K. Wimsatt and Monroe Beardsley, "The Concept of Meter," in Wimsatt's *Hateful Contraries* (Lexington: University of Kentucky Press, 1966), pp. 112–14, 122, 128–29.

8. Regarding low-mimetic verse, Frye says: "Wordsworth's theory that apart from metre the *lexis* of poetry and prose are identical is a low mimetic manifesto" (AC, 271). See Figure 2.

9. Frye has an extensive treatment of these two "generic seeds" in "Charms and Riddles," SM, 123–47.

10. *The Well-Tempered Critic* (Bloomington: Indiana University Press, 1963), p. 10. Hereafter cited as WTC.

11. On verse, prose, and associative rhythm, see also Frye's article "Verse and Prose," *Princeton Encyclopedia of Poetry and Poetics,* pp. 885–90.

12. Frye himself points to the similarity between his and Arnold's procedure at this point, adding that, despite the value judgments involved, a community of readers can still "feel that Arnold's taste, within obvious limits, is accurate and that his quotations are accurate" (WTC, 106–7).

13. The clarity of Frye's argument is not enhanced by the fact that he uses "species," "genre," "type," and "specific form" interchangeably. Generally, by "species" he means one of the five main kinds of drama we have outlined. But see AC, 282, where the *auto* is called a "genre."

14. It also represents some of Frye's earliest thinking about theory of literature, incorporating material developed in the early 1940s on the "anatomy" as a prose form. See "The Anatomy in Prose Fiction," *Manitoba Arts Review* 3 (Spring 1942): 35–47.

15. "Novel and Anatomy: Notes Toward an Amplification of Frye," *Criticism* 10 (1968), 153–65. Stevick refers to Frye's fourfold scheme as "the single most significant and influential event in the criticism of prose fiction in the last twenty years" (p. 153). Robert Scholes also observes that Frye's discussion of the four forms of prose fiction is "one of the most widely read and influential portions of the *Anatomy,*" yet he finds it "far less useful than [Frye's] theory of modes." See his critique of the four forms in *Structuralism in Literature,* pp. 125–28.

16. Since the three human cycles are also analogues of the Messianic cycle, they too are apparently a source for the analogical epic ("apparently" because Frye's argument is not altogether clear on this point).

17. Perhaps the most obvious reason for this is that the Bible—a paradigmatic cyclical work—has become less and less a literary influence on the encyclopaedic writer since the time, say, of Milton. We do encounter cyclical models in low-mimetic and ironic works, as Frye points out. But either their thematic range is much less limited than in mythical or romantic works or else the cycle is not particularly encyclopaedic.

18. The symmetry of this grand design is not so fearfully perfect as one might be led to conclude from my discussion. *Epos,* for example, which has the status of a separate genre in the first part of the Fourth Essay, gets lumped together with lyric in the last part. There are other disquieting matters for the reader who seeks in Frye a system of perfect parallels and correspondences; though it should be added that when the abstract categories precede their particular illustration, as is most often the case, we sometimes come to expect a more regular pattern of classification than Frye actually delivers.

19. The schema is perhaps the best example in the *Anatomy* of what Frye calls the mandala vision. See "Forming Fours," CL, 118–19, and SM, 117.

20. *The Return of Eden: Five Essays on Milton's Epics* (Toronto: University of Toronto Press, 1965), p. 9. Hereafter cited as RE.

21. AC, 325–26. See also "History and Myth in the Bible," in *The Literature of Fact: Selected Papers from the English Institute,* ed. Angus Fletcher (New York: Columbia University Press, 1976), pp. 1–19.

Chapter 5

1. Frye would not like the word "reconciliatory." "I wish we could throw away the notion of 'reconciling,'" he says, "and use instead some such conception as 'interpenetration.' Literature itself is not a field of conflicting arguments but interpenetrating visions. . . . The genuine critic works out his own views of literature while realizing that there are also a great number of other views, both actual and possible, which are neither

reconcilable nor irreconcilable with his own. They interpenetrate with him, and he with them, each a monad as full of windows as a Park Avenue building" ("Letter to the English Institute," p. 29).

2. AC, 3. Despite the fact that I have spoken often of "Frye's theory," he cautions against regarding the *Anatomy* as *his* system. Rather it should be considered, he says, as "an interconnected group of suggestions," parts of which are expendable if they are "of no practical use to anybody" (AC, 3). It offers critics a "new perspective," not a "new program" (AC, 341). And even though the large claims of Frye's enterprise are offered with confidence, he is careful to emphasize that the undertaking is provisional, not apodictic. The *Anatomy* "can only be offered to a reader," he says, "who has enough sympathy with its aims to overlook, in the sense not of ignoring but of seeing past, whatever strikes him as inadequate or simply wrong. I am convinced that if we wait for a fully qualified critic to tackle the subjects of these essays, we shall wait a long time" (AC, 29).

3. AC, 7. Thus Frye can speak of Allen Tate as being a "religious determinist" and Sir Herbert Read as a "psychological determinist . . . with latent political implications" (CL, 134). See also SeS, 25.

4. "Because I found the term 'archetype' an essential one," Frye remarks in *The Critical Path*, "I am still often called a Jungian critic, and classified with Miss Maud Bodkin, whose book I have read with interest, but whom, on the evidence of that book, I resemble about as closely as I resemble the late Sarah Bernhardt" (p. 16). On Frye's relation to Jung, see SM, 116–17.

5. *The Fantastic*, p. 16.

6. "Pandora's Box Revisited," p. 472.

7. One might also reply to Todorov's critique (1) that Frye does use these categories in a special literary sense; (2) that these are by no means Frye's primary categories; and (3) that no critic can escape from relying on general philosophic principles. Todorov's own work, based upon a Saussurean linguistic model, is a case in point. There is no difference between the nonliterary status of his categories (e.g., spatial/temporal, projection, isomorphism, vision) and Frye's. See my "Todorov and the Linguistic Model," *Language Sciences*, no. 45 (April 1977), pp. 1–5. A brilliant analysis of the necessity of general philosophic principles in criticism is Richard McKeon's "The Philosophic Bases of Art and Criticism."

8. "I have read [several hundred books in psychology] for whatever help they could give me as a literary critic: they interpenetrate my critical work but keep their own context in their own discipline. For a contemporary critic interested in Freud or Wittgenstein or Lévi-Strauss, such writers, like medieval angels, do not travel through space from another subject: they manifest themselves from within his subject" (SM, 107).

9. Especially in the Second Essay, where Frye distinguishes between centrifugal (descriptive) and centripetal (his own version of "literal") meaning.

10. See, for example, Richard Kuhns, "Professor Frye's Criticism," *Journal of Philosophy* 56 (1959): 745–55; John Casey, "A 'Science' of Criticism," in *The Language of Criticism* (London: Methuen, 1966), pp. 140–45; John Holloway, "The Critical Zodiac of Northrop Frye," in *Colours of Clarity*, pp. 153–60; Monroe K. Spears, "The Newer Criticism," in *Dionysus and the City* (New York: Oxford University Press, 1970), pp. 197–228; Paul Sporn, "Empirical Criticism: A Summary and Some Objections," *Poetic Theory/Poetric Practice*, ed. Robert Scholes (Iowa City: Midwest Modern Language Association, 1969), pp. 16–31; Raman Selden, "Objectivity and Theory in Literary Criticism," *Essays in Criticism* 23 (1973): 292–94.

11. *The Languages of Criticism and the Structure of Poetry*, p. x.

12. "Literary Criticism," in *The Aims and Methods of Scholarship in Modern Languages and Literatures*, pp. 61–62. This essay contains a good summary of Frye's views on evaluation.

Another succinct account is in "On Value Judgements," in SS, 66–73. See also SS, 23, 77–80; FI, 8, 128–29, 149; "An Indispensable Book," *Virginia Quarterly Review* 32 (1956): 313–14; "The Study of English in Canada," *Dalhousie Review* 38 (1958): 4–5; "Blake's Treatment of the Archetype," in *Discussions of William Blake*, p. 16; "Expanding Eyes," in SM, 99–107; and "Reflections in a Mirror," in *Northrop Frye in Modern Criticism*, pp. 135–36.

13. "Toward a Theory of Cultural Revolution," *Canadian Literature*, no. 1 (Summer 1959), p. 59.

14. On this aspect of Frye's work—his effort "to democratize criticism and demystify the muse"—see Geoffrey Hartman, "Ghostlier Demarcations," in *Northrop Frye in Modern Criticism*, pp. 109–31.

15. Hayden Carruth, for example, in commenting on the split between art and experience occasioned by the New Critics' concept of literary function, says that "Frye has resolved the split by denying the moral factor altogether. For him art is simply and totally conventional, and has neither a moral content nor a moral application" ("People in a Myth," *Hudson Review* 18 [1965–66]: 609). Similar judgments have been advanced by Gerald Graff, *Poetic Statement and Critical Dogma* (Evanston: Northwestern University Press, 1970), pp. 73–78; V.G. Hanes, "Northrop Frye's Theory of Literature and Marxism," *Horizons: The Marxist Quarterly*, no. 24 (Winter 1968), pp. 62–78; Fred Inglis, ":Professor Northrop Frye and the Academic Study of Literature," *Centennial Review* 9 (1965): 319–31; Gabriel Josipovici, *The World and the Book* (Stanford: Stanford University Press, 1971), pp. 264–69, 289–93, 303–5; Bernhard Ostendorf, *Der Mythos in der Neuen Welt* (Frankfurt am Main: Thesen Verlag, 1971), pp. 140–41; Richard Poirier, *The Performing Self* (New York: Oxford University Press), pp. 78–80; and Brian Robinson, "Northrop Frye: critique fameux, critique faillible," *Revue de l'Université d'Ottawa* 42 (1972): 608–14.

16. *New York Review of Books*, 26 February 1970 and 12 March 1970. Reprinted with only slight alterations in *Psychoanalysis and Literary Process*, ed. Frederick Crews (Cambridge, Mass.: Winthrop Publishers, 1970), pp. 1–24, and in *Out of My System* (New York: Oxford University Press, 1975), pp. 63–87. References within parentheses in my text are to the first reprinted edition.

17. This pragmatic orientation, as I have described it abstractly, does not differ significantly from the way one could describe any number of critical theories from Plato to Kenneth Burke. Crews's interest in psychic function, however, distinguishes his theory of literature from other pragmatic or rhetorical theories.

18. *Critics and Criticism* (1952), pp. 8–9.

19. It is interesting that when Crews does speak of value judgments his position is not at all different from Frye's. Frye would be in perfect agreement with the following statement by Crews on Conrad: "Predictions about the future rankings of authors should be made with the greatest tentativeness or not at all. In retrospect it is easy to see that literary value in any given age has been glimpsed through the haze of ideology. . . . The academy, that home of disinterested taste, cannot be appealed to as a referee. . . . Those of us who are involved in the quaint modern industry of explaining literature are assailed sometimes by a doubt as to whether we know what we like. To say what some future generation would like is quite beyond our power" ("The Power of Darkness," *Partisan Review* 34 [1967]: 507).

20. The confusion could be removed, it seems to me, if Crews would grant that not all critical methods attempt to answer the same kinds of questions.

21. AC, 113. This position is anticipated in the Polemical Introduction: "Ethical criticism [is based on] the consciousness of the presence of society. As a critical category this would be the sense of the real presence of culture in the community. Ethical criticism, then, deals with art as a communication from the past to the present, and is based on the conception of the total and simultaneous possession of past culture. An exclusive

devotion to it, ignoring historical criticism, would lead to a naive translation of all cultural phenomena into our own terms without regard to their original character. As a counterweight to historical criticism, it is designed to express the contemporary impact of all art, without selecting a tradition" (AC, 24–25).

22. New York: Oxford University Press, 1967. Hereafter cited as MC.

23. Most of the essays, for example, collected in Part I of *The Stubborn Structure*.

24. This tripartite division of poetic theories derives from Richard McKeon, "The Philosophic Bases of Art and Criticism," Part I, pp. 466–90.

25. Their ideas on the power of the imagination to create an ideal world are, however, similar. Compare, for example, Frye's views on anagogy in the Second Essay with Kant's statement that "the poet ventures to realize to sense, rational ideas of invisible beings, the kingdom of the blessed, hell, eternity, creation, etc.; or even if he deals with things of which there are examples in experience—e.g., death, envy and all vices, also love, fame, and the like—he tries, by means of imagination, which emulates the play of reason in its quest after a maximum, to go beyond the limits of experience and to present them to sense with a completeness of which there is no example in nature. This is properly speaking the art of the poet, in which the faculty of aesthetical ideas can manifest itself in its entire strength. But this faculty, considered in itself, is properly only a talent (of the imagination)" (*Critique of Judgment*, Part 49, trans J.H. Bernard [New York: Hafner, 1951], pp. 157–58).

26. Published originally in *The American Journal of Psychiatry* 119 (1962): 289–98; reprinted in FI, 151–67.

27. On the imagination as a vital force, see FS, 55, 83, 230, 235; FI, 80–81; as a unifying and synthesizing force, see FS, 56, 88; EI, 38.

28. "Myth, Fiction, and Displacement," in FI, 29–30. See also "The Developing Imagination," in *Learning in Language and Literature* (Cambridge: Harvard University Press, 1963), pp. 37–38. In another essay Frye says, "The imagination is instrumental in Coleridge: it is the power that unifies, but not the thing to be unified, the real coordinating principle" (CL, 175).

29. Ben Howard, "Fancy, Imagination, and Northrop Frye," *Thoth* 9 (Winter 1968): 31.

30. *Modern Literary Criticism: 1900–1970*, p. 184.

31. For a summary of Frye's views on the imagination as a perceptive faculty, see Iqbal Ahmad, "Imagination and Image in Frye's Criticism," *English Quarterly* 3 (Summer 1970): 15–24.

32. *The Languages of Criticism and the Structure of Poetry*, p. 31.

Chapter 6

1. Practical criticism is often associated with the kind of activity begun by I.A. Richards in the 1920s—the close analysis of specific works considered as poetic wholes. Frye's approach usually assumes a much broader perspective. He is closer to Coleridge, whose studies of Wordsworth and Shakespeare have caused some historians to refer to him as the father of practical criticism, than he is to the various New Critics who have practiced close rhetorical analysis.

2. Toronto: Anansi, 1971.

3. See Part I of my *Northrop Frye: An Enumerative Bibliography* and Section A of "Northrop Frye: A Supplementary Bibliography," *Canadian Library Journal* 34 (June 1977): 181–97.

4. "I hold to no 'method' of criticism," Frye says, "beyond assuming that the struc-

ture and imagery of literature are central considerations of criticism. Nor, I think, does my practical criticism illustrate the use of a patented critical method of my own, different in kind from the approaches of other critics" (SS, 82). J. Wilson Knight had a formative influence on Frye's ideas about the central considerations of criticism. See SM, 12–13.

5. Harold Bloom says that Frye "has Platonized the dialectics of tradition, in its relation to fresh creation, into what . . . turns out to be a Low Church version of Eliot's Anglo-Catholic myth of Tradition and the Individual Talent" (*A Map of Misreading*, p. 30).

6. See especially "Blake After Two Centuries," in FI, 138–50; "The Drunken Boat: The Revolutionary Element in Romanticism," in SS, 200–217; and "The Romantic Myth," in SER, 3–49.

7. References to at least twenty-four of Milton's other works give some indication of the scope of Frye's study.

8. There *is* a rough analogy between these orders and the hierarchy of fictional modes in the First Essay. Apparently, however, Frye does not intend to draw the parallel; or if he does, we are confronted with an inconsistency. The hero of *Paradise Lost,* he says, is Christ, "because as the agent or acting principle of the Father, he is ultimately the only actor in the poem" (RE, 24). Therefore, in terms of the "power of action" criterion, *Paradise Lost* would be in the mythical mode. But it is clear Frye considers it as a high-mimetic work.

9. Joseph H. Summers says that Frye's remarks on Galileo are, if not "just wrong," at least "mistaken in emphasis" (*Journal of English and Germanic Philology* 66 [1967]: 148).

10. "Introduction," *Paradise Lost and Selected Poetry and Prose,* ed. Northrop Frye (New York: Holt, Rinehart and Winston, 1951), p. xviii.

11. SS, 158. On Milton's relation to the Romantic tradition, see also CP, 77–78, and SeS, 6.

12. Insofar as the Age of Sensibility essay was published in 1956, a year before the *Anatomy,* it would be somewhat misleading to say that the essay applies principles found in that book. But the dates are not really important for my purpose, which is to show how Frye's principles, whenever they first made their way into print, are used in a particular kind of critical study. Of course, a large part of the *Anatomy* incorporates earlier published material, some as early as 1942.

13. FI, 134–35; cf. AC, 37: "The words pity and fear may be taken as referring to the two general directions in which emotion moves, whether towards an object or away from it."

14. Still, he is quite aware of the exceptions to the rule, qualifying his generalities by such expressions as "normally" and "typically." The implications of his title ("Towards Defining . . . ") suggest the original meaning of the word "essay," a trial or incomplete attempt.

15. He has been rather harshly criticized, for example, by the Spenser specialists. The attack begins with Frank Kermode's "Spenser and the Allegorists," in *Proceedings of the British Academy: 1962* (London: Oxford University Press, 1963), pp. 261–79, and is continued by Rudolf B. Gottfried's "Our New Poet: Archetypal Criticism and *The Faerie Queene,*" *PMLA* 83 (1968): 1362–77. For the controversy surrounding Gottfried's essay, see Carol Ohmann, "Northrop Frye and the MLA," *College English* 32 (1970): 291–300; Rudolf B. Gottfried, "Edmund Spenser and the NCTE," *College English* 33 (1971): 76–79; and Carol Ohmann, "Reply to Rudolf B. Gottfried," *College English* 33 (1971): 79–83.

16. An earlier and considerably shorter version of this chapter appeared as "The Drunken Boat: The Revolutionary Element in Romanticism," in *Romanticism Reconsidered: Selected Papers from the English Institute,* ed. Northrop Frye (New York: Columbia University Press, 1963), pp. 1–25; reprinted in SS, 200–217.

17. SER, v–vi. Frye's chief aim in the last three chapters is to show how the structure

and imagery of Beddoes, Shelley, and Keats break with the language and symbolism of the older paradigm.

18. To see it as having a historical center of gravity, he says in another essay, "gets us at once out of the fallacy of timeless characterization, where we say that Romanticism has certain qualities, not found in the age of Pope, of sympathy with nature or what not, only to have someone produce a poem of Propertius or Kalidasa, or, eventually, Pope himself, and demand to know if the same qualities are not there" (SS, 200).

19. On Frye's interpretation of Beddoes, see Ross G. Woodman, "Letters in Canada: Literary Studies," *University of Toronto Quarterly* 38 (1969): 371–72.

20. Because Frye's analysis of social myths appears to result mainly from an application to other matters of his critical theory, it has seemed more appropriate to consider that analysis in this chapter rather than in the previous one.

Chapter 7

1. The phrase belongs to Frye, one of his ironic jibes directed toward deterministic critics.

2. See *Critics and Criticism* (1952), p. 9, and *The Languages of Criticism and the Structure of Poetry*, p. 31.

3. *The Languages of Criticism and the Structure of Poetry*, p. 26.

4. This is another way of arguing for a pluralism of critical methods. I am not suggesting, however, that there is no disputing about paradigms. The issues involved in judging whether critical theories are equally valuable is raised by Wayne C. Booth, "Meyer Abrams: Historian as Critic, Critic as Pluralist," *Critical Inquiry* 2 (Spring 1976): 411–45. See also Abrams's own essay, "What's the Use of Theorizing about the Arts?" in *In Search of Literary Theory*, ed. Morton W. Bloomfield (Ithaca: Cornell University Press, 1972), pp. 1–54. For the continuing discussion about pluralism, see note 45, chapter 1.

5. "What's the Use of Theorizing about the Arts?" p. 24.

6. *The Structure of Scientific Revolutions*, 2d ed. (Chicago: University of Chicago Press, 1970), p. viii.

7. Ibid., p. 96.

8. "The Function of Dogma in Scientific Research," in *Readings in the Philosophy of Science*, ed. B.A. Brody (Englewood Cliffs, N.J.: Prentice-Hall, 1970), pp. 360–61. This essay, first published in 1963, represents a condensed form of the first third of *The Structure of Scientific Revolutions*.

9. For an evaluation of Kuhn's ideas, see *Criticism and the Growth of Knowledge*, ed. Imre Lakatos and Alan Musgrave (Cambridge: Cambridge University Press, 1970), a symposium devoted to his work.

10. *Conjectures and Refutations* (London: Routledge and Kegan Paul, 1963), p. 192; see also p. 128.

11. *Philosophy of Natural Science* (Englewood Cliffs, N.J.: Prentice-Hall, 1966), p. 15.

12. See note 3, chapter 1.

13. "The Critical Zodiac of Northrop Frye," pp. 154–55.

14. Ibid., pp. 155–56. The passage from Frye, slightly misquoted, comes from AC, 177. Emphasis is Holloway's. Robert Scholes also analyzes the possibilities of Frye's modal scheme, coming to a similar conclusion about the selective and unsystematic nature of the taxonomy: "There are many fictions which cannot be accurately classified according to Frye's system. Some myths, for instance, are about animals with supernatural powers. This makes them superior to man's environment, but are they superior to man? In kind or degree? Are demons, witches, and so forth superior to man in degree or only in kind? Frye's use of the word 'hero' has allowed him to ignore myths in which the central figure

is a magic animal or demon, wicked or mischievous, whose exploits are recounted with horror or pleasure" (*Structuralism in Literature,* pp. 119–20).

15. *The Logic of Scientific Discovery* (New York: Harper & Row, 1968), p. 34.

16. Ibid., pp. 41–42, 78–92.

17. *The Language of Criticism* (London: Methuen, 1966), pp. 141–42.

18. "Anatomy of Criticism," *University of Toronto Quarterly* 27 (1959), 194–95. Although Abrams's remark suggests an uncritical acceptance of Popper and the hypothetico-deductive model, generally he would not embrace this kind of scientism. In a recent essay he specifically separates the principles of criticism from those which depend on the models of logical calculi. See "What's the Use of Theorizing about the Arts?" especially Part IV, where he says: "Rather than to exaggerate the commonalty of method in science and criticism, it would be more profitable to say that while criticism involves the use of logic and scientific method, it must go far beyond their capacities if it is to do its proper job" (p. 52).

19. *The Structure of Scientific Revolutions,* especially chapter 2.

20. Ibid., p. 50.

21. Ibid., chapter 11.

22. Ibid., p. 150. Compare Kuhn's "Postscript—1969," pp. 174 ff., where he clarifies his idea of paradigm and qualifies his conception of the scientific community by indicating the various levels at which it exists.

23. "Anatomy of Criticism," *University of Toronto Quarterly* 28 (1959): 194.

24. *Meaning in the Visual Arts* (Garden City, N.Y.: Doubleday, 1955), p. 21.

25. *The Languages of Criticism and the Structure of Poetry,* especially section 5.

26. I believe this issue can also be fruitfully discussed in terms of E.D. Hirsch's distinction between intended meaning and significance. "*Meaning* is that which is represented by a text; it is what the author meant by the use of a particular sign sequence; it is what the signs represent. *Significance,* on the other hand, names a relationship between that meaning and a person, or a conception, or a situation, or indeed anything imaginable" (*Validity in Interpretation* [New Haven: Yale University Press, 1967], p. 8). Frye is a great adder of significances that authors never suspected.

27. "Anatomy of Criticism," *University of Toronto Quarterly* 28 (1959): 194, 195.

28. "The Use of Criticism in the Teaching of Literature," *College English* 27 (1965): 6.

29. Neither Abrams nor Booth would now entirely support the positions they were taking more than a decade ago. Even in Abrams's *The Mirror and the Lamp* (New York: Norton, 1953), written before his review of the *Anatomy,* he argues that although good aesthetic theories are "empirical in method," aesthetic facts "turn out to have the curious and scientifically reprehensible property of being conspicuously altered by the nature of the very principles which appeal to them for support. Because many critical statements of fact are thus partially relative to the perspective of the theory within which they occur, they are not 'true,' in the strict sense that they approach the ideal of being verifiable by any intelligent human being, no matter what his point of view" (p. 4). In "What's the Use of Theorizing about the Arts?" Abrams discusses the difference between critical and scientific theories. See also "Rationality and Imagination in Cultural History," *Critical Inquiry* 2 (Spring 1976): 447–64, where he asks rhetorically, "After reading certain books that violate calculi modeled on logic and the exact sciences, which would do more violence to my sense of what is rational and my intuition that I have learned new truths—to decide these books don't yield knowledge, or to decide that calculi are inappropriate to the procedures of discovery and demonstration that their authors have in fact employed?" (p. 448). Booth's recent views on dogmas about fact and truth are presented with great skill in *Modern Dogma and the Rhetoric of Assent* (Chicago: University of Chicago Press, 1974).

30. The example is John Casey's. See "A 'Science' of Criticism," *The Language of Criticism,* pp. 17–18, 143–44. Some of my discussion here is indebted to Casey's essay.

31. "A 'Science' of Criticism," p. 143.

32. Literature and Ideology Monograph, 1 (Montreal: Progressive Books and Periodicals, 1969). Equally incompetent are the review essay by J.D.S., "Northrop Frye and Reactionary Criticism," *Literature and Ideology*, no. 2 (1969), pp. 104–10, and the anonymous publication entitled *Objective Idealism as Fascism: A Denunciation of Northrop Frye's "Literary Criticism," Ideological Forum* [Montreal], No. 3, n.d.

33. In *Northrop Frye in Modern Criticism*, pp. 75–107.

34. "Criticism as Myth," p. 102.

35. Ibid., pp. 102–3.

36. On Wimsatt's view of Frye, see also Angus Fletcher "Northrop Frye: The Critical Passion," *Critical Inquiry* 1 (June 1975): 741–56.

37. See "The Philosophic Bases of Art and Criticism," pp. 522–45; "Literary Criticism and the Concept of Imitation in Antiquity," *Critics and Criticism* (1952), pp. 147–75; and "Imitation and Poetry," in *Thought, Action, and Passion* (Chicago: University of Chicago Press, 1954), pp. 102–221.

38. Frye does change the term "myth-play" to *auto*.

39. "The Critical Zodiac of Northrop Frye," p. 158.

40. "Blake's Treatment of the Archetype," p. 15.

41. Review of W.B. Stanford, *The Ulysses Theme*, and Cleanth Brooks, ed., *Tragic Themes in Western Literature, Comparative Literature* 9 (1957): 182, emphasis mine. In SM, 118, Frye also says that myths are archetypes.

42. "The Critical Zodiac of Northrop Frye," pp. 158–59.

43. "Dreadful Symmetry," *Hudson Review* 10 (1958–59): 617.

44. *Modern American Criticism* (Englewood Cliffs, N.J.: Prentice-Hall, 1963), pp. 254–55.

45. "The Juggler," *The Nation*, 17 January 1959, p. 58.

46. "Dreadful Symmetry," p. 617.

47. See, for example, Hazard Adams, *The Interests of Criticism* (New York: Harcourt, Brace & World, 1969), pp. 122–31; Fred Inglis, "Professor Northrop Frye and the Academic Study of Literature," *Centennial Review* 9 (1965): 319–31; Joseph Margolis, "Critics and Literature," *British Journal of Aesthetics* 11 (1971): 378–80; Monroe K. Spears, "The Newer Criticism," *Shenandoah* 21 (1970): 110–37; W.K. Wimsatt, *Hateful Contraries*, pp. 17–20; and Raman Selden, "Objectivity and Theory in Literary Criticism," pp. 292–94.

48. "Mr. Frye and Evaluation," *Cambridge Quarterly* 2 (1967): 116.

49. Frye is correct, I think, in maintaining that "comparative evaluations" always appeal to *a priori* criteria, based on subjective preferences.

50. *The Languages of Criticism and the Structure of Poetry*, p. 143.

51. Ibid., pp. 154, 155, 166. See also *Critics and Criticism* (1952), pp. 15–16, where Crane says that considering poems as wholes "involves asking ourselves, first, what the specific constitution and power of the whole the writer has achieved or aimed at really is. . . . Having done this, we may then ask, in the second place, to what extent and with what degree of artistic compulsion, any of the particular things the writer has done at the various levels of his writing . . . can be seen to follow from the special requirements or opportunities which the kind of whole he is making presents to him." The implied mode of reasoning here illustrates what Crane means by saying that "the conception and the method can hardly be separated" (*The Languages of Criticism and the Structure of Poetry*, p. 154).

52. *The Languages of Criticism and the Structure of Poetry*, p. 167. See also p. 174.

53. Ibid., p. 177.

54. Ibid., p. 181.

55. Ibid.

56. The past several decades have witnessed a host of arguments against any kind of absolute disjunction between facts and values. For a good annotated account of some of these, see Wayne C. Booth, "Two-Score and More Witnesses against the Fact-Value Split," *Modern Dogma and the Rhetoric of Assent,* pp. 207–11.

57. *Hamlet and the Philosophy of Literary Criticism* (Cleveland: World Publishing Co., 1966), pp. 277–78.

58. Ibid., p. 279.

59. For another well-reasoned alternative, see Elder Olson, "On Value Judgments in the Arts," *Critical Inquiry* 1 (September 1974): 71–90, reprinted in *"On Value Judgments in the Arts" and Other Essays,* pp. 307–26.

60. See, for example, the following reviews of Frye's book: J.M. Patrick, *Seventeenth-Century News* 24 (1966): 2; William G. Madsen, *Criticism* 8 (1966): 390–91; and Patrick Crutwell, "New Miltonics," *Hudson Review* 19 (1966): 501.

61. "The Philosophic Bases of Art and Criticism," especially section 2.

62. Frye's formal phase is an attempt to remove the antithesis between delight and instruction, or between the literal phase, which tends to erase all connection with life, and the descriptive phase, which tends explicitly to make such connections. But his argument is not convincing because of the ambiguity involved in saying that poetry is typical in two ways: that it is more philosophical than history, on the one hand, and more historical than philosophy, on the other. We can see how these ideas relate generally to event and idea, to *mythos* and *dianoia*. And we can see that there is some measure of truth in the statements if taken separately. But it is difficult to see how they can both be true at the same time; and if they cannot, then the antithesis Frye hopes to avoid still remains.

63. "The Critical Zodiac of Northrop Frye," p. 156.

64. See, for example, Robert M. Adams, "Dreadful Symmetry," p. 615.

65. As Frye himself remarks, "To make valid comparisons you have to know what your primary categories are. If you are studying natural history, no matter how fascinated you may be by anything that has eight legs, you can't just lump together an octopus and a spider and a string quartet" ("Sir James Frazer," in *Architects of Modern Thought,* 3d and 4th series [Toronto: Canadian Broadcasting Corporation, 1959], p. 27, reprinted in CL, 89).

66. "Letter to the English Institute," p. 27.

67. Ibid., p. 29.

68. "Current Opera: A Housecleaning," *Acta Victoriana* 60 (October 1935): 12–14.

69. "Ballet Russe," *Acta Victoriana* 60 (December 1935): 5. The same concepts appear in "Frederick Delius," *Canadian Forum* 16 (August 1936): 17. See also "Music in Poetry," *University of Toronto Quarterly* 11 (1942): 167–79. Edward Said is one of the few readers who have understood the centrality of music as a structural analogy in Frye's thought. See *Beginnings* (New York: Basic Books, 1975), p. 376. Frye, incidentally, understood the "harmonic" (vertical) and "melodic" (horizontal) ways of visualizing literature some twenty years before Lévi-Strauss was to speak of reading the Oedipus myth paradigmatically as well as syntagmatically.

70. "Wyndham Lewis: Anti-Spenglerian," *Canadian Forum* 16 (June 1936): 21–22.

71. *A Map of Misreading,* p. 30. Bloom echoes Geoffrey Hartman's remark about Frye: "What we need is a theory of recurrence (repetition) that includes a theory of discontinuity." See "Structuralism: The Anglo-American Adventure," in *Beyond Formalism,* p. 17.

72. SeS, 163. As Frye points out, these words were written before the appearance of Bloom's *A Map of Misreading* (SeS, 193). On Frye's discussion of continuity in another context, see "The University and Personal Life," in *Higher Education: Demand and Response*

(San Francisco: Jossey-Bass, 1970), 35–51, reprinted in SM, 27–48. This essay examines the positive and negative features resulting from the meeting of continuous and discontinuous views of the world. There can be no doubt about Frye's indebtedness to Eliot's ideas about the order of literature and about tradition and the individual talent, but *The Modern Century*, to cite another example, is an entire book about the interplay between continuity and discontinuity.

73. In response to essays by Angus Fletcher and Geoffrey Hartman, Frye says: "Both . . . emphasize the fact that my work is designed to raise questions rather than answer them, and that my aim is not to construct a *Narrenschiff* to keep future critics all bound in by the same presuppositions, but to point to what Mr. Fletcher calls the open vistas and Mr. Hartman the still closed doors of the subject. A critic who has been compelled by such ambitions to write on far too broad a front is particularly vulnerable to objections on points of detail" ("Reflections in a Mirror," p. 134).

74. "What's the Use of Theorizing about the Arts?" p. 25.

75. For example, Frank Kermode's review of the *Anatomy* in *Review of English Studies* 10 (1959): 317–23; and Homer Goldberg, "Center and Periphery: Implications of Frye's 'Order of Words,' " pp. 1–12. See also chapter 2, note 4.

76. See, for example, Florence E. Bennee, "Selected Applications of Frye's Academic Criticism in the Senior High School Years" (Ed.D. dissertation, Columbia University, 1971); Robert D. Foulke and Paul Smith, "Criticism and the Curriculum," *College English* 26 (1964): 23–37; Eli Mandel, *Criticism: The Silent Speaking Words* (Toronto: Canadian Broadcasting Corporation, 1966); Glenna Davis Sloan, *The Child as Critic: Teaching Literature in the Elementary School* (New York: Teachers College Press, Columbia University, 1975); W.T. Jewkes, "Mental Flight: Northrop Frye and the Teaching of Literature," *Journal of General Education* 27 (Winter 1976): 281–98; W.T. Jewkes, ed., *Literature: The Uses of Imagination*, 11 vols. (New York: Harcourt Brace Jovanovich, 1973). Frye's manual for this last series of texts is *On Teaching Literature* (New York: Harcourt Brace Jovanovich, 1972).

77. See George Bowering, "Why James Reany Is a Better Poet (1) Than Any Northrop Frye Poet (2) Than He Used To Be," *Canadian Literature*, no. 36 (Spring 1968), pp. 40–49; Desmond Pacey, *Essays in Canadian Criticism: 1938–68* (Toronto: Ryerson Press, 1969), pp. 202–5, 211; James Reaney, *Alphabet*, no. 1 (September 1960), pp. [2]–4; Lloyd Abbey, "The Organic Aesthetic," *Canadian Literature*, no. 46 (Autumn 1970), pp. 103–4; and Frank Davey, "Northrop Frye," in *From There to Here* (Erin, Ontario: Press Porcepic, 1974), pp. 106–12.

78. "Criticism and Other Arts," *Canadian Literature*, no. 49 (Summer 1971), p. 4.

79. "I have long ceased to view the *Anatomy of Criticism*," he says, "as a handbook of real practical value to the critic."

80. *Review of English Studies* 10 (1959): 323.

81. Hough, *An Essay on Criticism* (New York: Norton, 1966), p. 154; Levin, *Why Literary Criticism Is Not an Exact Science* (Cambridge: Harvard University Press, 1967), p. 24; Wellek, *Discriminations* (New Haven: Yale University Press, 1970), pp. 257–58.

82. "Reflections in a Mirror," p. 136.

83. G.C. Simpson, *Principles of Animal Taxonomy* (New York, 1961), p. 5, as quoted in Claude Lévi-Strauss, *The Savage Mind* (Chicago: University of Chicago Press, 1966), pp. 9–10, 13.

84. *The Savage Mind*, p. 13.

85. "Myth and Interpretation," *New Literary History* 3 (1972): 341.

86. Ibid., p. 342.

87. "Anatomy of Criticism," *University of Toronto Quarterly* 28 (1959): 196. The analogies Abrams refers to are found in AC, 183, 190, and 46 respectively.

88. Abrams, ibid., and Holloway, "The Critical Zodiac of Northrop Frye," pp. 159–60.

89. "The Future of Metaphysics," in *The Future of Metaphysics,* ed. Robert E. Wood (Chicago: Quadrangle Books, 1970), pp. 304–5.

90. "The Critical Zodiac of Northrop Frye," p. 159.

91. "Toward a Theory of Cultural Revolution: The Criticism of Northrop Frye," *Canadian Literature,* no. 1 (Summer 1959), p. 58.

92. "Reflections in a Mirror," p. 134.

Index

Numbers in italics refer to charts and diagrams. A list of these appears on page xiii.

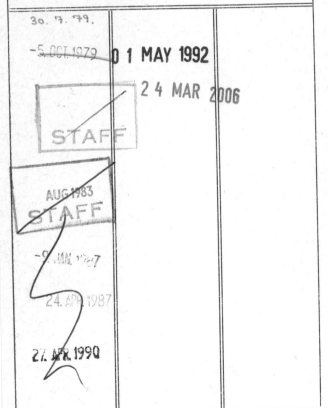